Economic Development and Planning in Egypt

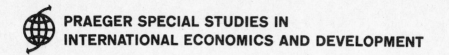

PRAEGER SPECIAL STUDIES IN
INTERNATIONAL ECONOMICS AND DEVELOPMENT

Economic Development and Planning in Egypt

Magdi M. El-Kammash

**Foreword by
Joseph J. Spengler**

FREDERICK A. PRAEGER, Publishers
New York · Washington · London

The purpose of the Praeger Special Studies is to make specialized research monographs in U.S. and international economics and politics available to the academic, business, and government communities. For further information, write to the Special Projects Division, Frederick A. Praeger, Publishers, 111 Fourth Avenue, New York, N.Y. 10003.

FREDERICK A. PRAEGER, PUBLISHERS
111 Fourth Avenue, New York, N.Y. 10003, U.S.A.
77-79 Charlotte Street, London W.1, England

Published in the United States of America in 1968
by Frederick A. Praeger, Inc., Publishers

© 1968 by Magdi M. El-Kammash

Library of Congress Catalog Card Number: 68-14158

Printed in the United States of America

To My Mother
and the Memory of
My Father

FOREWORD

This study is about economic planning and the progress of economic development in Egypt. The author suggests that one or the other or both of two relative shortages retard economic development, a relative shortage of productive factors, or a relative shortage of aggregate demand. One is left with two impressions, however, that a shortage of inputs is overriding, and that Egypt's longer-run as well as its short-run economic future turns on whether its population ceases to grow.

Let us consider the agricultural prospect, discussed in Chapters 2 and 9. W. A. Lewis has observed that the "overall rate of growth achievable in an underdeveloped economy depends primarily on what happens to its agriculture." This statement implicitly points up the difficulties faced in Egypt where current per capita calorific deficiency has been put at about 8 per cent. First, even given additional water for irrigation, the augmentability of cultivable land is limited. In fact, it is unlikely, given current population growth, that the per capita availability of cropland will increase, even as a result of completion of the Aswan High Dam in 1973. Second, it will not be easy to continue to increase yields per acre greatly, since some yields already approximate high Japanese levels. Third, the acreage available for food production is limited, since cotton, the source of over one-half the nation's foreign exchange, occupies about one-third of the cultivable acreage. Fourth, since agricultural and related shipments account for more than four-fifths of Egypt's export values, nonagricultural shipments are not currently capable of easing Egypt's current shortage of food grains. In the recent past shortage has been averted only through the food imports provided under the United States Public Law 480 programs.

Egypt's nonagricultural resource-structure reflects very limited productive potential, the author reports (Chapter 2). Exploitation of such potential as exists has only recently been effectively encouraged. Population growth, in excess of 2 per cent per year, steadily increases the pressure of numbers upon this limited resource-structure just as it increases pressure upon the limited stock of cultivable land.

Is Egypt capable of substituting capital equipment and human skill, together with applied science, for land and resources and thus easing its shortage of land and other natural resources? The statistical data assembled by Dr. El-Kammash are not very conducive to optimism. Although investment is reported as approximating 15 per cent of national income, per capita real income has risen only about 10 per cent since 1950. Moreover, the occupational structure was not markedly different in 1960 from what it had been in 1927; only public employment seems to have risen notably. Literacy has increased appreciably since 1950, however, as has the fraction of the population located in urban centers where it is easier to acquire literacy. Enrollment in educational institutions has increased much faster than population, though perhaps with too little emphasis upon secondary education and too much upon university education. Moreover, too few of those graduating from institutions of higher education are specializing in such areas as science and engineering.

Egypt's capacity to draw on external sources for products and capital is limited. Its balance of trade is quite unfavorable, with growth of exports currently limited by the growth of its agriculture. In the 1950's foreign loans, aid, etc., approximated 8 per cent of Egypt's income. Yet, as noted above, average income grew very slowly in this interval. That foreign funds will continue to flow in at this rate is doubtful.

The student of the Egyptian economy finds himself pressed to the conclusion that, unless population control becomes very effective very shortly, average income will persist at low levels. Up to now, however, little evidence of such impending control is manifest.

Other than demographic factors play roles in the Egyptian economy, as Dr. El-Kammash shows. They do not, however, outweigh the combined influence of a high rate of population growth and a relatively inexpandible natural-resource equipment. Economic planning must, therefore, aim at halting Egypt's population growth. Even then, average output will grow slowly unless free enterprise is given greater scope and political barriers to growth are dissolved.

The present study furnishes an informative background for the assessment of Egypt's conditional economic prospect.

Duke University   Joseph J. Spengler
Durham, North Carolina

PREFACE

This book is a revised and updated version of my Ph.D. dissertation, which was submitted to Duke University in the fall of 1965. It was written under the supervision of Professor Frank A. Hanna, to whom I am immeasurably indebted for all his help and advice in completing the study. I am also extremely grateful for the assistance I received from Professors Calvin B. Hoover and Robert Smith during my years of graduate study at Duke University.

Professor Joseph J. Spengler, who kindly wrote the foreword, read an early draft of the book. I sincerely appreciate his criticism and helpful comments, on which most of the revision was based. In addition, several of my colleagues at North Carolina State University reviewed portions of the manuscript and were kind enough to give me the benefit of their comments. Particular thanks are due Ernst W. Swanson for his scholarly criticism of the entire manuscript. Needless to say, responsibility for the final product is mine.

I wish to express my gratitude to my colleagues C. E. Bishop, former chairman of the Department of Economics, and W. D. Toussaint, present chairman, for putting at my disposal the many talents and resources of the department to help in producing the final typescript. Particular thanks are due Mrs. Sylvia Edwards and Miss Carol Cook for the typing, Mrs. Teddy Kovac and Harry Daniel for drafting and producing the charts and figures, and Miss Ruth Good for editing. Thanks also are due Mrs. Harriet Pasqualone for typing the final corrections.

Above all, I am indebted to my wife, Gloria. She worked with me during the difficult task of finishing the book and attended to all of the details of proofreading and indexing. I want to thank her for her marvelous patience, support, and help.

Oxford University   Magdi M. El-Kammash
December, 1967

CONTENTS

PART II.   SOME ASPECTS OF DEVELOPMENT
OF THE EGYPTIAN ECONOMY

LIST OF TABLES

LIST OF FIGURES

PART I

THE FRAMEWORK OF THE STUDY

CHAPTER 1 INTRODUCTION

The nineteenth century witnessed a marked contrast among the rates of economic development of the different regions of the world. While countries such as the United States, the United Kingdom, and Germany made rapid strides in development, large areas of the world remained in a condition of relative economic stagnation. During the twentieth century the gap widened progressively. In fact, the disparities in the standards of living between developed and underdeveloped areas continued to increase until now two-thirds of the world's population receive less than one-sixth of world income.

ECONOMIC DEVELOPMENT

This disparity in the rates of growth has provoked a great deal of discussion in recent economic literature. In fact, the question of development and growth has become crucial to all countries, developed as well as underdeveloped. While the latter are obviously concerned with launching their programs of development, the highly developed countries are interested in maintaining or increasing their rates of growth. It should be noted that we differentiate here between "growth" and "development." "Economic growth" is associated with a rise or an increase in some economic quantity, while "economic development" implies change. Thus "development" means a considerable structural change in the economy, while "growth" could take

1

place without such change. In other words, development implies growth but not the other way around. As Byé argues, developed countries are capable of strong growth with little structural change, while modest growth in underdeveloped countries is only possible by means of considerable structural change.[1]

There has, of course, been a great deal of theoretical work dealing with development, most of it based on the experience of the already developed countries. There is, however, a tendency for economists concerned with development to think that the underdeveloped countries of today pose a problem quite different in nature from that which existed in the predevelopment periods of some of the presently advanced economies. While it is true that the problem in both cases is basically one of development, it exerts itself diversely in each type of economic situation. These differences are results of varying characteristics, structures, and environments, all of which in some way influence the process of development. Because of these differences, the course of development which existing underdeveloped countries must undergo, if nowadays subjected to development programs, will no doubt be different from the process of development that took place in the nineteenth century in those countries which are now industrially developed.

As a case in point, take the role of technological advancement in economic development in the nineteenth century. Development in the industrially advanced countries took place in large part as a result of the introduction of innovations, new techniques, and products. In the now underdeveloped countries the emphasis will be on adaptation rather than on the creation of new techniques and innovations. That is to say, development in these countries will proceed, not only by the way of new techniques and innovations, but principally through the adoption of already established ones. Thus, in analyzing development, though the main focus is on the special problems of the region in question, both the degree of advancement of the already advanced countries and the general state of technology must not be overlooked or even minimized.

Although the problem of maintaining the rates of growth in the industrially developed countries is quite vital, this work concerns itself only with one of those areas which are called "underdeveloped" countries (sometimes "backward" or "poor" countries). These countries are generally characterized by low levels of per capita income and a phenomenal rate of population growth. Moreover, there is little incentive to invest capital in the introduction of the modern efficient methods of large-scale production because of the low levels of income. When income is low, the demand for goods and services is too small to make any large-scale operation profitable, thus limiting the size of the market.

These and many other factors have combined to keep the economies of these countries in a low-level equilibrium state--that is, trapped in the vicious circle of poverty. Scattered efforts in the past have failed in most cases to break the economic deadlocks found in these countries. These failures have directed the attention of many economists to an investigation of whether the underdeveloped countries are capable of initiating development, under what circumstances and through what mechanism. Two principal lines of thought are apparent in these approaches: First, there are those economists who stress the role of the relatively deficient supply of productive factors in the underdeveloped economies; second, there are those economists who feel that they have found the key to the problem on the side of aggregate demand.

APPROACHES TO DEVELOPMENT

Actually a great deal of the thought on underdeveloped countries is concerned with the supply side of the problem, that is, with the deficiency or lack of certain factors of production which are considered strategic to the process of development. It is said that the lack of capital and the lack of technical knowledge in underdeveloped countries are the two chief impediments to accelerating development. An increase in the supply of these factors would help underdeveloped countries initiate development and convert their stationary economies into dynamic systems, possibly capable of self-generating expansion.

The supply approach to economic development finds its origins in the writings of the classical and neoclassical economists such as Smith,[2] Mill,[3] and Marshall.[4] Though no formal theory of development may be found in their writings, they introduced the basic concepts. It was not until 1928 that the supply approach was revised by Allyn Young in his well-known article[5] in which he coupled Smith's "division of labor and the extent of the market" with Marshall's "external economies." His main conclusion was that division of labor depends on the extent of the market, but the extent of the market depends upon the division of labor.

The supply approach to economic development has been advocated recently by several outstanding economists. Careful analysis, however, shows that in many cases they really argue vehemently in favor of a single aspect of the problem. This approach results in the "big push," "balanced growth," or "minimum effort" thesis, such as we find in the writings of Rosenstein-Rodan,[6] Nurkse,[7] and Leibenstein,[8] respectively. On the other hand, the supply approach has been attacked by other economists, such as Fleming,[9] Hirschman,[10] and Singer.[11] They elect to look at the problem from its demand side, and consider the deficiency in demand as the main obstacle to development. It should be noted that in most cases advocates of the demand approach took the defensive side and concentrated mainly on critically analyzing the supply approach. This gave rise to the unbalanced growth doctrine. Advocates of the supply approach generally accept the thesis which implies that in order for underdeveloped countries to break the vicious circle and to escape the low-level equilibrium, a big "balanced push" is needed. This "big balanced push," which cannot be below a "minimum quantum of investment," is required to get these economies off the ground in the initial stage of development. Once they break the deadlock, growth will become self-sustaining. This is very well illustrated by a statement to be found in a paper presented to a special Senate Committee to study the foreign aid program. "...launching a country into self-sustaining growth is a little like getting an airplane off the ground. There is a critical ground speed which must be passed before the craft becomes airborne; to taxi up and down the runway at lower speeds is a waste of gasoline. Debate is possible as to precisely what level of aid is required to get a country over this minimum of threshold. We suspect that for many countries it is above recent levels of development assistance."[12]

THE PROBLEM STATED

The question to be posed here is: What are the factors which, if mobilized, will set the economy on its development path? Is it a lack of effective demand that results from low levels of income and productivity? Or does the problem lie on the supply side as represented by the deficiency or shortage in some factor supply such as capital, labor, and entrepreneurship? A third alternative may be offered--that the shortage in the supply of certain productive factors acts to produce a low level of income which in turn limits the size of effective demand. Thus there is no more room for improvement in the quantity or quality of productive resources, and income is kept at a low-level equilibrium. In other words, we have here a case of a supply-demand vicious circle.

It is true that each underdeveloped economy has its own problems which stem from the nature of the country, its economic structure, political organizations, and social institutions. A close examination of such economies should reveal some of the underlying factors behind the process of development of these countries. Moreover, such factors are common, if not

to all, to most of them, even though these factors may
manifest themselves in different forms. However, this
study will not attempt to undertake such a tremendous
task. We propose rather to analyze the economy of a
single underdeveloped country which in recent years
has embarked on a course of development. An analysis
of the two contrasting periods which this country has
experienced, its underdeveloped period and the developing period, should shed light on the factors that
have been mobilized in order to start the economy on
its upward path. The case to be analyzed is the economy of Egypt. Egypt is formally known now as the United Arab Republic. The name United Arab Republic came
into being with the union between Egypt and Syria in
1958. From this date the U.A.R. consisted of two regions: The Egyptian region or the southern region
(formerly Egypt) and the Syrian region or the northern
region (formerly Syria). However, after the unity was
dissolved in 1961, the name U.A.R. was reserved for
Egypt. Throughout this study, the name Egypt will be
used since we are concerned with the Egyptian region.

By one classification scheme, Egypt was an underdeveloped country during the first half of the
twentieth century.[13] With the beginning of the second
half of the century, the country entered another stage
of its political and economic life; this stage has
brought it more sharply into world focus. After the
Revolution of 1952, a monarchy which had lasted over a
century was replaced by a republic. Besides major political reforms, efforts to change the economic and
social structure of the country were begun and these
have been continued. To be sure, during the years
following the 1952 Revolution these actions and plans
were not given any systematic form. Beginning in 1959
and 1960, however, economic development took the form
of a ten-year plan to be executed in two five-year
phases.

In this study, we propose to examine some
structural aspects of the Egyptian economy, such as
population, resources, and basic patterns of economic
organization. An analysis of the development process

in Egypt will be provided. In analyzing the process up
to 1950, we shall be mainly concerned with the salient
factors in the economy during that period and ask
whether they retarded its development. Moreover, emphasis will be placed on the factors which contributed
to the development of the 1950's.   The transformation
of the traditional and mainly subsistence economy to a
modern economy constitutes a basic characteristic of
economic development in Egypt.   In other words, the
Egyptian economy is to be analyzed in the light of
some of the theories of development advanced by contemporary economists, and in particular those advoca-
ting the supply approach to economic development.

The supply approach to economic development
offers a useful conceptual framework by means of which
the generalization derived from the experience of the
developing nations may find its place.   In order to
formulate a tentative hypothesis, three factors of
economies which contribute a great deal to the process
of development have been chosen as the core of the
analysis.   These three factors are:

(1) Increasing returns accrue to the firm as
it and the industrial system as a whole grow in size.

(2) Since inducement to invest is limited by
the size of the market, certain economies may be reaped
from a scheme of "balanced development."

(3) Most underdeveloped economies lack "social overhead facilities" which are held to be a prerequisite to development in general and to the industrial sector in particular.   They tend to render the
cost of creating new industries or expanding the existing ones less costly and thus more feasible.

In analyzing the process of development of the
Egyptian economy, emphasis will be placed on the role
of these three factors in accelerating the rate of
growth during the second half of the twentieth century.   To validate the hypothesis about the supply

approach, such international comparisons will be entered into the analysis as may be needed. It should be noted that the model presented above is consciously derived from the Egyptian experience and is built to serve the Egyptian case, although it is hoped to have wider application and hopefully more general value. No model can be expected to be equally relevant to all cases.

External capital is an integral part of the supply approach to economic development of underdeveloped countries. The Egyptian economy has been subjected to several political changes that interfered with its flow of external capital. Thus, in addition to analyzing investment allocation and priorities both during the development and the planning periods, the role of external capital in the development of the Egyptian economy will be examined. An attempt will also be made to estimate the growth of the economy in the absence of external capital.

The transformation of an underdeveloped economy into a rapidly growing one introduces certain arguments about the role of the state in economic development. As Spengler writes, "Economic growth is influenced indirectly, on the whole rather than directly by a society's social structure and its apparatus of state."[14] Mason also refers to the role of the state in economic development. His argument is based on the early experience of the United States.[15] Also using the American experience in development in the early nineteenth century, Nurkse emphasized the place of government activity on the investment side particularly in the building of social overhead facilities.[16] Thus we find that an evaluation of the role of the state in the development of the Egyptian economy is indispensable especially when the domain of the public sector has been expanding to include major economic activities. The drive toward "Socialism" which is stated explicitly in the 1958 Constitution has changed the economy into a mixed private-government economy. While foreign trade, basic industries, and transportation fall in the domain of the public sector, retail trade, agriculture, small-scale industry, and professions are still in private hands.

METHODOLOGY

The present study is intended to be both theoretical and empirical. The theoretical discussions are bound by the practical situations prevailing in underdeveloped areas. In fact, development of underdeveloped countries is treated as a special case in the general theory of growth. Such an approach takes into account the special characteristics of underdeveloped economies. It will obviously be necessary to use statistical data from both developed and underdeveloped countries. Though our chief concern is with the Egyptian economy, comparisons with other developed and underdeveloped countries will be used as a frame of reference.

Naturally it would have been extremely helpful if statistical data had been available whenever needed. Unfortunately, this is seldom the case with underdeveloped countries. All too often, inadequacy of statistical information for many underdeveloped countries places severe limitation on analysis. Much of the existing data are scanty, a fact which renders the limits of error, at best, very wide. For this study, the data needed for analysis or comparison will be obtained from a sample of countries representing the underdeveloped regions of the world--that is, the geographical distribution of underdeveloped countries over all the world. The availability of statistical information will be given priority in deciding upon which countries should be included in the sample. Consequently, the lack of complete data does not necessarily invalidate the generality of the indexes and models to be constructed or the comparisons to be made.

Development is a complex process which depends on human assets and human behavior as much as on natural resources. Social, religious, and political institutions certainly have implication for the process of development in a given area and they,too, must have a place in our economic analysis.[17] In this study, I shall consider the roles played by such institutions in the development of a country, particularly when they are subject to a certain degree of quantification. Moreover, the economist's observations (especially if he identifies himself psychologically and politically with the region under consideration) have a place in economic analysis and certainly should be drawn upon and used where applicable. While the theory should be as objective as possible, such observations can be used in formulating and supporting the arguments.

Because of the unreliable nature of the data available and because of the inaccuracy and the wide margin of error involved in collecting such data, we shall not resort to any rigorous statistical techniques in analyzing them. The results of such statistical tests cannot, at best, be more accurate than the data used in them. Therefore, most of the statistical analysis in this work will draw on the nonparametric method. A concerted attempt will be made to adapt it to economic data.

Notes to Chapter 1

[1]See Maurice Byé, "The Role of Capital in Economic Development," in Howard S. Ellis (ed.), _Economic Development for Latin America_ (New York: St. Martin's Press, 1961), p. 110.

[2]Smith considered the process of development and growth as one determined mainly by the increasing specialization and widening of the market. Adam Smith, _An Inquiry into the Nature and Causes of the Wealth of Nations,_ Cannan's Edition (New York: Random House, 1937), pp. 2, 3, 16, 17, 259.

[3]J. S. Mill had the nucleus of a theory of underdevelopment--or backwardness--with the deficiency

in capital accumulation as its cornerstone. While not underestimating the importance of social overhead costs in development he stressed the role played by the extent of the market. John Stuart Mill, Principles of Political Economy, 5th London Edition (New York: D. Appleton and Co., 1872) I, 13, 218, 237, 242-44, 250.

[4]In addition to introducing the concept of economies, both internal and external, Marshall discussed the role of improved transport on the extent of the market. Alfred Marshall, Principles of Economics, 8th Edition (New York: The Macmillan Co., 1948) Book IV, especially Chapters VIII, IX, X and XI. Also his Industry and Trade (London: Macmillan Co., Ltd., 1919), pp. 6-8 and 35-39. For an analysis of Marshall's generalized but historical approach and the influence of the German Historical School and his philosophical background on his approach to development see, A. J. Youngson, "Marshall on Economic Growth," Scottish Journal of Political Economy, III (February, 1956), 1-18.

[5]Allyn A. Young, "Increasing Returns and Economic Progress," Economic Journal, XXXVIII (December, 1928), 527-42.

[6]P. N. Rosenstein-Rodan, "Problems of Industrialization of Eastern and South-Eastern Europe," Economic Journal, LIII (June-September, 1943), 202-211.

[7]Ragnar Nurkse, Problems of Capital Formation in Underdeveloped Countries (Oxford: Basil Blackwell, 1953).

[8]Harvey Leibenstein, Economic Backwardness and Economic Growth (New York: John Wiley and Sons, 1957).

[9]J. Marcus Fleming, "External Economies and the Doctrine of Balanced Growth," Economic Journal, LXV (June, 1955), 246. Reprinted in A. N. Agarwala and S. P. Singh (eds.), The Economics of Underdevelopment (Bombay: Oxford University Press, 1958), pp. 272-94.

[10]Albert O. Hirschman, The Strategy of Economic Development (New Haven: Yale University Press, 1961).

[11]Hans Singer, "The Concept of Balanced Growth and Economic Development: Theory and Practice," in Eastin Nelson (ed.), Economic Growth (Austin: University of Texas Press, 1960), pp. 71-86.

[12]Center for International Studies, Massachusetts Institute of Technology, The Objectives of United States Economic Assistance Program (Washington, 1957), p. 70.

[13]Magdi M. El-Kammash, "On the Measurement of Economic Development Using Scalogram Analysis," Papers and Proceedings, Regional Science Association, XI (1963), pp. 309-334.

[14]Joseph J. Spengler, "Social Structure, the State, and Economic Growth," in Simon Kuznets, Wilbert E. Moore, and Joseph J. Spengler (eds.), Economic Growth, Brazil, India, Japan (Durham, North Carolina: Duke University Press, 1955), p. 364; also see his "The State and Economic Growth: Summary and Interpretation," in Hugh G. J. Aitken, The State and Economic Growth (New York: Social Science Research Council, 1959), pp. 353-382.

[15]Edward S. Mason, "The Role of Government in Economic Development," papers and proceedings of the Seventy-Second Meeting of the American Economic Association, American Economic Review, L (May, 1960), 636-641.

[16]Nurkse, op. cit., pp. 152-154.

[17]For a detailed discussion of the role of these factors in development, see Joseph J. Spengler, "Theory, Ideology, Non-Economic Values, and Politico-Economic Development," in Ralph Briabanti and Joseph J. Spengler (eds.), Tradition, Values and Socio-Economic Development (Durham, North Carolina: Duke University Press, 1961), pp. 3-56.

2

THE BACKGROUND
OF THE ECONOMY

Egypt is situated in the northern part of the African continent. Its area of a little over one-third of a million square miles is bounded on the north by the Mediterranean, on the south by the Republic of Sudan, on the west by the Libyan desert, and on the east by the Red Sea. This geographical situation at the junction of three continents (Europe, Asia, and Africa) which comprised the old world made her the object of the large colonial powers bent on conquest. While Egypt was a part of the Turkish Empire, she was occupied by the British in 1882. This was done under the pretext of saving the ruling dynasty and restoring the Sultan's authority. Actually, the British interest was to gain control of the most vital waterway in the world and the shortest route for trade between Europe and the Far East--the Suez Canal.

GENERAL CHARACTERISTICS

The Nile River, the second largest river in the world, measuring approximately 4163 miles, has its main source in Lake Victoria. It branches at Cairo into two parts which form the fertile area of the Delta. Thus, Egypt, by its nature, became an agricultural economy, depending largely on the Nile as the main source of water for irrigation. Agricultural development was enhanced in the beginning of the nineteenth century by the introduction of cotton planting by the French. Since that time the Egyptian economy has been an

13

agrarian one, with cotton the principal crop and the major component of national output.

Geographically, Egypt consists of five main parts: the Delta, the Nile Valley, the Eastern Desert, the Western Desert, and the Sinai Peninsula. Although the area of Egypt is 386,870 square miles (one million square kilometers),only a small fraction is inhabited. The inhabited areas are restricted to those which have access to water supply and, as a result, the people are crowded into that thin green ribbon of Nile watered land and its fertile Delta which has produced Egypt's food since the dawn of history. This picture can be seen clearly from Figure 1 which shows a map of the cultivated areas in Egypt. There is also some cultivation in the oasis to the west of the Nile. However, this is carried on on a small scale and depends on irrigation from underground water by primitive methods. In addition, the lack of means of transportation makes it isolated from the rest of the country.

The increase in population and the increase in arable land has not been proportionate. The inhabited areas for the period 1937-60 rose by only about 3 per cent. With the tremendous population increase from 16 to 25 million during the same period, the density of population increased by almost 69 per cent. The cultivated areas, which are the source of income for the majority of the population, increased only by about 10 per cent in the same period. Without industry to absorb the increase in population, this imbalance in growth led to disguised unemployment and low productivity of farm workers. It also reduced the per capita share of the limited services available, such as health and education, which in turn reduced productivity and depressed the level of income even further. According to United Nations estimates, annual average per capita national product for the period 1952-54 was only $120[1] For purposes of comparison, Table 1 shows average per capita national product for selected countries during the period 1952-54. Egypt's per capita national product of $120 is less than one-tenth that of Canada, Switzerland, New Zealand and

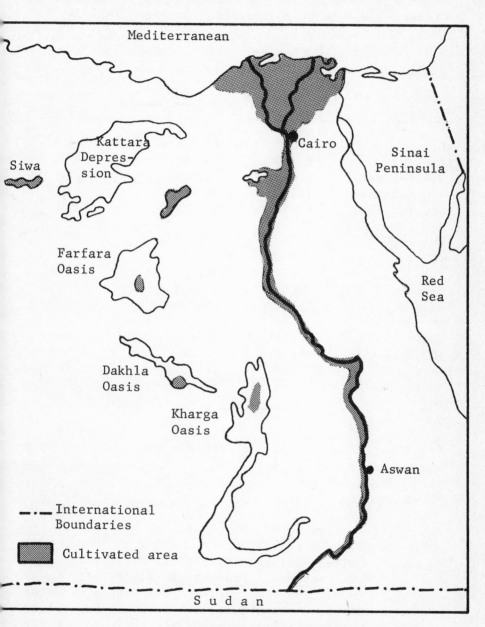

FIGURE 1.   CULTIVATED AREAS IN EGYPT

Table 1. Per Capita National Product of Selected
Countries, in U. S. Dollars (Average 1952-54)[a]

Country	Per capita national product	Country	Per capita national product
U.S.A.	1,870	Argentina	460
Canada	1,310	Puerto Rico	430
Switzerland	1,010	Austria	370
New Zealand	1,000	Malaya	310
Australia	950	S. Africa[c]	300
Luxembourg	890	Colombia	250
Belgium	800	Brazil	230
U.K.	780	Mexico	220
Denmark	750	Turkey	210
France	740	Guatemala	160
Norway	740	Egypt	120
Finland	670	Ceylon	110
Germany[b]	510	Pakistan	70
Netherlands	500	India	60

[a]Simple arithmetic mean of annual per capita product
estimates.

[b]West Germany

[c]Union of S. Africa

Sources: United Nations, Statistical Office, Per Cap-
         ita National Product of Fifty-Five Coun-
         tries, 1952-54, Statistical Papers, Series
         E, No. 4 (New York, 1957), pp. 8-9; United
         Nations, Statistical Office, National and Per
         Capita Income, Seventy Countries, 1949, Sta-
         tistical Papers, Series E, No. 1 (New York,
         1950), pp. 14-16.

the United States, whose averages are over $1,000. Compared with some countries which are in the process of development, such as Argentina, Malaya, Union of South Africa, Turkey, and Puerto Rico, per capita national product of Egypt is still very low, amounting to a little over one-third the average for these countries. This shows the wide gap which existed between Egypt and some of the other countries at the turn of the second half of the twentieth century, and gives an indication of the magnitude of development needed to raise per capita income to a level comparable to the more developed nations.

It was observed that the most densely populated areas are those around the Delta and the Nile River where agriculture, the dominant industry, makes use of water from the Nile.[2] Actually, a large part of the land in Egypt is desert where life rarely exists except for the nomad Arabs who settle in the oases along the Mediterranean, the Red Sea, in Sinai Peninsula, and the Western Desert. The number of these nomad Arabs is negligible. According to the 1937 census they counted to only 12,000 and in 1947 they numbered 55,037. The truly inhabited area of Egypt consists of the narrow strip of land which extends on both sides of the River Nile and its Delta, called the Nile Valley. The area of Egypt, excluding deserts, which can be called the inhabited area was 13,205 square miles in 1937. This increased to 13,668 square miles by 1960, an increase of only 3.5 per cent during a period of a quarter of a century. In 1960, the inhabited area amounted only to 3.5 per cent of the total land area.

In spite of the smallness of the inhabited area, the fertile land on which cultivation is feasible is still smaller. Table 2 shows the cultivated area, population density per square mile of cultivated area, crop surface, and the ratio of crop surface to cultivated area during the period 1882-1960. The cultivated area, which was 7,708 square miles in 1882, amounted then to only 2 per cent of the total area of Egypt. By 1960, it had increased by 22.8 per cent to 9,467 square miles, or what amounted to 2.4 per cent of the total

Table 2. Cultivated Area, Crop Surface, and Population Density of Egypt (1882-1960)

| Year | Cultivated area | | Crop surface | | Ratio of crop surface to cultivated area |
	Square miles	Pop. density[a]	Square miles	Pop. density[a]	
1882	7,708	870	7,718	869	1.00
1897	8,008	1,203	9,997[b]	964	1.25
1907	8,753	1,278	12,412	902	1.42
1917	8,617	1,476	12,813[b]	993	1.49
1927	8,981	1,579	14,031	1,010	1.56
1937	8,555	1,861	13,540	1,176	1.58
1947	9,333	2,032	14,851	1,277	1.59
1960	9,467	2,755	16,680	1,564	1.76

[a]Number of people per square mile.

[b]Estimated by interpolating from the ratios of crop surface to cultivated area for the years 1882,1907,and 1927.

Sources: Calculated from Egyptian Federation of Industries,Yearbook 1950-51 (Cairo: S.O.P. Press, 1956); Central Committee for Statistics, Collection of Basic Statistics (Cairo: S.O.P. Press, 1962), pp. 20-21; El-Shafie, M. Ahmed, "Population Pressure on Land and the Problem of Capital Accumulation in Egypt," unpublished Ph.D. dissertation, The University of Wisconsin, 1951.

area of Egypt. From this trend it can be seen that the process of land reclamation was very slow during the period 1882-1960. The major reason for this slow development is that cultivation depends entirely on irrigation from the Nile, and is thus limited by the

amount of water that can reach the land by the canals
and other expansions in the irrigation system.

During the last quarter of the nineteenth century Egyptian agriculture followed a one-crop-a-year
system. Cultivation, which naturally depends on irrigation from the Nile, was only feasible once a year.
By the turn of the century, however, several improvements were introduced: reservoirs on the Nile, canals
and drainage facilities, and extensive control of flood
waters. This made possible the cultivation of one more
crop on a given piece of land a year. In itself, this
improvement is considered equivalent to an increase in
the cultivated area. In other words, we may define a
crop surface as distinguished from the cultivated
area. The former is the total area cultivated during
the different seasons of the year. From Table 2 it can
be seen that since the turn of the century the crop
surface averaged around 50 per cent more than the cultivated area, but with an upward trend. While the cultivated area increased by one-fourth during the period
1882-1960, crop surface more than doubled during the
same period.

Now, we may compare population density in terms
of the cultivated area and the crop surface, for it
makes a significant difference which area is used in
the denominator. Population density per square mile of
cultivated area was 870 in 1882, but the density more
than tripled by 1960 to 2755 per square mile, as a result of the population pressure with no corresponding
increase in land. Since about 99 per cent of the Egyptian population lives in the Nile Valley, that is, the
cultivated area, and since more than one crop can be
cultivated on the same piece of land in one year which
could be considered equivalent to the increase in the
cultivated area, crop surface might be used to obtain
the population density. This adjustment reduces the
otherwise large increase in population density that
would be obtained by using the cultivated area. Actually, the figures were not significantly different
during the last part of the nineteenth century. The
difference, however, becomes larger over time. In

1960, population density was 1564 per square mile of crop surface as compared with 2755 per square mile of cultivated area.

NATURAL RESOURCES

While Egypt is well endowed with human resources, it is far less endowed with natural resources. Apart from agricultural land, which is limited by the access to water available from the Nile for irrigation, resources are, indeed, extremely limited. Moreover, the resources available were not fully exploited until the development period.

It has been said repeatedly that Egypt is, by its nature, an agricultural country. However, if it were not for the water from the Nile, cultivation would have been impossible. The climate in Egypt falls into two distinct seasons : a winter from November to April and a summer from May to October. However, there is no climatic break between the two seasons, since there is no rainfall during the summer and, except for a small amount along the coast, practically none during the winter months. Thus cultivation depends solely on irrigation from the River Nile and is practiced under the threat of seasonal floods that come between July and December. Then the average rise in the level of the river registers 25 feet at Aswan and 15 feet at Cairo. The rest of the country is barren desert where cultivation is impossible except where occasionally underground water is available.

Egypt does not have any waterfalls to facilitate the generation of the hydro-electric power. On the other hand, it is moderately endowed with alternative resources for power, such as oil. Table 3 shows the production of crude oil, gasoline, kerosene, and heavy oils for selected years during the period 1938-52. The production of crude oil only doubled during the ten-year period of 1942-52. The same moderate increase could be observed with respect to the production of petroleum products. However, the production of

Table 3. Production of Petroleum
and Petroleum Products, 1938-52

Year	Crude oil	Gasoline	Kerosene	Heavy oils[a]
		(Thousand metric tons)		
1938	[b]	95	18	168
1939	[b]	105	52	387
1940	[b]	130	71	519
1941	[b]	157	61	800
1942	1162	167	58	712
1943	1278	170	61	725
1944	1347	186	66	844
1945	1341	176	68	737
1946	1278	196	67	762
1947	1332	198	72	772
1948	1889	194	94	1347
1949	2266	213	119	1626
1950	2349	195	151	1761
1951	2358	208	210	1715
1952	2352	189	219	1843

[a]Consists of diesel and fuel oil.

[b]Not available.

Sources: Department of Statistics and Census, Annuaire Statistique 1959 (Cairo: Government Press, 1960); Central Committee for Statistics, Collection of Basic Statistics (Cairo: S.O.P. Press, 1962), pp. 98-100; Egyptian Federation of Industries, Yearbook 1955-56 (Cairo: S.O.P. Press, 1956), pp. 322-23.

gasoline, kerosene, and heavy oils fell short of consumption during the period, necessitating importation
of these products and imposing a limitation on industrialization. In 1946, production of gasoline, which
amounted to 196,000 metric tons, exceeded a consumption of only 189,000.[3] Beginning in 1947, consumption
exceeded production by a small amount until in 1952
domestic production could meet only 77 per cent of
consumption needs.

Due to the deficiency in the supply of electric power, kerosene was widely used for household
purposes in addition to its use in some light industries. Thus in 1946 we find that production amounted
to 17 per cent of consumption, and as production increased from 67,000 to 219,000 metric tons during the
period 1946-52, consumption almost doubled, thus still
leaving a wide gap between consumption and production.[4] The situation was somewhat better with respect
to heavy oils, which consisted of diesel and fuel oil.
Production was short of consumption until 1952 when it
began to catch up with consumption.

Such a state of affairs is due mainly to government policy that considered most mining and extractive industries as strategic industries which were
dealt with under complete restriction. The result was
a number of laws and regulations which prolonged and
complicated the process of obtaining a permit for exploration or oil drilling, a matter that slowed down,
if not discouraged in most cases, the process of exploitation.

Since there was been no encouragement to drilling and mining, whether in the process of issuing the
permits, exploration, or exploitation, there has been a
decline in the number of companies in the process of
exploration from 13 to 9 by 1950.[5] The same trend can
be detected in the number of companies in the process
of exploitation, which dropped from 23 companies in
1945 to 21 by 1950.[6]

The same state of affairs could be observed in

Table 4. Production of Phosphate, Manganese,
Salt and Cement, Selected Years,1939-52

Year	Phosphate	Manganese	Salt	Cement
	(Thousand metric tons)			
1939	543	120	--	353
1945	349	--	9	444
1946	294	--	7	588
1947	371	--	46	648
1948	377	60	126	768
1949	350	139	364	889
1950	379	152	567	957
1951	501	155	607	1074
1952	527	195	498	947

Sources: Central Committee for Statistics, Collection
of Basic Statistics (Cairo: S.O.P. Press,
1962),pp. 98-100; Egyptian Federation of Industries, Yearbook 1952-53, and Yearbook
1953-54 (Cairo: S.O.P. Press, 1953, 1954);
Department of Statistics and Census, Ten
Years of Revolution, Statistical Atlas,
(Cairo: S.O.P. Press, 1962), Table 37.

the field of production of other raw materials such as
phosphate, manganese, salt, and cement. Table 4 shows
the production of these basic materials for selected
years during the period 1939-52 in thousands of metric
tons. The figures of this table indicate the stagnant
state of affairs that prevailed in mining. The production of phosphate declined considerably during the
period 1939-49,and while it started increasing in 1951
and 1952, it still remained below the 1939 level. The
production of manganese, which stopped during the period 1945-47, again began to increase and reached a
level of 195 thousand metric tons by 1952.

Egypt is endowed with several salt mines that stretch along the Mediterranean. Salt is an export commodity to the European markets, in addition to being a commodity with a considerable domestic demand. With practically no output during the years 1939-46, salt production began to increase, reaching a level of 498 thousand metric tons by 1952. The same trend took place with respect to cement, a commodity with a high domestic demand for the purpose of construction, in addition to being an export commodity to the neighboring Arab countries. The production of cement increased from 353,000 metric tons in 1939 to 947,000 by 1952. However, the production of these commodities would have expanded by higher percentages had the Egyptian government adopted a policy that would have provided the environment to render the entry in the industry less complicated.

The process of obtaining a permit to explore was under several governmental departments and agencies, a matter that prolonged the process and rendered it difficult. This discouraged several corporations from venturing in such an investment. On the other hand, the mining industry was subject to the same regulation as are other industries and without regard to the special circumstances that pertained to them. Mining industries are usually located in remote desert areas where living and transportation facilities are deficient. This was not taken into consideration in specifying the regulations governing these industries. Moreover, explosives, essential to mining operations, were under tight government control and the difficulty of obtaining them caused the mining industry to suffer.

With respect to competition, these industries were at a disadvantage. The passage fees through the Suez Canal were prohibitive. It was, however, the only available means of transportation. There was a lack of roads from the eastern desert where these industries are located adjacent to the Red Sea. This increased the cost considerably and rendered it impossible for these industries to compete in the American and European markets. Actually, the lack of roads and the deficiency in the means of transportation in general was an obstacle to exploiting the mines on the Gulf of Suez and along the Red Sea which are rich with iron, copper, and lead.

This situation was somewhat improved with the change that took place in the Mining and Quarrying Laws and Regulations in 1950. Although the passage fees through the Suez Canal were not reduced, the other changes which reduced the steps involved in obtaining the permits resulted in some encouragement to the industry, as can be seen from the 1951 figures in Table 4. However, such encouragement did not last long because of the War of Palestine, an affair that presented great obstacles to the industry because of its closeness to the war fields. Moreover, the political unrest prior to 1952 contributed to a general decline in industrial production.

EVOLUTION OF THE LAND TENURE SYSTEM IN EGYPT

As noted earlier, agriculture has been the major industry and the chief occupation in Egypt for centuries. It contributed more than 35 per cent of gross domestic product in 1954, besides absorbing more than half of the labor force.[7] It also constitutes a large part of the natural wealth. In 1945, two-thirds of the capital invested in Egypt was found in agriculture and particularly in agricultural land, per se.[8]

The dominance of agriculture as the chief occupation and the major source of income, coupled with the dependence on a single crop, cotton, has some important implications to development of the economy. In the first place, farming in Egypt has been characterized by two extremes of land ownership: numerous small holdings on the one hand and few larger estates at the other end of the spectrum. Small holdings sometimes render farming uneconomical. This diversity, in conjunction with the scarcity of capital and the low levels of income, puts the farmer at a competitive disadvantage in the money market. Furthermore, the dependence on the single crop, cotton, subjects the economy to wide fluctuations resulting from severe changes in prices and occasional failures in crop yield.

The wide disparities in land holdings are the result of the changes over time in the land tenure system since the early days. Actually, the developments in the land tenure system gave rise to the many characteristics that dominated the economy for decades.

Here a review of the historical developments in the land tenure system, and in particular the rights of private ownership, is in order. At the time of the Ottoman Empire, and following the conquest of Egypt by the Turks, Sultan Selim--ruler of the Turkish Empire-- claimed all the land as his personal property. Then he granted large estates to the soldiers who stood by him during the war. Such estates were called the "Riska" (Grants) and were given mainly to the "Mamelukes" (Princes) of Egypt who had absolute rights on such land.

As the Ottoman Empire grew weaker and began to have less control over its territories, the Mamelukes gradually took possession of the land. Eventually they broke away both from Cairo and Constantinople.[9] Amid such confusion, some Egyptian farmers seized the opportunity and took possession of the land they cultivated. This could be considered, for the first time, the beginning of land ownership in Egypt, although it did not last long. Tax receipts were considered documents of ownership. And during the seventeenth and eighteenth centuries the farmer could dispose of his property to his offsprings through inheritance, a form of prima geniture. In fact, the farmer gradually acquired the right to dispose of his property by selling it after informing the tax collector, who was called "Moultazim," about such a transaction. The Moultazims, who were responsible for collection of land tax on an area which consisted of a number of villages, were allowed a tax-free land called "Wissiya." In addition, the Moultazims had the right to recruit farmers from

their area to work on their land free. All these privileges were handed from father to son.[10]

The third type of land possession that existed
under the Turkish Rule is the "Wakf" land. This is
tax-free land established for the use of religious
foundations. The revenue from this land was allocated
for the perpetual benefit of either charitable organizations or individuals. This type of land could not be
alienated and the government had no power over it.

When Mohamed Ali came into power in 1805,[11] he
found that the land tenure system in general and the
"Iltzam" or tax collection system in particular represented an obstacle to his development plans for the
country. Thus in 1808, he proceeded by requesting the
Moultazims to give an estimate of the annual return on
their operations. Being suspicious that Mohamed Ali
might tax their profits, they gave the lowest possible
estimate. When the ruler received their estimates, he
abolished the Iltzam system and compensated the Moultazims by granting them a lifetime pension, based on
their own estimates of their profits. And the government took over the function of collecting taxes for
the first time.

The Wissiya land, which was the tax-free land
of the Moultazims, was left in their hands to be exploited during their lifetime; also it remained exempt
from taxes. The land was to go to the government following the person's death. However, when the Mamelukes
were completely defeated in 1811, their private estates,as well as the Wissiya land in Upper Egypt, were
confiscated. All these were the initial steps toward
accomplishing Mohamed Ali's goal, that is, to become
the sole owner of practically all the land in Egypt.
In addition, the government took over the "Wakf" land
to manage and granted a monetary compensation to the
previous managers.

Starting in 1813, Mohamed Ali ordered a survey
of all agricultural land. He then had traced the

borders of each village and divided the areas of villages into plots. According to D'jabarti, "...in the
...year 1229 Higry[12] (1813 A.D.) he (Mohamed Ali)
started surveying the land. This caused many farmers
and peasants to flee, leaving behind their homes and
fields; at harvest time nobody could be found to ex-
ecute the orders of the state in this respect."[13]   In
the same year he published a Decree according to which
he became the sole owner of the land throughout the
country. Mohamed Ali followed this by dividing the
land among the farmers in plots ranging from three to
five acres. About 4 per cent of the land of the village was given to the Shiekh of the village (the en-
derman) tax-free in return for his official duties.
The manner in which Mohamed Ali administered the land
can best be seen from an account of the period by Amin
Samy:

> In 1241 Higry (1825 A.D.) Mohamed Ali di-
> vided the country into new provinces in-
> tended to encourage progress and the devel-
> opment of agriculture. But as he detected a
> certain derelection of duty on the part of
> "Mamours" (administrative agents) in some
> parts of the country, particularly their
> failure to supervise properly the cultiva-
> tion of new imported crops, he decided to
> visit all parts of the country himself. He
> threatened to gather all the government of-
> ficials of any area in which he might find
> traces of negligence, and order the digging
> of a big ditch to bury them all alive.[14]

Mohamed Ali exercised also a great deal of
control over the cultivation of land. "...during 1231
Higry (1815 A.D.) the Pasha (Mohamed Ali) seized the
crops of farms belonging to the peasants who were paying land tax...he fixed prices for the crops...but
when they wanted to retain a portion of the crops,
they had to buy them back at higher fixed prices."[15]
Actually, the farmer was financed by the government
who provided him with all the inputs needed for production,such as livestock,seeds,tools, and fertilizers

needed to cultivate the crops designed by the government. The farmer was not allowed to sell the yield from his land, but rather, he had to deliver it to the State Grainaries where it was evaluated at the prices fixed by the government. After deducting the land tax, as well as all the expenses advanced to the farmer during the season, the rest constituted the return to the farmer. This portion, however, was not usually handed to the farmers in the form of money but instead was paid to them in terms of state bonds. A portion of these bonds was ordinarily withheld as an advance towards payments of the taxes due during the coming year. If, after all the deductions, there was still something due to the farmer, it was paid in kind from the surplus products of the state at prices higher than those at which they sold their crops to the government.

It can be seen from this brief historical treatment that Mohamed Ali's schemes did not provide the rights of private ownership, although it was a first step. It is true that the farmer's name was inscribed on the official registers, but that did not really mean ownership since the ownership of all the land was vested in the government. The farmer had no right to dispose of his land by sale or mortgage, and the land could be taken from him by the government at any time without having to specify a reason or to pay him a compensation. In other words, the farmer had usufructuary rights only, although usually he was permitted to use and exploit the land so long as he paid his taxes.

Although Mohamed Ali accomplished his goal to be the sole owner of practically all the land of Egypt, he was inclined to distribute some of the land among the foreign notables,[16] military, and administrative officials in order to strengthen and maintain his rule. But such distribution was discriminatory. To some, he granted fallow land to reclaim and bring under cultivation. This land, which was known as "Abadiat,"[17] amounted to about 20,760 acres.[18] To others, mainly members of his family, he granted the most fertile land which was most accessible to irrigation. This was known as "Shafaalek," referring to estates given as grants. In other words, Mohamed Ali created a new class of land aristocracy.

The principle of private property was developed later, when, under the rule of Abbas --who ascended to Egypt's throne in 1848--a law was issued abolishing state ownership of land and establishing a certain degree of rights of property. The main provisions of this law were:

(1) Those who were exploiting the land had the right to dispose of the right of exploitation to others, provided that the transaction was registered in the presence of witnesses.

(2) The farmer lost the right of exploitation if he failed to pay his taxes.

(3) If the farmer neglected the land, or ceased to live in the vicinity, the state had the right to exploit the land. However, in the event of his return, he was entitled to regain the right of exploitation.[19]

This procedure was furthered in 1854 when Said introduced some changes both in the registration and inheritance systems. A new decree stated that all transfers of land must be made by a legal document issued at the "Moudirieh," which is the Provincial Governorate. The heirs had the right to take possession of the land which they inherited, and thus the principle of family inheritance was legalized. Moreover, legal processes affecting land rights were valid for 15 years.

The rights of private property were finally affirmed in 1858 by Said's famous statutes which declared that those who utilize the land had the right to rent, mortgage or sell it, and the heirs had the right to inherit these prerogatives without distinction of sex. This arrangement was in accordance with

the Islamic law. However, article 4 of that statute
stipulated that the farmer who abandoned his land for
more than five years was deprived of the right of exploitation. Land holders were also exempted from the
payment of their tax arrears which amounted to over
two million dollars.[20]

Some minor changes took place in the procedure
of registration and concerning the person who should
inherit the land. However, in 1875 registration procedure was completed by the establishment of the mixed
courts, and in 1881 a decree was issued to reaffirm
inheritance according to the Islamic law.

From this brief historical review of the developments in the tenure system in Egypt, we can see
that the Egyptian farmer did not gain the rights of
private property until the second half of the nineteenth century. That development led to still other
important implications, since it resulted in characteristics that dominated Egyptian farming for a long
time and stood in the way of progress.

In the first place, though agriculture was the
main source of income, the government, which considered
land as a source of income made little improvement in
agriculture. Cultivated area increased only by 5 per
cent during the period 1897-1937. On the other hand,
the farmer's income was too low to allow any important
improvement. Besides, the instability in the rights of
private property did not encourage the land holder to
undertake capital improvements. Second, we find a dichotomy in the product of land: first, the one single
important crop, cotton, and second, cereals and foodstuffs that were used to satisfy the farmer's needs.
Actually, cotton dominated Egyptian agriculture to the
extent that the country had to import wheat for domestic needs. Third, and most important, is the very
skewed distribution of land. At one extreme there were
the large estates which Mohamed Ali started with his
grants to his sons, notables, and officials, while at
the other there were the small holders who lived on
less than five acres. As we shall see in the following

section,the number of small holders has increased tremendously.

LAND DISTRIBUTION, 1896-1950

As we observed in the last section, there was
a tremendous change in the land tenure system during
the nineteenth century, a matter that affected the
distribution of land ownership among Egyptian farmers.
This can be seen from Tables 5 and 6.   Table 5 shows
the number and percentage distribution of landowners
by size of ownership for selected years, 1896-1950.
Table 6 shows the total areas owned and the percentage
distribution by size of ownership for the same period.

The number of farmers who possessed less than
five acres of land amounted to 611,100 in 1896 or
about 80 per cent of all landowners. At the other end
of the spectrum, only 1.6 per cent of the landlords
held 43.8 of total land area. This in itself is an extremely skewed distribution of land. Consequently, not
only did the situation not improve, there was also a
tendency toward further inequality in land ownership
during the first half of the present century. By 1950,
93.9 per cent of landowners possessed only 33.5 per
cent of total land, leaving the larger part, 66.5 per
cent, in the hands of a minority, which amounted to
only 6.1 per cent of owners.   Actually, in 1950 over
one-third of the land was owned by one-half of one per
cent of landlords who had in their hands 2,218,700
acres. A further breakdown shows that 21 per cent of
the land was in the hands of only 0.08 per cent of the
landowners.[21] In other words, during this period the
situation was not corrected; to the contrary, there
was a tendency toward further skewness in land distribution. This inequity can easily be seen in Figure
2, in which a Lorenz curve is fitted to the cumulative
percentage distribution of the number of owners and
total area owned. In spite of the fact that the curve
for 1896 is far to the right of the 45-degree diagonal
line which represents the most equitable distribution,
the curve for 1950 had moved further to the right.

Table 5.   Number and Percentage
Distribution of Land Ownership by Size
of Ownership, Selected Years, 1896-1950

Size of ownership	1896	1906	1916	1936	1950
		(1,000 owners)			
Less than one acre	--	--	1006.9	1677.5	1874.7
1-5	611.1	1084.0	473.7	564.7	599.2
5-10	80.8	76.9	76.7	84.6	83.2
10-21	41.3	37.0	36.9	39.6	41.5
21-52	22.2	20.0	19.9	21.8	21.2
Over 52	11.9	12.7	12.3	12.5	12.1
Total	767.3	1230.3	1626.3	2400.7	2631.9
		(Per cent)			
Less than one acre	--	--	61.9	69.9	71.2
1-5	79.6	88.1	29.1	23.5	22.7
5-10	10.5	6.3	4.7	3.5	3.2
10-21	5.4	3.0	2.3	1.7	1.6
21-52	2.9	1.6	1.2	0.9	0.8
Over 52	1.6	1.0	0.8	0.5	0.5
Total	100.0	100.0	100.0	100.0	100.0

Sources: Compiled and calculated from: Central Com-
mittee for Statistics, Collection of Basic
Statistics (Cairo: S.O.P. Press, 1962), pp.
75-76; "Socio-economic Aspects of Agrarian
Reform in the United Arab Republic," in
Agrarian Reform and Land Development, a spe-
cial issue of The Scribe, The Arab Review
(July, 1964) VIII, p. 18, and Sayed Marei,
Agrarian Reform in Egypt (Le Caire: Impri-
merie de l'institut Francais D'archéologie
Orientale, 1957), pp. 17, 27.

Table 6. Total Area Owned
and Its Percentage Distribution by Size
of Ownership, Selected Years, 1896-1950.

Size of ownership	1896	1906	1916	1936	1950
		(1,000 acres)			
Less than one acre	--	--	445.8	714.8	718.8
1-5	1031.7	1341.9	1059.7	1191.6	1262.5
5-10	587.3	558.5	548.7	582.6	591.9
10-21	595.9	531.7	529.4	548.4	582.4
21-52	701.3	634.9	630.1	682.0	667.2
Over 52	2274.9	2570.1	2446.0	2339.4	2218.7
Total	5191.1	5637.1	5659.7	6058.1	6104.5
		(Per cent)			
Less than one acre	--	--	7.9	11.8	12.8
1-5	19.9	23.8	18.7	19.7	20.7
5-10	11.3	9.9	9.7	9.6	9.7
10-21	11.5	9.4	9.4	9.0	9.5
21-52	13.5	11.3	11.1	11.3	10.9
Over 52	43.8	45.6	43.2	38.6	36.4
Total	100.0	100.0	100.0	100.0	100.0

Sources: Compiled and calculated from: Central Com-
mittee for Statistics, Collection of Basic
Statistics (Cairo: S.O.P. Press,1962), pp.
75-76; "Socio-economic Aspects of Agrarian
Reform in the United Arab Republic," in
Agrarian Reform and Land Development, a spe-
cial issue of The Scribe, The Arab Review
(July, 1964) VIII, p. 18, and Sayed Marei,
Agrarian Reform in Egypt (Le Caire: Impri-
merie de l'institut Francais D'archéologie
Orientale, 1957), pp. 17, 27.

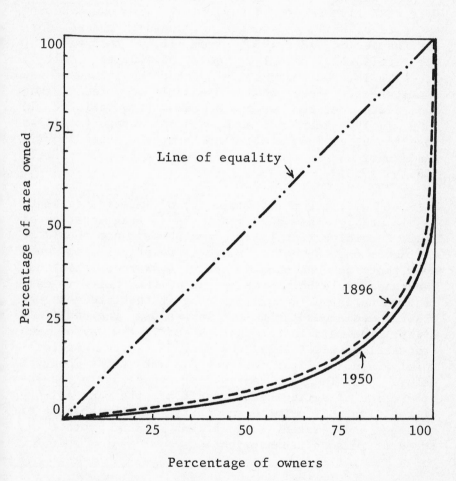

FIGURE-2.   LORENZ CURVE FOR THE DISTRIBUTION
OF LAND OWNERSHIP IN EGYPT
IN 1896 AND 1950

Naturally this is a consequence of the demographic pressure. During this period population more than doubled.

Let us now compare the number of owners of less than five acres and the total area owned during the period. While the number of owners increased, during the period 1896-1950, from 611,100 to 2,473,900, the total area rose only from 1,031,700 to 1,981,300 acres. In other words, a further splitting of the small areas of less than five acres occurred. This took place over time as can be seen from Table 6. In 1896 and 1906 there was no one in the category of less than one acre. Such a class of farmers started in 1916 and continued to increase, amounting to about 2 million by 1950.

Sometimes the Islamic law of inheritance is to be blamed for the subdivision and fragmentation of land. According to this law, the inheritance should be divided among the heirs. There is no stipulation, however, that each one should receive a share of the land. The land could be bought by one of the heirs in case it is not large enough, as long as the proceeds are distributed according to the law among the beneficiaries. The main factor that stood in the way of such transactions was the lack of a credit system. Agricultural financial institutions did not exist in Egypt before 1880. The main reasons for the delay in the introduction of agriculture credit are the instability of the rights of private property and the absence of mortgage and related legislations which protect the investor in such transactions.

Notes to Chapter 2

[1]United Nations, Statistical Office, Per Capita National Product of Fifty-Five Countries, 1952-54, Statistical Paper, Series E, No.4 (New York, 1957), p. 9.

[2]In 1954 agriculture contributed more than one-third (35 per cent) of gross domestic product. This

is a relatively high percentage, even when compared with some countries oriented toward agriculture, such as Argentina,Austria, and Puerto Rico, where the share of agricultural sector in gross domestic product ranges from 14 to 19 per cent only. Cf. United Nations, Department of Economics and Social Affairs, Statistical Yearbook, 1957 (New York, 1957), pp. 486-489.

[3]Central Committee for Statistics, Collection of Basic Statistics (Cairo: S.O.P. Press,1962), p.100.

[4]Ibid., p. 100.

[5]Egyptian Federation of Industries, Yearbook, 1951-52 (Cairo: S.O.P. Press, 1952), p. 261.

[6]Ibid., p. 261.

[7]United Nations, Department of Economic and Social Affairs, Statistical Yearbook 1957 (New York, 1957), p. 487; International Labor Office, Yearbook of Labor Statistics (Geneve, 1959), p. 14.

[8]Department of Agriculture, "The Economic Structure of Egypt," Mimeographed. (Cairo, 1951),p. 1.

[9]For a detailed history of this period, see Mohamed Fahmy Leheita,Modern Economic History of Egypt (Cairo, 1938), A. E. Crouchley, Economic Development of Modern Egypt (London: Longman, Green and Company, 1958), and Philip K. Hitti, The Near East in History (Princeton, N. J.: D. Van Nostrand, 1961), Chs. V, XII, XXI, XXIX, XXXI, and XXXVI.

[10]Sayed Marei, Agrarian Reform in Egypt (Le Caire: Imprimerie de l'institut Francais d'Archeologie Orientale, 1957), Ch. 1.

[11]Mohamed Ali turned the throne over to his son Ibrahim in 1848. Ibrahim died that same year and was succeeded by Abbas.

[12]Higry refers to the Flight of the Prophet Mohamed from Mecca to Medina in Heghaz Arabia on Friday, July 16, 622 A.D. This date marks the beginning of the era on which the Arabic lunar calendar is based.

[13]D'jabarti Abd-Al-Rahman B. Hassan Al-Hanafi, Adjaib Al-Athar fi Taradjim-wal-Akhbar (The Great History of Egypt in the 12th and 13th Moslem Centuries), (Government Press: 1297 Higry /1880 A.D./) as quoted in Marei, op. cit., p. 5.

[14]Amin Samy, The Nile Almanac (Egypt: Government Press, 1915), as quoted in Marei, op. cit., p. 6.

[15]D'jabarti, quoted in Marei, op. cit., p. 6.

[16]Although foreigners were not allowed ownership of land, sometimes they were granted "Abadiat." The right of foreigners to hold land was confirmed by an Imperial Decree from Constantinople in 1867.

[17]This is the name of "Excluded Estates,"a name which is a familiar one in the rural areas of Egypt up to the present time.

[18]Marei, op. cit., p. 10.

[19]Leheita,Modern Economic History of Egypt, op. cit., pp. 148-150.

[20]Ibid., pp. 165-67.

[21]"Socio-economic Aspects of Agrarian Reform in the United Arab Republic," Agrarian Reform and Land Development, a special issue of The Scribe, The Arab Review, VIII (July, 1964) 19. Moreover, G. Said states that while there existed 60 landlords with an average area owned of 4,717.9 acres, there were two million farmers and each owned on the average less than one half of an acre. G. M. Said, The Road to Socialism (Cairo: Arab Renaissance Press, 1962), p. 309.

CHAPTER 3   THE ECONOMY PRIOR TO THE DEVELOPMENT ERA

The Egyptian economy was exposed to several attempts at development during the nineteenth century and the first half of the twentieth century. Such attempts ultimately proved abortive and did not succeed in setting the economy on a self-sustaining growth path. The economy always reverted to the old low-level equilibrium. These attempts, however, were not entirely futile for they did prepare the economy for the development that took place in the 1950's following the Revolution.

PREDEVELOPMENT STAGES DURING THE PERIOD 1800-1950

At the beginning of the nineteenth century, Mohamed Ali became the ruler of Egypt in 1805 while it was yet part of the Turkish Empire. He tried to achieve political independence from the Turkish Empire through building a strong army. Since this required dependence on national industries to provide the increasing needs of a well-equipped strong army, he started to develop the Egyptian economy to make it self-sufficient.

Mohamed Ali's program called for the simultaneous development of both agriculture and industry. The latter was regarded as the best outlet for agricultural products, while at the same time it would reduce the dependence of the economy on outside markets.

His program was based on state ownership and management of all the projects which he initiated throughout the country. The state provided all inputs to the producing units in agriculture and industry, with the understanding that these units would sell their output to the state.

Besides promoting the production of sugar, Mohamed Ali introduced the cultivation of cotton to the Egyptian economy.[1] Soon Egyptian cotton became one of the widely used raw materials, making Egypt the main supplier of the European textile industry. Under Mohamed Ali, considerable efforts were also directed toward utilizing these agricultural products in the domestic industries. In all the industries he created, Mohamed Ali depended largely on importing machinery, technical knowhow, and skilled labor from Europe. Besides, 300 students were sent to Europe, and several times as many studied in the newly opened Egyptian schools of medicine, engineering and languages, and in the military and naval colleges.[2]

The first sugar refinery was established in Ryramon in 1818[3] by an Englishman.[4] He urged the government to establish other refineries, and four more were built during the period 1840-45. However, most of the efforts in the area of industrialization were concentrated on the textile industry. In an attempt to displace importation, the first textile factory was completed in 1816 in Cairo with skilled workers brought from Florence, Italy, for weaving silk and other fine materials. By 1829 there were several textile mills designed mainly for cotton ginning, spinning, and weaving in the majority of the cities in lower Egypt. It is estimated that there were 145 workers engaged in the production of regular yarn and 1,919 in the production of fine yarn. The daily production of regular yarn amounted to 14,500 pounds during the summer months and 8,640 pounds during the winter months. The number of looms used was estimated at 1,215.[5]

Several other industries were created and

developed on a smaller scale. These included the weaving of linen and wool, the production of dyes, leather, pottery, oil, flour, rice, glass, chemicals, and some metal industries. The total number of industrial workers engaged was estimated at 31,000 workers. In construction there were 40,000 workers. Before 1840, the number of animals used to run the machinery was estimated at 12,000.

This attempt at industrialization in particular and economic development in general met with little success, however, and came to an end by 1840 after Mohamed Ali's military defeat. Several ultimate factors contributed to the failure of Mohamed Ali's program. In the first place, the cost of production was high in spite of the low cost of labor and domestic raw materials. This was due mainly to the bureaucracy connected with the centralization policy adopted in managing these industries, a matter that resulted in waste and low-grade supervision. As a consequence of the high cost of production and noncompetitive prices, domestic products could not withstand the competition of imported goods which had the advantage of paying only a uniform tariff of 3 per cent. With the Treaty of Commerce in 1838 between England and the Porte, English merchants were granted the right to import from any part of the Ottoman Empire at a uniform duty of 12 per cent.[6] Thus, the Treasury had always to meet the loss resulting from selling at a price lower than cost in order to keep producing units in operation. Another important factor which contributed to the failure of this attempt was the agricultural labor shortage which resulted from industrialization. With the close of the second half of the nineteenth century, the population of Egypt did not exceed two and one-half million,[7] a figure which clearly indicates that Egypt was not then overpopulated. The shift of labor from agriculture to industry led to a decline in agricultural production, a decline that was not compensated by a concurrent increase in industrial production. Moreover, the use of livestock as a source of power in industry also constituted a loss to agriculture, which had depended on the livestock in cultivation.

There was some balance between agriculture and industry at the beginning of this development experience. However, Mohamed Ali had started these industries without building the infrastructure or creating the social overhead investments which should come first. Without roads, canals, power, and other social overheads, the new industries could survive only as long as they had state support.

Mohamed Ali's successors found that the state monopoly over industry and its continuous protection was an obstacle to trade, especially to the main crop, cotton, which became widely used in the textile industry in Europe. At the same time, the steam engine was being used in industry and in transportation in other parts of the world, a matter which encouraged the building of considerable railway transportation systems. Hence, after 1840 we find a shift from the development of industry to the promotion of foreign trade. Most efforts were concentrated during this period toward the development of trade and commerce via the improvement of the transportation system. The first railway system between Cairo and Alexandria was completed in 1857, and another one, linking Cairo with Suez, in 1859. This period also witnessed the improvement of water transportation with the use of the steam engine on newly constructed canals and waterways. The Suez Canal, a vital international waterway, was opened for navigation in 1869. This in turn helped to promote new industries, but still on a limited scale.

In fact, if the order of these two stages, i.e., Mohamed Ali's period and his successors, had been reversed, it would have set the Egyptian economy on possibly the same development path which some of the European countries embarked on at that time. Building of the infrastructure of the economy could have helped the economy to embark on its development path, but such development was abortive. The financial troubles resulting from extravagance in the building and opening of the Suez Canal forced the government to borrow from foreign bankers. Hence the government was left without any capital to initiate or even stimulate industrial growth.[8] In the meantime, these circumstances gave the British the opportunity to interfere in Egypt resulting in British occupation in 1882. After this, the British managed to keep Egypt as a source for cotton, to supply their industries, while making it a market for their manufactured products, mainly textiles. This unsuccessful experience of industrialization brought with it the conviction that Egypt is the gift of the River Nile. It suggested that, by its nature, it should remain an agricultural country; it did not possess the requirements for industry.

That concept lasted until the beginning of the twentieth century. With the First World War, Egypt entered a new phase of economic change. The impediments to foreign trade which resulted from the war compelled the country to depend on its own resources in supplying the goods and services which had previously been imported. This led to the initiation of some local industries under the leadership of Bank Misr, which was established in 1920 with domestic capital. The aim of this bank was to encourage investment in Egyptian industries with local capital.

However, there was an obstacle to the development of local industries. Trade agreements with foreign countries gave them the privilege of exporting to, and importing from, Egypt with little or practically no tariffs. Up to 1930, they prevented the government from helping the infant industries. By 1939 the government managed to terminate all such foreign privileges according to the 1939 treaty thus enabling it to impose direct taxes for the first time.

Although the 1930 depression affected the Egyptian economy, the creation of those few industries after the first war paved the way for the change which came with the Second World War. Circumstances of war stopped the importation of many commodities on which the economy used to depend. In addition, armed forces stationed in Egypt required large amounts of consumer goods. This situation encouraged and made profitable the creation of several small industries. One industry

which especially flourished during the war period and
continued to flourish after the war was the textile
industry and all its related processes.

This movement toward industrialization was reflected in national income figures. During the period
1939-47, national income, at constant (1953) prices,
increased at an average rate of 3.4 per cent annually.[9] Even if we take into account the tremendous increase in population that took place during the same
period, the per capita income increased at a rate of
one and a half per cent.[10] If we take the figures for
the period 1939-49, the rates become 4.7 per cent for
national income at constant prices and 2.8 per cent
for per capita real income.[11]

When the war began in 1939, Egypt had reason
to be grateful for the progress that took place in
some industries which otherwise would not have flourished. In a report prepared for the Economic Development Section of the Division of Economic Stability and
Development in the United Nation's Department of Economic Affairs, M. A. Refaat gives an illustration of
the notable extension of economic activities and especially the industrial progress during that period. He
provides the following percentages which indicates the
degree to which local production covered local requirements at the outbreak of war.[12]

Commodity	Per cent of requirements	Commodity	Per cent of requirements
Sugar	100	Soap	90
Methylated		Furniture	80
spirits	100	Matches	80
Cigarettes	100	Beer	65
Edible salt	100	Vegetable	
Flour		oils	60
milling	99	Caustic	
Cotton yarn	96	soda	50
Shoes	90	Cotton	
Cement	90	textiles	40

It is natural that the Second World War brought some prosperity to the nation's economy in the industries created by the demands of the armed forces stationed in Egypt. Employment increased and prices went up, but when the war ended the high level of employment could not be maintained. Industries created as a result of the circumstances of the war could not survive. The textile industry was an exception. This industry which had begun in the early 1930's became stronger during the war period. With the vertical expansion of this industry, it managed to survive after the war. However, it became self-contained and did not have any appreciable effects on the expansion of other industries of the economy.

With the end of the war, the Egyptian economy entered another phase. Most of the countries which were involved directly or indirectly in the war, and even those which were almost totally destroyed, embarked on programs of development and reconstruction. The Egyptian economy suffered from inflation, an increase in population, and unemployment. The cost of living more than tripled during the period 1939-52, with the index (1948 = 100) rising from 36 to 113.[13] The annual average rate of increase in national income (at constant prices of 1953) was only 1 per cent during the period 1947-52. Taking into account the increase in population during this period, we note that the per capita income at constant prices decreased by 1.5 per cent.

To sum up, five phases in the Egyptian economy's development can be distinguished:

First, the industrialization period, begun in 1805, but which declined by the middle of the century, with the defeat of Mohamed Ali;

Second, the period characterized by the improvement in one type of social overhead--transportation--ended by the financial troubles resulting from the opening of the Suez Canal in 1869 and then the British Occupation in 1882;

Third, Egypt as a predominantly agrarian economy, a period that lasted until the beginning of the First World War;

Fourth, a period of industrialization after the First World War, dependent on domestic capital, was initiated by Bank Misr and affiliated industries. This movement managed to bring about legislation favorable to the establishment of new industries and protection of important ones. It also paved the way for the prosperity of the Second World War.

The fifth period was one of stagnation which immediately followed the Second World War and lasted until 1952.

The year 1952 marks the beginning of the development period of the Egyptian economy following the change in government. The struggle among political parties to seize power coupled with corruption in administration led the economy into a declining state characterized by low levels of income and high price levels. This state of economic conditions led to dissatisfaction among the majority of the population and especially the armed forces. In 1952 a bloodless military coup took place. The King was expelled and the New Republic established under Mohamed Naguib who, in 1954, was replaced by Gamal Abdul-Nasser.

AGRICULTURAL PRODUCTION

Before 1952 there had been a slowing down of economic expansion, especially in agriculture, the major sector of the economy. At the same time, population increased at a rate of over 2 per cent annually. The inefficient means and traditional ways of cultivation, coupled with the land tenure system discussed in the last chapter, led to an exhaustion of the soil. The situation became worse with the outbreak of World War II, particularly because of the difficulty in importing fertilizers. Before the war two-thirds of the fertilizers were imported from Chile and the rest from

Germany and the United Kingdom. While importation from Chile did not cease, it was reduced considerably. Importation from Germany stopped and at the same time the war made it difficult to import from the United Kingdom. Total imports of fertilizers fell from 471,000 tons in 1939 to 158,000 tons in 1943.[14] Cotton acreage, furthermore, was reduced owing to the difficulties encountered in exporting cotton,[15] and also because emphasis was placed on the production of food to meet both domestic demand and the needs of the armed forces stationed in Egypt at that time.

This state of affairs is reflected in the productivity of agriculture, as can be seen from the yield of the major agricultural crops in Egypt before and during the war period. The yield here is defined as the number of tons per acre and is taken as a measure of productivity. Table 7 shows yield indexes for the important agricultural crops in Egypt for selected years during the period 1920-44. A glance at this table shows a steady increase in the yield of these crops, including the major crop of the country, cotton, following World War I and up to the year 1939. The index number for the yield of wheat, taking 1913 as the base year, increased from 96 to 117 during the period 1920-39. A similar trend took place with respect to the yield of rice, which increased from 87 in 1920 to 108 in 1939. Barley also showed a considerable increase, while corn and beans showed only some increase. Beginning with 1940, with the exception of cotton, a considerable change occurred in the yield of these crops. This trend continued until 1944. From a high level of 117 in 1939, the index number for the yield of wheat (1913 = 100) dropped to 73 by 1944, that of corn from 111 to 94, and that of barley from 129 to 97 during the same period. The index numbers for beans and rice also showed the same trend, but with less severity. In the meantime, the index number for the yield of cotton increased from 74 in 1920 to 120 in 1939 and to 123 by 1944.

With the exception of cotton, trends in the yield of all crops in Table 7 reflect the typical

Table 7. Yield Indexes for Important
Agricultural Crops in Egypt, Selected
Years, 1920-44 (1913 = 100)

Year	Wheat	Corn	Barley	Beans	Rice	Onions	Cotton
1920	96	108	99	81	87	79	74
1930	94	110	98	78	87	75	89
1935	106	120	120	82	100	75	115
1939	117	111	129	93	108	90	120
1940	115	112	128	92	85	87	123
1941	95	95	117	90	84	89	115
1942	102	83	122	90	91	73	132
1943	86	80	107	87	69	71	113
1944	73	94	97	89	65	65	123

Source: Department of Statistics and Census, Annuaire
Statistique (Cairo: National Press, 1948).

backward-bending supply curve. In addition to domestic
needs, there was, moreover, an increased demand for
foodstuffs to meet the needs of the armed forces. The
result is a noticeable increase in the prices of products such as wheat, rice, corn, barley, beans, and onions. This increase in prices, however, did not lead
to an increase in production. Actually, production of
all these crops declined. During the war period, the
production of wheat declined by 22 per cent, corn by 8
per cent, beans by 6 per cent, rice by 3 per cent, and
that of barley by 29 per cent. This took place while
the cultivated area of these crops did not show any
significant increase.[16] This condition resulted in the
decline in the yield of these crops as shown in Table
7. Knowing that the war situation was temporary, farmers tended to reap the quick profits of this period.
Few improvements were made on agricultural land,
especially because of the difficulty of importing

fertilizers. The reduction in applying fertilizers in the production of these crops contributed to the decrease in yields. Thus land was exhausted and yields decreased. However, the loss in productivity was compensated for by the rising prices of agricultural products, leaving the producers always in a better situation.

The trend in yield of cotton was opposite from that of the other crops during the war period. While other crops showed a decrease in their yield,the yield of cotton showed an increase. Owing to the difficulty in exporting cotton, cotton acreage, however, was reduced. Moreover, because of the rising prices of foodstuffs, agricultural land was transferred from the production of cotton to the production of foodstuffs. This limitation on the land available for growing cotton served as an inducement to improve its production, hence a corresponding rise in its yield. In 1947-48 the yield of cotton showed an increase of about 12 per cent over its level in 1938-39.[17]

FLUCTUATIONS IN THE MAJOR CROP

Although cotton was not cultivated, it has existed in Egypt since antiquity. Its production was introduced in Egypt after the experimentations of Jumel, a French scientist who came with the French expedition at the outset of the nineteenth century. Since then, Egyptian agriculture has been characterized by one major crop, cotton. The production of cotton which started with 1130 tons in 1823 increased to 36,000 tons by 1850 due to the successful efforts of Mohamed Ali to secure economic independence from the Turkish Empire.[18] However, the event that established Egypt as a major cotton producer was the American Civil War. The blockade of the Confederate States ports by the Union fleets enabled Egypt to export 82,000 tons of cotton to Europe in 1862. By 1865 cotton exports had increased to a quarter of a million tons. Even after the war and return of the United States to the market, Egypt still exported to the European markets, because

the improvement in quality of the Egyptian cotton during the war period enabled her to withstand American
competition.

Egypt is the sixth largest producer in the
world, providing 2 to 5 per cent of the world's cotton.
As for quality of its fiber, she is, practically speak-
ing, at the top of the list with her long staple cotton. The government of Egypt insures the continuous
production of new varieties of cotton through the extensive research conducted in the laboratories of the
"Cotton Research Board." Moreover, a good part of the
efforts of the Ministry of Agriculture are directed
toward the improvement of cotton production. For example, the "Sakellaridis" and "Wafir," which were the
most famous cotton fibers for a long time after the
war, were replaced by "Giza 7" and later on by "Kar-
nak." These are among the long staple variety and
reach 40 millimeters and more. Among the short fiber
varieties are "Achmouni" and "Zagora," to mention a
few. These are between 25 and 35 millimeters and are
comparable to American cotton.

The yield of Egyptian cotton is on the average
very high compared with that of other countries. The
yield per acre amounts to about 500 pounds on the average. This is equal to the average yield for the
United States and far exceeds that of India, two of
the large cotton producing countries. Such a yield is
reached in Egypt in spite of the frequent attacks by
the cotton worm, the boll weevil, which require a
large financial outlay to control. The improvement in
yield can be seen from Table 8, which also shows prices
and the total value of Egyptian cotton for selected
years during the period 1920-52. Figure 3 illustrates
the wide fluctuations in these figures.

There has been an upward trend in the average
yield per acre with some fluctuations that result from
weather conditions and the frequent attacks by the
boll weevil. The gain in productivity during the second quarter of the century is considerable and reached
its highest level in 1948. On the other hand, there have

Table 8. Average Yield per Acre, Price, and Total Value of Egyptian Cotton Crop, Selected Years, 1920-52

Year	Average yield		Average price		Value of the crop	
	Lbs. per acre	Index	Dollars per 100 lbs.	Index	Million dollars	Index
1920	327	100	16	100	96	100
1922	369	113	14	87	95	99
1924	403	123	18	113	132	137
1926	425	130	10	63	76	79
1928	459	140	12	75	96	100
1930	393	120	6	37	51	53
1932	448	137	6	37	31	32
1934	432	132	7	44	50	52
1936	526	161	8	50	68	71
1938	462	141	5	31	44	46
1940	539	165	7	44	65	68
1942	594	182	13	81	53	55
1944	539	165	19	119	85	89
1946	496	152	20	125	118	123
1948	611	187	26	163	226	235
1950	426	130	58	363	497	513
1952	499	153	28	175	280	292

Source: Compiled and calculated from Department of Statistics and Census, *Annuaire Statistique, 1959* (Cairo: Government Press, 1960), pp. 250-251.

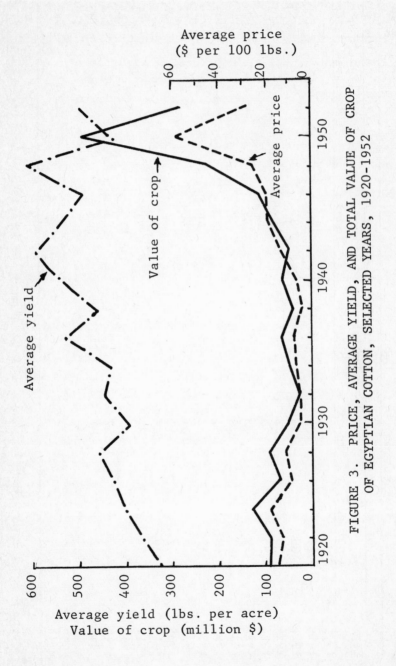

FIGURE 3. PRICE, AVERAGE YIELD, AND TOTAL VALUE OF CROP
OF EGYPTIAN COTTON, SELECTED YEARS, 1920-1952

been wide fluctuations in cotton price,which, in turn,
caused similar fluctuations in the total value of the
crop. From Figure 3 we can see that the change in average prices reflects the same variation as the total
value of the crop.

THE INFLATIONARY PRESSURE

The splitting of land ownership, coupled with
the population pressure, increased the demand on agriculture which in turn led to an increase in prices of
agricultural land without a corresponding increase in
the real value of agricultural products. While the
monetary value of agricultural products increased by
1949 to five times its level in 1938,the real value of
agricultural products increased on the average by 14
per cent. This increase in the value of agricultural
products is primarily a result of the increase in demand.

To give an illustration of the high value of
land, the following comparison is made. For the United
States, in 1945, average value per acre of farm land
was $40.63.[19] This amounts to about ten times the av-
erage farm wage per day in 1945, which was $4.12. Ac-
cording to a study by the Fellah Department in 1945,
the corresponding figures for Egypt were $690 per acre
and $.207 average farm wage per day. This gives a ra-
tio of 3333 for Egypt as compared with ten for the
United States.[20]

Several reasons could be pointed out as contributing to the phenomenon of land being the most
preferred form of investment:

(1) Usually land benefits from the improvements in irrigation and drainage undertaken by the
state.

(2) Taxes are considerably lower on land.

(3) Land yield is high when compared with other

investments.

(4) Prestige is bestowed on the landowner in agrarian underdeveloped communities.

(5) The position of the farmer is that the risk in agriculture (which he knows and has experienced) is less than that in industry (which is unknown to him).

(6) There is a high degree of liquidity. As Keynes pointed out in the General Theory, "The possession of land has been characterized by a liquidity premium in the minds of the owners of wealth."[21]

The land tenure system enhanced the increase in rent. In most cases, land on the large estates was rented to small farmers who fell in one or the other of the following four classes of tenants in the agricultural ladder: (1) cash renters, (2) cash and share renter, (3) share renters who pay to the owners fixed amount of the product, (4) share renters who pay to the owner a percentage amount of the product. Thus we find an increasing trend in rent of agricultural land. Rent per acre in Egypt's North Delta Region almost doubled during the period 1928-46. The same increase applies to the fertile areas of Middle Egypt. Even in the less fertile areas of the South Delta, rent per acre about doubled during those 18 years. For the entire agricultural area, the figures in Table 9 show the increase in average rent per acre over the period 1939-47. During a period of seven years (1939-46), the rent per acre more than tripled. It went down only in 1947 at the end of the Second World War.

To give another illustration of the conditions before 1952, an index of the inflationary pressure has been calculated. Inflationary pressure is considered to arise from the discrepancy between aggregate demand as represented by current expenditure on consumption and investment and aggregate supply as represented by the value, at constant prices of available output

Table 9. Average Rent Per Acre
of Agricultural Land in Egypt,
1939-47

Year	Average rent per acre (U.S. dollars)	Index of rent per acre (1939 = 100)
1939	31	100
1940	40	129
1941	47	150
1942	67	214
1943	80	257
1944	84	271
1945	102	329
1946	102	329
1947	91	293

Source: "Socio-Economic Aspects of Agrarian Reform in
the United Arab Republic," in Agrarian Reform
and Land Development, a special issue of The
Scribe, The Arab Review, VII (July, 1964),
21.

produced domestically, and by capital inflow and re-
mittances from abroad. Table 10 shows an estimate of
the inflationary gap in Egypt during the war period,
1939-45.[22] The inflationary gap is defined as the
range between aggregate supply and aggregate demand
and is measured here by the percentage ratio of that
difference to aggregate supply. Since prices were controlled during this period, aggregate supply is taken
as the value at the prices of 1939, of the total domestic output plus the net import surplus. The current
value of agricultural production, industrial production, and value of output of the rest of the economy
were deflated by prices indices for each of these
groups. Aggregate demand is represented by total private and government consumption in addition to private

Table 10. Estimation of the Inflationary Gap in Egypt
During the Period 1939-45
(Million U. S. dollars)

	1939	1940	1941	1942	1943	1944	1945
Aggregate supply:[a]							
Domestic production	386.4	366.8	363.9	381.3	354.7	365.3	373.5
Net import surplus	+1.8	+3.5	-3.7	-21.1	-17.3	-19.1	-23.4
Total supply	388.2	370.3	360.2	360.2	337.4	346.2	350.1
Aggregate demand:							
Total consumption	370.0	363.4	418.6	575.0	716.6	763.6	874.0
Total investment	18.2	75.9	17.3	174.8	179.4	303.6	280.6
Total demand	388.2	439.3	535.9	749.8	896.0	1067.2	1154.6
The inflationary gap[b]	0	18.6	48.8	108.2	165.6	208.3	229.8

[a] In prices of 1939.

[b] Inflationary gap is measured by the distance between aggregate supply and aggregate demand. The percentage ratio of this difference to supply is used here.

Sources: Compiled and computed from Mohmoud A. Anis, A Study of the National Income of Egypt (Le Caire: Societe Orientale de Publicité, 1950), pp. 669-89 and Mohmoud A. Anis, The National Income, Output and Expenditure of Egypt for the Years 1937-1945 (Cairo: Nile Printing House, 1950), pp. 11-23.

and public investment. The index of the inflationary pressure is calculated by taking the difference between aggregate demand and aggregate supply as a per cent of the latter.

The figures on the inflationary gap at the bottom of Table 10 are self-evident. The index increased tremendously during the period, rising from 18.6 in 1940 to 229.8 by 1945. It should be noted that aggregate supply during the period showed a slight decline.

In conclusion, the Egyptian economy was exposed to several attempts at development during the nineteenth century and the early part of the twentieth century. Such attempts did not succeed in launching the economy on an upward trend. The Second World War brought some prosperity, but it ended with the close of the war. The Egyptian economy reverted again to a standstill by the end of the first half of the twentieth century. While those countries which were involved directly or indirectly in the war, and even those which were almost totally destroyed, began their development and reconstruction, Egypt was suffering from inflation, an increase in population, and unemployment. The economy was still dependent on the cotton crop, whose price was determined outside the Egyptian economy and which is subject to wide fluctuation. All these lead to a considerably reduced level of real per capita income and actually resulted in a negative annual rate of growth of real per capita income (-1.54) during the postwar period (1947-52).

Notes to Chapter 3

[1]He introduced the production of cotton "Gomel" which was considered to rank better than the "Sea-Island."

[2]Charles Issawi, Egypt in Revolution (London: Oxford University Press, 1963), p. 23.

[3]André Eman, "L'Industrie Egyptienne Sous La Dynastie De Mohamed Ali," in <u>Livre D' or De La Federation Egyptienne De L'Industrie</u> (Le Caire: Imprimerie Schindler, 1948), pp. 81-85.

[4]He was succeeded by two Italians.

[5]Eman, <u>op</u>. <u>cit</u>., p. 82.

[6]A. E. Crouchley, "The Development of Commerce in the Reign of Mohamed Ali," <u>Egypte Contemporaine</u>, XXX (February-March, 1937), 310-11.

[7]John Bowing, a report on Egypt as mentioned in André Eman, <u>op</u>. <u>cit</u>., p. 83.

[8]Ahmed Al-Hitta, <u>Economic History of Egypt</u> (Cairo, 1957), p. 201.

[9]Tables 31 and 32, pp. 173 and 174, <u>infra</u>.

[10]<u>Ibid</u>.

[11]<u>Ibid</u>.

[12]United Nations, Department of Economic Affairs, <u>Domestic Financing of Economic Development</u> (New York, 1950), p. 122.

[13]United Nations, Statistical Office, <u>Monthly Bulletin of Statistics</u>, VIII (June, 1954), 138.

[14]Institut National De La Statistique Et Des Etudes Économiques, <u>Mémento Économique</u>, <u>L' Egypte</u> (Paris: Presses Universitaires De France, 1950),p.60.

[15]Exports of cotton fell from 409 thousand tons in 1939 to 145 thousand by 1943. <u>Ibid</u>., p. 144.

[16]<u>Ibid</u>., p. 70.

[17]<u>Ibid</u>., p. 65.

[18]Ibid., p. 64.

[19]United States, Department of Commerce, Statistical Abstracts (Washington, 1948), p. 597.

[20]Hassan A. Dawood, "Economic Aspects of Land Tenure in Egypt" (Ph.D. dissertation, Michigan State College, 1950), pp. 126-129.

[21]John Maynard Keynes, The General Theory of Employment, Interest and Money (New York: Harcourt, Brace and Co., 1938), p. 241.

[22]The index is limited to this period only because of the unavailability of data for the postwar period. It should be noted that during this period there was price control.

PART II

SOME ASPECTS OF DEVELOPMENT OF THE EGYPTIAN ECONOMY

CHAPTER 4

DEMOGRAPHIC CHANGE

Among the Middle Eastern countries, Egypt is recognized as very advanced in census-taking and the collecting of vital statistics.[1] It has a history of reasonably accurate population censuses which can be traced to 1882. The population of Egypt was estimated several times during the first half of the nineteenth century, but mainly for military and tax purposes. As was mentioned in Chapter 3, during the time of Mohamed Ali, the population of Egypt was estimated at not over 2.5 million people. By the means of a census of housing, the Egyptian population was estimated at 4.5 million in 1846.[2] An official census, but not in the modern sense of census-taking, was conducted in 1859. It stated that the population of Egypt was then 5.25 million.[3]

The above collations mean that the Egyptian population doubled during the first half of the nineteenth century that is under the rule of Mohamed Ali (1805-1848). This raises some doubt about the accuracy of the estimate at the beginning of the nineteenth century, especially if we compare it with Egypt's population in the Pharonic, Roman, and early Arab times which is generally estimated between 6 and 7 million.[4] Two sets of explanations are offered by demographers for this heavy drop of population by the end of the eighteenth century. Cleland explains it by the misrule and exploitation of the people by the Mamelukes that lasted for centuries.[5] To this, Issawi adds the diversion of the trade routes linking Europe with India as causing the population to drop to about 2.5 million by the end of the eighteenth century.[6]

If we accept these explanations, then we may observe a new cycle of population growth, beginning with the rule of Mohamed Ali in which population doubled in about half a century. Mohamed Ali's rule of Egypt was characterized by a degree of prosperity generated by his concentrated efforts to initiate development programs both in agriculture and industry. More land was brought into cultivation and new crops were introduced. Among the latter, cotton is particularly important for it resulted in the establishment of the textile industry in Egypt. All of these factors, coupled with national security and the stability of the government, reduced emigration measurably and provided an atmosphere in which a larger population could be supported. All these factors, as Issawi puts it, set the population curve on an upward course from which it has not since deviated.[7]

The first official census using modern techniques was taken in 1882, when population amounted to 6.7 million. A factor always cited as contributing to the increase of population to that level is the rapid expansion of cotton cultivation during that period since cotton absorbs much labor, especially child labor. The production of cotton expanded further to meet world demand when the American Civil War stopped the exporting of American cotton to the European markets. The second census followed in 1897. Since that year censuses were taken decennially up until 1947. The date was then changed in order to allow international comparisons. The most recent census was taken in 1960, and the plan is to take the census decennially.

Egypt has experienced a really tremendous growth in population since the last quarter of the nineteenth century. This accretion results from a young population with high fertility rates and decreasing mortality rates, since migration has been negligible. Egypt has not experienced any sizable external migration into or out of the country in recent

history. Both Cleland and El-Badry consider the magnitudes of migration in Egypt negligible.   There has
been virtually no migration on the part of the Egyptians.   The number of Egyptian nationals residing
abroad have been estimated at 25,000 in 1937 and at
less than 100,000 at present. This consists mainly of
teachers and professionals in Arab countries.   In-
migration from abroad was very small, as we see from
the following figures:

Year	No. of foreigners (in thousand)	Proportion of total population (per cent)
1927	226	1.6
1937	187	1.2
1947	146	0.8
1960	143	0.5

It should be noted that immigration has been
decreasing and has little effect on population growth.
Thus El-Badry considered Egyptian population in his
model as "closed."[8]

Table 11 shows total population and the annual
rate of its growth for the period 1882-1964. In these
years the number of people quadrupled. But perhaps
more descriptive is the magnitude of increase from 6.7
million in 1882 to 26.9 million by 1961. Egypt's rate
of growth is extremely high when compared with most
other countries.   There is, however, a major discrepancy. It seems that the 1882 census was incomplete and
tended to undercount population. In 1917 the census
officials reviewed the results of that census. They
estimated at 7.6 million the population for 1882 instead of the less likely figure of 6.7 million.[9]

As may be seen from Figure 4, the rates of
growth in population have shown a consistently steady
increase. As explained above, the high rate of 2.91
per cent for the period 1882-97 is attributable to the
inefficiency in census taking in 1882.   An adjustment
for the new count of 7.6 million brings the growth

Table 11. Population Growth
of Egypt (1882-1964)

Year	Population (1,000)	Annual rate of growth (per cent)	Year	Population (1,000)	Annual rate of growth (per cent)
1882[a]	6,706		1949	19,888	2.02
1897[a]	9,635	2.91	1950	20,393	2.54
1907[a]	11,190	1.61	1951	20,872	2.35
1917[a]	12,718	1.37	1952	21,584	3.41
1927[a]	14,178	1.15	1953	22,103	2.40
1937[a]	15,921	1.23	1954	22,666	2.55
1938	16,295	2.35	1955	23,166	2.21
1939	16,588	1.80	1956	23,754	2.54
1940	16,887	1.80	1957	24,245	2.07
1941	17,190	1.79	1958	24,797	2.28
1942	17,499	1.80	1959	25,458	2.67
1943	17,814	1.80	1960[a]	25,984	2.07
1944	18,134	1.80	1961	26,716	2.82
1945	18,460	1.80	1962[b]	27,373	2.46
1946	18,792	1.80	1963[b]	28,030	2.40
1947[a]	18,967	0.93	1964[b]	28,721	2.47
1948	19,494	2.78			

[a]Census figures

[b]Preliminary

Sources: Compiled as follows, for the period 1882-
1951, Department of Statistics and Census,
Annuaire Statistique, 1959 (Cairo: Government Press, 1961). For the period 1951-59,
Central Committee for Statistics, Collection
of Basic Statistics (Cairo: S.O.P. Press,
1962), pp. 20-35, in Arabic. For the period
1960-64, U.A.R. Central Agency for Mobilization and Statistics, Statistical Handbook
1952-64 (Cairo: Dar Memphis, 1965), p. 11.

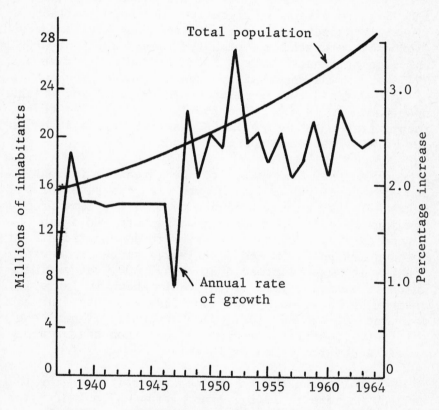

FIGURE 4.   POPULATION CHANGE AND ITS ANNUAL
            RATE OF INCREASE (1937-64)

rate down to 1.75 instead of the earlier 2.91 per
cent. The new rate is more in line with the rates of
growth for the periods following 1897. Until 1937, the
rate was a little over 1 per cent, when it suddenly
rose to 2.35 per cent in 1937-38. This high rate again
results from the method of estimation. With the exception of the period 1937-47, the intercensus years
were obtained by adding births and subtracting deaths,
ignoring the effect of migration which is negligible.
Since birth and death registration was neither complete nor accurate, it resulted in the apparent accumulation at census years. It should be noted that the
1947 census was somewhat overestimated, a consequence
of Second World War experience and a rationing census
undertaken in 1945:   When the 1947 census was taken,
people tended to overestimate their families so as to
get more of rationed consumer goods.

Another exception to the steadily increasing
annual rate of population growth is the rate for the
years 1951-52, when it jumped to 3.41 per cent from a
previous rate of 2.35 per cent, then dropped again to
a rate of 2.40 per cent. There were some variances in
the population estimated for 1952, since in certain
sources it was estimated at 21,473,000, an estimate
which is somewhat less than that shown in Table 11.
However, even if we accept that last estimate, the annual rate of growth for 1951-52 becomes 2.9 per cent;
this rate is still somewhat higher than the previous
levels and warrants an explanation.

Following the Palestine Repartitioning by the
United Nations in 1948, Arab refugees moved to the
neighboring countries, especially Jordan and Egypt.
When the refugees arrived in Egypt they were placed in
camps isolated from the rest of the population for
health reasons and until arrangements could be made to
settle them in the country. After this was accomplished, the refugees began to seek employment where
they settled. Having been accepted by the communities,
because of a common religious and social background,
they intermarried with the Egyptians and thus perhaps
accelerated population growth. Since this settlement

process took two to three years, we find that its effect on population first shows up in 1952. This could account for the upsurge in population growth in 1952.

The rate of population growth has been accelerating for a quarter century as the following figures suggest:

Period	Rate of population growth (per cent)
1917-27	11
1927-37	12
1937-47	19
1947-60	30*

*Adjusted for ten-year period.

Thus, the recent rate is more than double what it was in 1917-37. The rate for 1947-60, which is equivalent to an annual rate of increase of 3 per cent, is high in comparison with the rates of growth of world population and of the continent of Africa--2.1 and 2.4 per cent respectively, in 1960-62.[10] The rate is also high, compared to that of some underdeveloped countries such as India with a rate of 2.3 per cent, and South Africa with a rate of 2.6 per cent.[11] Compared with the countries having almost the same social structure and religious background, the annual rate of population growth in Egypt is still higher, say, than the rate for the Moslem population in Algeria, which was 2.4 per cent, in Pakistan with a rate of 2.1 per cent, and in Tunisia with a rate of 1.4 per cent in 1958-62.[12]

The increase in the rate of Egyptian population growth after 1947 is associated with an improvement in health conditions and a consequent decline in mortality, especially infant mortality, as well as with the rise in the birth rate. Improvement in public health, particularly in the field of infant care, has permitted infant mortality to drop from an average of

139 per 1,000 in 1945-49 to 108 by 1961.[13] The wide-
spread use of DDT and antibiotics supplemented the improvements in sanitation and personal hygiene. The
Egyptian experience reflects the effectiveness of public health measures in reducing mortality.

Egypt appears to be in a transitional stage of
population growth. In his model of population growth,
Notestein identifies three stages or categories of
demographic development.[14] The first includes regions
of incipient population decline. The second consists
of regions of transitional growth. The third is com-
posed of the regions of high potential. The pattern of
the population growth of Egypt tends to place it in
the second category, i.e., the regions of transitional
growth with declining mortality while fertility is re-
sponding slowly to modernization and only reverts to a
decline with industrialization and urbanization.

So long as death rates fall faster than birth
rates the rate of growth of the Egyptian population
will rise. The Central Committee for Statistics fore-
casts a population of 34 million by 1970 and of about
46 million by 1980.[15] This agrees with the United Nations estimates which project the population of Egypt
at 34.5 and 46.7 million in 1970 and 1980 respectively.[16] This sizable advance in population is anti-
cipated for several reasons. In the first place the
improvements in health and sanitary conditions are
expected to continue and should effect a further reduction in death rates. This does not affect fertility
since disease control does not necessarily involve basic changes in social institutions or education. Moreover, on religious grounds the Moslems, a majority of
the population, does not favor birth control. Furthermore, a large percentage of the population is still
engaged in agriculture, an occupation with which attitudes favorable to large families are associated.

Spengler notes that "Economic change affects
fertility through its impact upon income, the price
structure and the cost and utility of children."[17] In
the light of these factors, the future population trend

in Egypt may be said to favor an increase in population. Spengler considers "an increase in average income, if unattended by other changes, would normally bring about an increase in fertility in the population of reproductive age."[18] To apply his hypothesis, improved living conditions for the average income earner in Egypt, which may be expected to be associated with industrialization and economic development, will in all likelihood lead to an increase in fertility. Yet the effect of the increase in family income on fertility which takes place in the first stages of development, "may prove temporary, and eventually be reversed if the overall family expenditure pattern is adjusted sufficiently upward,"[19] with urbanization and a rise in the cost of living, all of which are expected at a later stage in development, fertility may fall.

If we take one factor developed by Spengler, that is, the cost and utility of children, we find that it also may operate toward an increasing trend in population growth. Among the factors mentioned as favorable to high fertility, United Nations experts emphasize the heavy dependency on agriculture, isolation, and the fatalist attitude. All of these factors are believed to foster attitudes contributing to large families.[20] The utility of children is derived from the income they could produce and from the security they might supply their parents in old age.[21] In spite of the industrial development of Egypt, the agricultural sector remains, and will remain a major sector, especially after the completion of the Aswan Dam. Thus, until the time when a general increase in the level of income takes place and the time when the family no longer depends on the earnings of children and their work on the farms, and the cost of rearing children exceeds their utility, fertility of the agriculture population in all probability will remain high.

Within the new socialist framework of the Egyptian economy, the state is now responsible for the provision of such services as health and education free of charge. All stages of education in Egypt up to the university level are free of charge except for a nominal fee for books. As the cost of children falls, fertility tends to rise.[22] In such a society the desire to provide high standards of living and education to offspring will not operate effectively as a factor in reducing birth rates.

BIRTH AND DEATH DIFFERENTIALS

Increases in population, then, result primarily from the operation of two factors: births and deaths. Migration is considered negligible. While birth rates are high, mortality rates show a consistently downward trend. This net effect can be seen from Tables 12 and 13. Table 12 shows, for the period 1923 to 1963, the crude birth rates for urban areas, rural areas with health departments, rural areas without health departments, and for the whole country. Table 13 lists the crude death rates for the same areas during the same period. Birth rate is the number of live births per 1000 population, while death rate is the number of deaths per 1000 population. The rates in these two tables are calculated by the use of the demoninator of an estimate of population that is based on geometric intercensal growth rather than on the natural increase method.

Birth rates for the whole country were generally high throughout the period 1923-63. With a rate of over 40 per thousand, the rate in Egypt is thus higher than that for the whole world (37) and a little under that for India (40.9), a country with a high population growth rate.[23] Actually, except for the decline during the war years 1941-46, the rates average a little above 42 per 1000. Such a high rate could be explained by several factors pertaining to the economic structure, social background, religious and ethical value, and the cultural pattern. With a major agricultural sector, Egypt's economic structure favors large families. The nature of the Egyptian agriculture with cotton as the major crop is a labor-intensive operation which encourages large families. As to the

Table 12. Egypt's Crude Birth Rates
by Urban and Rural Areas,
With and Without Health Departments
(1923-63)[a]

Year	Urban areas	Rural areas		Whole country
		With health department	Without health department	
1923	--	--	--	43.1
1925	--	--	--	43.5
1927	--	--	--	44.0
1929	--	--	--	44.2
1931	--	--	--	44.5
1933	--	--	--	43.8
1934	44.4	49.1	41.0	42.2
1935	42.5	47.0	40.5	41.3
1936	45.1	50.9	43.4	44.2
1937	46.9	47.2	42.1	43.4
1938	44.7	46.3	42.4	43.2
1939	44.4	47.0	40.6	42.0
1940	42.5	47.5	40.2	41.3
1941	40.0	46.8	39.0	40.4
1942	40.7	41.1	36.0	37.6
1943	44.5	41.3	36.1	38.7
1944	48.0	42.6	36.0	39.8
1945	49.8	47.1	39.0	42.7
1946	49.1	43.9	37.3	41.2
1947	49.9	48.7	40.2	43.8
1948	49.5	45.0	39.2	42.7
1949	49.0	43.6	37.9	41.8
1950	51.0	45.2	40.6	44.4
1951	51.8	46.1	40.8	44.8

(continued)

Table 12 (continued)

Year	Urban areas	Rural areas With health department	Rural areas Without health department	Whole country
1952	51.2	46.7	41.6	45.1
1953	50.9	43.4	37.5	42.5
1954	50.7	43.3	37.6	42.4
1955	50.0	43.7	33.5	40.2
1956	48.1	39.2	36.0	40.6
1957	41.1	39.4	35.4	37.8
1958	43.9	42.2	39.0	41.1
1959	44.1	45.2	41.1	42.6
1960	--	--	--	42.9
1961	--	--	--	43.9
1962	--	--	--	41.2
1963	--	--	--	42.8

[a]Birth rate is the number of live births per 1,000 population.

--Not available

Sources: M. A. El-Badry, "Trends in the Components of Population Growth in the Arab Countries of the Middle East: A Survey of Present Information," Demography, II (1965), p. 144. Department of Statistics and Census, Annuaire Statistique, 1959 (Cairo: Government Press, 1960), Central Committee for Statistics, Collection of Basic Statistics (Cairo: S.O.P. Press, 1962), p. 202. U.A.R. Central Agency for Public Mobilization and Statistics, Statistical Indicators for the United Arab Republic 1952-64 (Cairo, 1965), p. 19.

Table 13. Egypt's Crude Death Rates
by Urban and Rural Areas
With and Without Health Departments
(1923-63)[a]

Year	Urban areas	Rural areas		Whole country
		With health department	Without health department	
1923	--	--	--	25.8
1925	--	--	--	26.5
1927	--	--	--	25.2
1929	--	--	--	27.6
1931	--	--	--	26.6
1933	--	--	--	27.5
1934	29.5	36.0	26.7	27.8
1935	27.7	34.1	24.7	26.4
1936	29.9	37.5	27.7	28.8
1937	29.8	31.5	26.0	27.1
1938	28.9	31.5	25.0	26.5
1939	27.8	31.5	24.6	25.9
1940	27.4	33.7	25.2	26.3
1941	28.1	32.7	24.0	25.7
1942	33.2	34.7	25.6	28.3
1943	33.2	33.1	24.7	27.7
1944	31.2	31.3	23.2	26.0
1945	31.2	34.1	25.3	27.7
1946	27.1	29.9	23.4	25.0
1947	23.5	27.0	19.8	21.4
1948	23.9	23.1	18.4	20.4
1949	24.1	24.1	18.4	20.6
1950	22.8	22.2	16.7	19.1
1951	23.2	22.1	16.8	19.3

(continued)

Table 13 (continued)

| Year | Urban areas | Rural areas | | Whole country |
		With health department	Without health department	
1952	20.7	20.3	15.8	17.7
1953	22.6	23.3	17.2	19.5
1954	20.8	20.8	15.6	17.8
1955	20.9	21.9	14.8	17.6
1956	18.1	18.8	14.6	16.3
1957	19.2	20.0	16.5	17.8
1958	18.0	19.7	15.0	16.6
1959	17.8	19.4	14.6	16.2
1960	--	--	--	16.9
1961	--	--	--	15.8
1962	--	--	--	17.8
1963	--	--	--	15.5

[a]Death rate is the number of deaths per 1,000 population.

--Not available.

Sources: M. A. El-Badry, "Trends in the Components of Population Growth in the Arab Countries of the Middle East: A Survey of Present Information," Demography, II (1965), p. 145. Department of Statistics and Census, Annuaire Statistique, 1959 (Cairo: Government Press), Central Committee for Statistics, Collection of Basic Statistics (Cairo: S.O.P. Press, 1962), p. 202. U.A.R. Central Agency for Public Mobilization and Statistics, Statistical Indicators for the United Arab Republic 1952-64 (Cairo, 1965), p. 19.

social background, the religious and ethical val
Kingsley Davis points to some factors contributing
high fertility in underdeveloped countries.[24] The
are: (a) effect of the composite family and join
household in which we find the economic factor is a
dominant one, (b) the segregation of male and female
roles, (c) family and kinship as principle basis of
social position. It should be noted that the economic
factor is also operating and lies behind these factors. The factors Davis singles out appear to have
been operating in the Egyptian economy.[25]

In the first place, the nucleus family of pro-
creation tends in the rural agricultural areas of
Egypt to be controlled by the parental families. That
is, the elder relatives govern the conduct and economic position of the family. The position of the
family in the community depends largely on its numbers, a matter that encourages large families which
tend to dwell close to and remain under the surveil-
lance of the "in-laws." The second factor concerns the
segregation of male and female roles in the agrarian
societies of Egypt. The institutional reduction of the
feminine sphere of influence reaches an extreme due to
a misinterpretation by the illiterate of the teachings
of the Moslem religion. Women are confined in the
household without any education, since it is considered unnecessary. The per cent of female population
literate in rural areas in 1957 was 7.7 as compared to
31.1 for urban areas. However, if we look at 1927 we
find that these percentages were 1.1 and 17.4, respectively.[26] The female role thus is largely identified
with reproduction.[27]

To consider a recent period, the birth rate
declined in the mid-fifties up to 1957. This may be
explained by the depressed economic conditions at that
time and the hardships that followed the Suez crisis
in 1956. In addition to the loss of lives, especially
males, the depressed economic conditions that resulted
from the economic blockade on Egypt by the major countries of the world were not favorable to an increase
in the number of children or marriages. Since this

situation, the birth rates gradually
a level of 43 per thousand by 1960.

other hand, the crude death rates show
decline over the period. From a rate
934 it declined to 15.5 by 1963, more than
n a period of 29 years. During this time
been a great improvement in health condi-
especially in rural areas. The number of per-
s per hospital bed declined from 892 to 713 during
the period 1952-62, and consumption of piped pure
water in rural areas doubled during the period 1956-
61.[28] Improvement in health conditions adds to the
population pressure but it also contributes to the reduction in morbidity, which in turn promises to raise
the health level and productive capacity.[29]

Religious Differentials. Egypt is one of the
leading Moslem countries with 92 per cent of its population Moslems.[30] Among the majority of the Moslem
population, in Egypt as well as in other countries, a
religious aversion is inherent that makes them resent
any attempt to control their numbers. Actually, there
is a strong conviction that a large family is encouraged by the teachings of the Islamic religion. Such
attitudes are evident from a study of total fertility
rates among the Moslems and Christians in the metro-
politan areas of Egypt. Total fertility rate--defined
as the number of children born to a cohort of 1,000
women passed through the childbearing age of 15-49--
was 6,675 among the Moslems as compared with 4,089
among the Christians.[31]

The Islamic religion is usually blamed for
such high fertility rates prevailing among the Moslems. The teachings of the religion, if literally
interpreted, could be construed to prohibit the limitation of the number of children or what we will refer
to as family planning or population control. This is
due to two main factors:

First, there is no direct verse in the Koran
(the Holy Book of the Moslems) that sanctions or

prohibits birth control. Rather, there are some verses in the Koran and sayings of the prophet that could be interpreted as favoring large families;

Second, by the end of the thirteenth century, Islamic jurisprudence and interpretation declined. With the passage of time the source became so distant that trivial matters regarding birth control soon swelled into independent streams and became rooted as part of the religions.

Appendix "A" provides an analysis of the Islamic legal framework and its stand with respect to family planning and population control. However, it suffices to give here the opinion of the Moslem jurists. They agree that birth control or family planning is permitted in the following cases:[32]

First, in case a woman might be capable of becoming pregnant immediately following a previous pregnancy; a matter that might affect the health of the mother and also the children;

Second, if either of the parents carries a hereditary disease that might be transmitted to the offspring;

Third, in the case when frequent pregnancies might endanger the health of the mother or delay her recovery from an illness;

Fourth, when the family income is too low to allow a large family. In other words, when more children may lower the standard of living of the family. In this connection we find Imam El-Gazaly emphasizes this point and gives his sanction to the practice of birth control since a large family causes poverty and poverty affects belief.[33]

Regional Differences. Figure 5 shows the crude birth and death rates for urban and rural areas and the nation for the period 1934-60. Looking at the curves for the whole country, we can see how, over

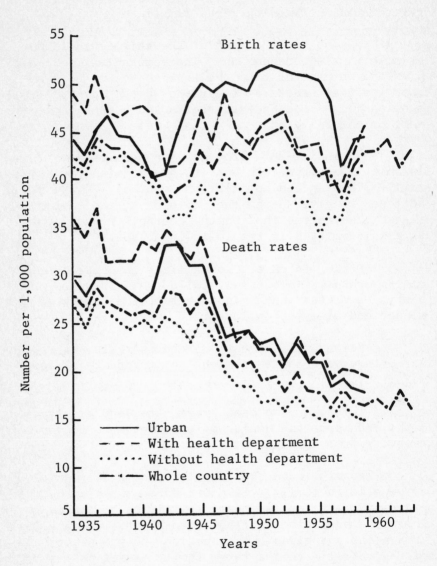

FIGURE 5.   CRUDE BIRTH AND DEATH RATES
1934-63

time, the gap is widening between the birth and the
death rates, the primary reason for the observed growth
in population.   This figure also indicates regional
differences.

National crude birth and death rates conceal
area differentials.   If we refer to Table 12 we find
that rural areas are subdivided into those with and
those without health departments. This has major implications on the efficiency with which births, deaths,
and other vital statistics are recorded. It should be
noted that, as for population censuses, vital statistics in Egypt have a much longer history than in other
countries of the Middle East. El-Badry reports that
death and birth registration in rural as well as urban
areas dates back to 1839, though it was made obliga-
tory only at the end of the last century.[34] A study
by Rizk shows that birth and death registration was
not made compulsory in Egypt until 1912.[35] Nevertheless, satisfactorily complete coverage is still lacking
especially in the rural areas without health departments.

Rural areas without health departments appear
to have a lower rate of births than those with health
departments. Such a phenomenon is contrary to experience. If we take the absence of health departments as
an indication of the state of urbanization and education, a higher birth rate is expected for rural areas
without health departments. The fact that this is not
shown in the statistics for Egypt is doubtless due to
the deficiency in birth registration in rural areas
without health departments. Several factors contribute
to this underestimation of births. In the first place,
some people tend not to register their children in an
effort to avoid their draft for military service. In
the second place, sometimes registration is delayed.
Thus, if the child dies soon after birth, his birth is
not registered, nor is his death reported. This also
explains the apparently high death rate in those rural
areas which have health departments as compared with
those which do not.   In addition, the high degree of

illiteracy in the rural area contributes to the deficiency in registration.

Birth rates for urban areas are higher than
for rural areas, although it is widely believed that
urbanization tends to lower birth rates. This could
also be due to a deficiency in birth registration in
the rural areas. It may also explain the fact that the
rates for the whole country, including rural areas,
are lower than for urban areas.

For crude death rates, the same difference is
observed between rural and urban areas. Table 13 shows
that rural areas without health departments, an indication of the low level of health services, have a
lower rate than rural areas with health departments.
Again, this is due to underreporting of deaths, since
some people in these areas tend not to report deaths
to avoid the inspection by the health department about
the cause of death.36 Births which were not registered
are not reported in the case of death. Such underreporting is especially revealed in the rates for rural
areas with health departments which have a somewhat
higher rate. The rate for rural areas with health departments is a little higher than those for urban
areas. It appears as if there was, as late as 1960,
still some deficiency in the reporting in rural areas.

In spite of the deficiency in birth and death
registration in rural areas without health departments, some basis for estimating the extent of nonre-
porting is afforded by the vital statistics given
separately for urban areas and areas with health departments. El-Badry obtained a correction factor by
dividing the total "natural increase" of rural population by its total "geometric growth." He used this
factor to adjust the reported birth and death rates in
rural areas without health departments.37 The adjusted
figures along with the resulting corrected natural
rate of increase are shown in Table 14 along with the
reported natural rate of increase calculated from
Tables 12 and 13.

Table 14. Adjusted Crude Birth Rates, Death Rates,
Rate of Natural Increase, and the Unadjusted Rate
of Natural Increase of the Egyptian Population,
Selected Years, 1934-59[a]

Year	Adjusted birth rate	Adjusted death rate	Rate of natural increase	
			Adjusted	Reported
1934	48.0	34.5	13.5	14.4
1935	45.9	32.5	13.4	14.9
1940	46.2	32.1	14.1	15.0
1945	47.9	33.3	14.6	15.0
1947	49.1	26.0	23.1	22.4
1949	45.3	24.1	21.2	21.2
1951	48.0	22.5	25.5	23.5
1952	48.2	20.5	27.7	27.4
1953	45.9	25.1	20.8	23.0
1954	45.7	20.7	25.0	24.6
1955	45.9	21.6	24.3	22.6
1956	42.3	18.6	23.7	24.3
1957	40.0	19.7	20.3	20.0
1958	42.8	19.1	23.7	24.5
1959	44.8	18.8	26.0	26.4

[a]For method of adjusting birth and death rates, see p. 82.

Sources: The first two columns: M. A. El-Badry,"Trends in the Components of Population Growth in the Arab Countries of the Middle East: A Survey of Present Information,"Demography, II (1965) pp. 144-45. The third column is obtained by subtracting column 2 from column 1 and the last column by subtraction from data in Tables 12 and 13.

Comparing the corrected birth and death rates
for the whole country (Table 14) with the reported
rates (Tables 12 and 13) we find, as El-Badry noted,
that the effect of adjustments have been generally
small in extent.38 Adjusted crude birth and death
rates are somewhat higher than reported rates. However, it should be noted that the gap has been nar-
rowing over time. In 1959 the adjusted birth rate was
44.8 as compared with a reported rate of 42.6. The
same trend is observed with respect to adjusted death
rates, which in 1959 was 18.8 as compared with a reported rate of 16.2. The main cause of such differences, it may be reiterated, is the underreporting of
births and deaths in the rural areas of Egypt, especially those without health departments.

Although there is a considerable difference
between the adjusted crude birth and death rates, the
difference between adjusted and reported rates of natural increase is somewhat narrower. In most cases the
adjusted rates are lower than the reported ones. In
other words, the adjustment of birth and death rates
is of such a magnitude that it leaves the rate of natural increase to a great extent unaltered. The adjusted rate still shows the same increasing trend,
especially beginning with the 1950's.

GEOGRAPHICAL DISTRIBUTION OF POPULATION

Population density is generally high in Egypt,
but the population is not evenly distributed over the
different parts of the inhabited areas of the country.
The sharp geographical dichotomy of the area between
the desert and the Nile not only describes the physical characteristics, but also sets the pattern for
population distribution. As Cook reports, population
density along the Nile, "is nearly three times that of
Japan, and more than twice that of the Netherlands,
England and Wales or Belgium."39

Egypt is subdivided administratively into governorates which fall into three regions (Figure 6).

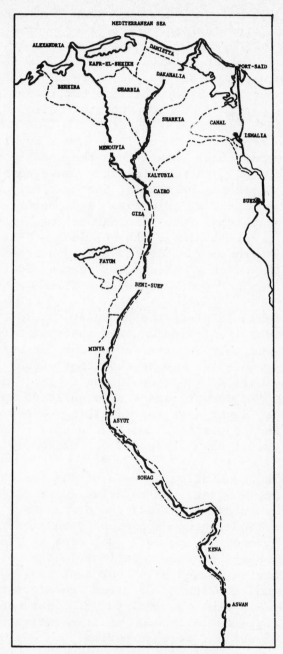

FIGURE 6.   ADMINISTRATIVE
DIVISIONS OF EGYPT

These governorates occupy more than 99 per cent of the land area; the rest comprises the Border Districts. Five of the governorates constitute the urban part of the country, which will be called in this study "Urban Governorates." These include Cairo, Alexandria, Suez, Ismalia, and Port-Said. The last two, Ismalia and Port-Said were parts of one governorate called Canal until October 1959 when this governorate was divided into two. The area which is called "Lower Egypt" includes eight governorates. Other than the urban governorates north of Cairo, there are eight governorates. They include Damietta, Dakahalia, Sharkia, Kalyubia, Kafr-El-Sheikh, Gharbia, Minufia, and Beheira. "Upper Egypt" is divided into another set of eight: Giza, Beni-Suef, Fayum, Minya, Asyut, Sohag, Kena, and Aswan. This group constitutes the less urbanized portion of the country which lies to the South of Cairo and mainly along the banks of the Nile.

Table 15 gives the population in each of the four regions and its percentage share in total population for the census years during the period 1882-1960. From this table, it can be seen that Lower Egypt held about one half of the population in 1882 and that it still has the larger share of population in 1960. In 1882, Upper Egypt was the dwelling place of 40 per cent of the population, while the urban governorates share of total population did not exceed 10 per cent.

The population of each of the regions has been increasing; however, the relative share of each region in total population has undergone changes. There has been a decline in the shares of both Lower and Upper Egypt. From 49.4 and 40.2 per cent in 1882, the respective shares of these regions in the total population became 41.9 and 35.4 per cent by 1960. For the same period the share of urban governorates doubled from 9.9 per cent in 1882 to 21.5 per cent in 1960. Border districts increased their share also in total population during the same period.

This structural change resulted in a different density of population for the three regions as can be

Table 15. Geographical Distribution of the Egyptian Population, 1882-1960

Region	1882	1897	1907	1917	1927	1937	1947	1960
				Number (in thousands)				
Governorates	663	973	1,112	1,357	1,808	2,209	3,363	5,598
Lower Egypt	3,313	4,687	5,446	6,126	6,565	7,179	8,244	10,933
Upper Egypt	2,693	3,932	4,578	5,187	5,710	6,423	7,199	9,240
Border districts	37	43	54	48	95	110	161	314
Total	6,706	9,635	11,190	12,718	14,178	15,921	18,967	26,085
				Per cent				
Governorates	9.9	10.1	9.9	10.7	12.7	13.9	17.7	21.5
Lower Egypt	49.4	48.6	48.7	48.1	46.3	45.1	43.5	41.9
Upper Egypt	40.2	40.8	40.9	40.8	40.3	40.3	38.0	35.4
Border districts	0.5	0.5	0.5	0.4	0.7	0.7	0.8	1.2
Total	100.0	100.0	100.0	100.0	100.0	100.0	100.0	100.0

Sources: Compiled from Department of Statistics and Census, Population Census of Egypt, 1947 (Cairo: Government Press, 1952), pp. 46-47; Central Committee for Statistics, Collection of Basic Statistics (Cairo: S.O.P. Press, 1962), pp. 26-35.

seen from the population map shown in Figure 7. Taking the inhabited areas in the three regions in 1960,
we find that the urban governorates comprise the most
populated regions with an average density of 3,002 per
square mile, where the land area is small.   Upper
Egypt had a density of 755, while Lower Egypt, which
has the largest land area of the three regions, had a
density of 514 in 1960.   This pattern of geographical
distribution is affected by migration.

INTERNAL MIGRATION

Although data on migration based on a complete
registration system are not available for Egypt, we
shall use the scanty and limited information available
from the censuses of population of 1927, 1937, and
1947 and some preliminary results of the 1960 census.
Data were collected in these censuses on movements of
population during the last ten years by place of emigration and immigration, for all governorates of Egypt
and the border district.   Out-migrants are considered
those enumerated outside the governorate of birth,
while in-migrants are those who were born outside the
region of enumeration.

For this study the data on the individual governorates were consolidated under four regions: urban
(5 governorates), Lower Egypt (8 governorates), and
Upper Egypt (8 governorates), in addition to the border district. The data in Table 16 show interregional
in- and out-migration for those four regions for the
census years 1927, 1937, and 1947.

The second column in Table 16 shows that the
number of out-migrants almost doubled during the period 1927-47. The largest movement out occurred in
Lower Egypt, which experienced an increase in out-
migration of more than 100 per cent during the years
1927-37.   Considering the small size of urban governorates, there has thus been a considerable outward
movement.

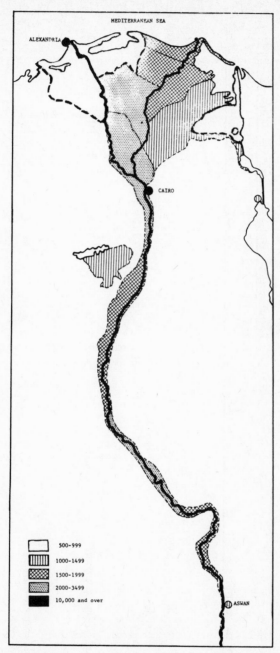

FIGURE 7.   POPULATION MAP OF EGYPT
(number per square mile)

Table 16.　Movement of the Egyptian Population by Region, Census Years, 1927, 1937, and 1947

Region of birth	Total emigrants[a]	Number enumerated outside the regions of birth			
		Urban governorates	Lower Egypt	Upper Egypt	Border districts
1927					
Urban governorates	75,659	---	45,829	27,991	1,839
Lower Egypt	253,844	226,558	---	25,069	2,217
Upper Egypt	324,869	267,903	49,660	---	7,306
Border districts	13,710	8,409	4,751	550	---
Total immigrants[b]	668,082	502,870	100,240	53,610	11,362
1937					
Urban governorates	79,522	---	43,742	32,434	3,346
Lower Egypt	328,712	296,491	---	29,148	3,073
Upper Egypt	329,733	283,801	37,493	---	8,439
Border districts	15,564	10,124	4,325	1,115	---
Total immigrants[b]	753,531	590,416	85,560	62,697	14,858

1947

Urban governorates	112,888	---	63,825	44,834	4,229
Lower Egypt	609,756	561,121	---	45,437	3,198
Upper Egypt	477,671	411,742	65,929	---	---
Border districts	31,963	13,214	3,359	1,399	13,991
Total immigrants[b]	1,232,278	986,077	133,113	91,670	21,418

[a]Emigrants are considered those enumerated outside the governorate of birth.

[b]Immigrants are those who were born outside the region of enumeration.

Sources: Compiled from Department of Statistics and Census, Population Census of Egypt, 1937, General Tables (Cairo: Government Press, 1942), pp. 72-73; Population Census of Egypt, 1947, General Tables (Cairo: Government Press, 1952), pp. 68-69.

Most of the migrants from the urban governorates go to Lower Egypt, but the outflow declined. The percentage of total emigrants from urban governorates to Lower Egypt which was 60.6 in 1927 became 56.5 in 1947. On the other hand, migrants from Lower and Upper Egypt go to urban governorates. About 90 per cent of emigrants in the case of the former and over 80 per cent of the latter went to urban governorates during the period 1927-37. Considering the size of out-migration from Lower and Upper Egypt, this accounts for the large number of migrants into the urban governorates. Advancing from about half a million immigrants in 1927, urban governorates received almost a million in 1947. The ratio and magnitudes of in-migration to Lower and Upper Egypt are not very high. This also could account for the high birth rates in urban areas as noted before.

A comparison of in- and out-migration can best be seen from Table 17 which shows in- and out-migration as a percentage of the population of each region for 1927, 1937, and 1947. Leaving aside the migration movement in and out of the border districts, since it is negligible, we find that in 1927 the highest in-migration occurred in the urban governorates (27.3 per cent) and the highest out-migration came from Lower Egypt (5.7 per cent). This pattern continued in 1947 when the figures became 28.9 and 6.8 per cent, respectively. Most of this increase is due to the movement that occurred during the Second World War and job opportunities opened around the cities working for the Armed Forces. In addition, a few industries developed during that period. In densely populated Lower Egypt, agriculture still remains the dominant industry, and the level of income is too low to support large rural families. Out-migration should have been directed toward the less-populated regions of the country. Urban governorates with their living facilities and general job opportunities are attractive to migrants.

Migration as a percentage of total population remained constant at 4.7 per cent during the period

Table 17. Out-migration and In-migration by Region as a Percentage
of Population of the Region, 1927, 1937, and 1947

Region	1927		1937		1947	
	Out-migration	In-migration	Out-migration	In-migration	Out-migration	In-migration
Urban governorates	4.1	27.3	3.5	26.3	3.3	28.9
Lower Egypt	3.9	1.5	4.6	1.2	7.4	1.6
Upper Egypt	5.7	0.9	5.1	1.0	6.8	1.3
Border districts	14.5	12.0	14.2	13.6	11.2	13.3
Total Egypt	4.7	4.7	4.7	4.7	6.5	6.5

Source: Data in Tables 15 and 16. Out-migration is computed by taking total emigrants as a percentage of total population for each region and the whole
country. In-migration is computed by taking total immigrants as a percentage
of total population for each region and the whole country.

1927-37. This constant and small magnitude of migration is due to the high private cost of migration which can be broken down to money and nonmoney costs. Sjaastad includes in money costs the out-of-pocket expenses of movement, while in the nonmoney costs he includes foregone earnings and the "psychic" costs of changing one's environment.[40] These two types of costs were high in Egypt and they operated to keep population movement at a low level. The lack of roads and means of transportation rendered the cost of movement considerably high. Studies on the cost of migration in the United States establish that the marginal costs of migration associated with additional distances are considerably high.[41] Moreover, we find that the structure of the agrarian society puts a still higher premium on movement by raising the nonmonetary costs. In the agrarian society which dominates Egypt, family ties are very strong. Even if the person managed to move away, he has to consider the "psychic" cost as represented by the trips he has to make home frequently. In addition to this fact, many nonmoney costs act as obstacles to movement in Egypt. First, the earnings foregone while traveling are high because inefficient means of transportation prolong travel time. Second, the earnings foregone while searching for and learning a new job are high because the high level of unemployment prolongs the time spent finding a new job. Another factor that impedes migration, is the lack of a free flow of information about employment opportunities in another place because of poor communications and the high degree of illiteracy among the majority of rural population.

It was not until the beginning of World War II that people started moving from Upper Egypt seeking jobs with the Armed Forces stationed mainly in Lower Egypt. As a result of this, by 1947 the percentage of migrants to total population increased by more than a third. It is expected that with rising industrialization, and the construction of roads and means of communication, such as is taking place in the Aswan area, population mobility will increase.

Data comparable to those in   Table 17 are not
available for 1960.   However, El-Badry provides some
data on migration by region   and sex in his study on
trends in the components of population   growth in some
Arab countries.[42] We used his data to compare the
trends and differentials in migration. Table 18 and
Table 19 show out-migration   and in-migration as a percentage of total population by sex   for the Egyptian
governorates in 1937 and 1960.

The increasing trend of in- and   out-migration
detected between 1927-47 continued to 1960 with two
exceptions.   First, out-migration from Damietta declined over time   due to the urbanization of this governorate during the 1950's.   The second   exception is
the   slackening of in-migration to the two major cities, Cairo and   Alexandria, and to some extent Suez.
These two major cities show a slight   decline in in-
migrants.   This is due mainly to the congestion of
these two cities and their inability to absorb more
people. On the other hand, there has been a considerable growth in the neighboring areas that began to
absorb some of the in-migrants.   It is noticeable from
the table that the per cent of population migrating to
Giza, which is very close to Cairo, increased from 8
to 22 for males and from 5 to 21 for females during
the period 1937-60. Furthermore, the industrialization
of the country helped to release the pressure on these
two cities, since people started to migrate to the
new areas with employment opportunities.   Aswan was
one of the highest "population exporting" governorates
in the country, where migrants traveled north to Cairo
and Alexandria to seek employment in the service industries. However, between 1937 and 1960 the percentage
of total population that migrated to this area increased from 12 to 16 for males and from 8 to 11 for
females.   This was enhanced by the employment opportunities created by the construction operations of the
High Dam, quarries, and iron ore mines.

Percentage differences between males and females who migrate are not very sharp.   A marked difference is observed between in- and out-migration.

Table 18.   Out-migration as a Percentage
of Total Population by Sex for the
Governorates of Egypt
in 1937 and 1960

	Males		Females	
	1937	1960	1937	1960
Upper Egypt				
Aswan	20	29	7	16
Asyut	9	14	6	11
Beni-Suef	5	9	4	8
Fayum	3	7	3	7
Giza	8	8	7	8
Kena	8	16	5	12
Minya	3	5	3	4
Sohag	10	17	6	13
Lower Egypt				
Beheira	6	7	4	8
Dakahalia	7	11	7	11
Damietta	36	12	38	14
Gharbia	{5	13	{5	13
Kafr-El-Sheikh		6		6
Kalyubia	8	14	7	13
Menoufia	12	23	9	22
Sharkia	6	10	5	9
Urban Governorates				
Alexandria	8	8	11	9
Cairo	9	10	8	10
Ismalia[a]	{10	14	{9	14
Port-Said[a]		16		17
Suez	14	15	13	15

[a]In 1957 the Canal Governorate was divided into two
governorates, Port-Said and Ismalia.

Source: M. A. El-Badry, "Trends in the Components of
Population Growth in the Arab Countries of
the Middle East: A Survey of Present Information," Demography, II (1965), pp. 160-63.

Table 19.   In-migration as a Percentage
of Total Population by Sex for the
Governorates of Egypt
in 1937 and 1960

	Males		Females	
	1937	1960	1937	1960
Upper Egypt				
Aswan	12	16	8	11
Asyut	2	3	1	2
Beni-Suef	4	4	4	3
Fayum	2	3	2	3
Giza	8	22	5	21
Kena	1	3	1	1
Minya	3	3	3	3
Sohag	1	2	1	3
Lower Egypt				
Beheira	6	7	7	6
Dakahalia	3	4	2	3
Damietta	10	10	9	9
Gharbia	{4	6	{3	6
Kafr-El-Sheikh		6		5
Kalyubia	5	11	3	9
Menoufia	1	3	1	2
Sharkia	5	4	3	4
Urban Governorates				
Alexandria	35	30	28	26
Cairo	40	39	36	36
Ismalia[a]	{44	40	{38	39
Port-Said[a]		31		31
Suez	49	47	42	45

[a]In 1957 the Canal Governorate was divided into two
governorates, Port-Said and Ismalia.

Source: M. A. El-Badry, "Trends in the Components of
Population Growth in the Arab Countries of
the Middle East: A Survey of Present Information," Demography, II (1965), pp. 160-63.

Out-migration of both sexes is generally higher than
in-migration for the governorates of Upper and Lower
Egypt with the exception of Giza. This governorate,
though administratively in Upper Egypt, is located in
the outskirts of Cairo, an urban governorate with a
high rate of in-migration. Therefore, with respect to
the migration pattern, we find Giza conforms to the
urban governorates which reflects a degree of in-
migration higher than that of out-migration.

Out-migration. In addition to the direction
of migration between regions, regional differentials
are observed not only among broad regions, but also
within them. Looking at the eight governorates in
Upper Egypt, a dichotomy is observed as to the percentage of out-migrants to total population both males
and females. The Southern governorates in this region
(Aswan, Asyut, Kena, and Sohag) have been experiencing
a large out-migration. On the other hand, the Northern
governorates of this region (Beni-Suef, Fayum, Giza,
and Minya) show that a smaller percentage of their
population move out. The difference within this region
is due mainly to the population pressure on the land
and the lack of employment opportunities.[43] The land
in Upper Egypt can only be irrigated once a year,
which puts a limitation of the expansion of the crop
area.

Out-migration from the governorates of Lower
Egypt is somewhat moderate except for those surround-
ing Cairo (Kalyubia and Menoufia). The same situation
is observed with regard to the urban governorates.
Among these governorates, Cairo and Alexandria are the
lowest of the "population exporting" governorates.
The per cent of population migrating out of the governorates along the Suez Canal was somewhat high in
1960, possibly because of the stagnant economic conditions that followed the Suez crisis and the consequent
closing of the canal.

In-migration. With the exception of Aswan and
Giza, migration into the governorates of Upper Egypt
was and still is very small. This is due to the lack

of opportunities   in the   region,   in addition   to its
remoteness from the other parts of the country and the
deficiency in transportation.   All this   tends to increase the money and the nonmoney   costs of migration.
As said above, the considerable   migration to Aswan is
explained by the   employment   opportunities created by
the construction of the   High Dam and   the development
of extractive industries.   Giza, being close to Cairo,
absorbs those   migrants   who find employment   in Cairo
but reside in Giza.   This also   explains the decrease
in   the percentage   of   people   migrating   to Cairo in
1960.   The governorates of Lower   Egypt experienced a
somewhat moderate in-migration.

Migration into the urban governorates has been
so heavy that the percentage of its population born in
governorates   other than   urban ranges   between 26 and
47.   These   governorates   are the urban   areas   of the
country and act as a "Mecca"   for everyone.   This partially explains   the overurbanization   of the two cities, Cairo   and Alexandria.   Davis   and Golden explain
this   overurbanization by the   movement   of productive
nonagriculturists   or nearly everybody not involved in
farming to the cities.[44]   This degree of overurbanization creates   problems. These   are   treated   in the next
section.

URBANIZATION

The migration movement toward the major cities
of the urban   governorates of Egypt   creates new problems, especially   those   arising   out of urbanization.
Although countries in the early   stages of development
have   a tendency   to be "overurbanized,"   Davis   and
Golden consider   that Egypt "has far   more urbanization
than its degree of economic   development would lead us
to expect."[45]   In comparing   Egypt with some countries
which are   higher   in the scale   of industrialization,
they found Egypt definitely   overurbanized.   The percentage of population in cities with   100,000 inhabitants and over   was 19.3   in Egypt   in 1947,   which is
higher than that of Sweden with 17.4 (1945) and France

with 16.6 (1946), although it is less than that of
Switzerland with 20.6 (1950). On the other hand, the
percentage of population in cities with 200,000 inhabitants and over in Egypt is not much less than for
these three countries, which are far more industrialized than Egypt.

The urbanization movement is not undesirable
in itself, since it largely reflects the progress of
industrialization and social change.[46] There are several economic aspects of urbanization. In the first
place, urban areas are characterized by occupational
diversification, the result of changes in the occupational structure of the working force in favor of nonagricultural or industrial activities. Urbanization
thus reflects technological change and new forms of
economic organization, and creates employment opportunities as well as social mobility. Second, urbanization results in the creation of external economies due
to the growth in tertiary industries. The growth of
urban areas tends to attract several servicing activities such as retail trade, transportation, and domestic
services, all of which create external economies. A
third aspect of urbanization is the internal economies
of scale made possible by the increasing income and
increase in demand of the growing population in urban
areas. Fortunately, urbanization may lead to increases
in demand for agricultural products needed to feed the
growing urban population, and this may enhance agricultural development. If we add to this the fact that
those who move to the cities come from rural areas, we
can see that this may cure the disguised unemployment
prevailing in this rural area and raise productivity
in agriculture. Furthermore, urban areas require heavy
investments in the infrastructure, such as public
utilities and housing, especially when urbanization is
outpacing the rate of economic development. This might
serve as a push factor and lead to increasing capital
formation in order to meet requirements for urbanization.

The definition of "urban population" is somewhat arbitrary and varies from one study to another.[47]

For the purpose of this analysis urban places are considered to be any settlement with at least 20,000
inhabitants. Apart from being a definition that ap-
proximates the official Egyptian definition, it permits comparison with data from United Nations.[48]

Although Hoselitz came to the conclusion that
industrialization and urbanization are effective means
of economic advancement, he warns that this process
should not be looked upon as one of unmixed blessings
due to the social consequences of the growth of urban
centers in underdeveloped countries. He does not consider those urban centers in underdeveloped countries
as really genuine industrial cities compared to those
of western Europe which were the chief centers of social change and which played an important role in
"strengthening the new technical order based on ra-
tional allocation of resources,competitive markets,and
the pursuit of self-interest in economic action."[49]
Thus urbanization reflects economic progress and industrialization but it could become a problem when
it outpaces the rate of economic development. In such
a case the nation faces overurbanization. The overurbanization of Egyptian large cities and the two main
cities is emphasized by J. Abu-Lughod and Davis and
Golden.[50] Between 1937 and 1960 the share of urban
population in the total population in Upper Egypt increased from 12 to 20 per cent. The same trend is in
Lower Egypt from 12 to 19 per cent.[51] This resulted
in the increase of the share of urban population in
total population of Egypt from 24 to 37 per cent during the period 1937-60. This, of course, is higher
than that for the two rural regions of Egypt (Lower
and Upper Egypt) since it includes the inhabitants of
the urban governorates. These are all urban people and
they showed a considerable increase in number. Actually, while urban population in Egypt experienced an
increase of 104 per cent during the period under consideration, rural population increased only by 35 per
cent.

Cities are sometimes taken as an indication of
urbanism. The word "city" is generally identified as

both antecedent to and consequent upon modern western civilization.[52] The increase in urban population tended to change the size and number of Egyptian cities which are considered urban. For 57 cities which are considered urban according to the 1947 census, the rates of population increase were as follows:[53]

Period	Percentage Increase
1897-1927	15.7
1927-1937	12.3
1937-1947	19.1
1947-1960	28.8*

*Adjusted for ten-year period.

Apart from the considerable increase at the beginning of the twentieth century, the figures show that urbanization is a postwar phenomenon. We shall therefore concentrate on the period 1947-60. Table 20 shows the regional distribution of Egyptian cities and towns by size in 1947 and 1960. This table reflects the tremendous increase in the population of cities with at least 20,000 inhabitants. While their number increased from 57 to 86, their population almost doubled between 1947-60. Most of the increase is due to the increase in the urban population of the cities located in upper Egypt, and the two primates, Cairo and Alexandria. Actually, these figures show the wide gap between the size of these largest two cities and the size of the other urban communities of secondary importance. This is an indication of the pattern of imbalanced urbanization which tends to create problems for the overurbanized areas and the consequent drain of resources from the secondary urban communities, in addition to the sociological impact created by urbanization and its concomitant, the introduction of mechanized industry.[54] Hoselitz distinguishes three types of patterns. The first is the need for adjustment to a new environment since the city in an underdeveloped country "is an inhospitable environment for many actual or potential laborers."[55] The second impact is

Table 20. Regional Distribution of Egyptian Cities and Towns by Size
in 1947 and 1960

Size (1,000)	Upper Egypt		Lower Egypt		All Egypt	
	Number of cities	Popula-tion (1,000)	Number of cities	Popula-tion (1,000)	Number of cities	Popula-tion (1,000)
1947						
Primates	2	3010	0	0	2	3010
Cities of 50 plus	5	357	9	931	14	1288
Large towns (25-49.9)	13	424	13	417	26	841
Small towns (20-24.9)	8	178	7	158	15	336
Total	28	3969	29	1506	57	5475
1960						
Primates	2	4859	0	0	2	4859
Cities of 50 plus	9	955	12	1721	21	2676
Large towns (25-49.9)	18	589	21	725	39	1314
Small towns (20-24.9)	12	271	12	263	24	534
Total	41	6674	45	2709	86	9383

Source: Calculated from data in Janet L. Abu-Lughod, "Urbanization in Egypt: Present
State and Future Prospects," Economic Development and Cultural Change, XXIII
(April, 1965), 318-32.

the replacement of handicraft work by machine work that results from the introduction of new technology. The third is "the impact of new forms of social structure and the requirements of new types of social behavior appropriate to large-scale production in the factory."[56] Enke also points to an equally important factor, that is, the increase in the real cost of expanding industry that results from urbanization. Extra workers employed in town to provide extra housing and other utilities that are a peculiar cost to urban living, represent a cost that should be included in the economy's transformation function from agriculture to industry.[57]

The build-up of the infrastructure in these twin magnets, Cairo and Alexandria, attracted industries to these two centers. Both capital and human resources move toward these two cities, leaving the other areas without any potential growth. Another factor that enhances such movement is that these two cities (mainly Cairo) are the seats of government in addition to being the location of the four largest universities in the country, other institutions of higher learning, and research centers.

It was only recently that the Egyptian government tried to redistribute the new projects all over the country in order to create more urbanized centers and attract people to them. Examples of this are the developments of the Aswan area, where population increased from 26,000 to 48,000; Ismailia, which increased from 68,000 to 276,000; Giza, 66,000 to 250,000; Port-Said, 178,000 to 244,000; and Suez, 107,000 to 203,000 during the period 1947-60. Another factor that is promoting the urbanization of areas other than Cairo and Alexandria is the redistribution of the institutions of higher education all over the country instead of being concentrated in Cairo and Alexandria. These last two are the location of the two oldest universities in Egypt and now the largest four universities in the country in addition to several institutes. The location of institutions of higher learning in new areas is resulting in the movement of population to seek employment in service industries. This shift is seen in the growth of places such as Port-Said, Asyut, and Al-Mansura, where higher institutions of education and branches of the universities are now located. The population of Asyut increased from 90,000 to 122,000 and Al-Mansura from 102,000 to 152,000 during the period 1947-60.

Notes to Chapter 4

[1] Egypt is considered "one of the few economically underdeveloped countries with reasonably accurate census data," see Robert C. Cook, "Egypt's Population Explodes," Population Bulletin, XII (July, 1956), 59.

[2] Clyde V. Kiser, "The Demographic Position of Egypt," Demographic Studies of Selected Areas of Rapid Growth (New York: Milbank Memorial Fund, 1944), p. 98. This study also appeared in Milbank Memorial Fund Quarterly, XXII (October, 1944), 384-85.

[3] George L. Beer, "Egyptian Problems," in African Questions at the Paris Conference (New York: Macmillan, 1923), pp. 308-309.

[4] Charles Issawi, "Population and Wealth in Egypt," Milbank Memorial Fund Quarterly, XXVII (January, 1949), 99. Reprinted in J. J. Spengler and O. D. Duncan (eds.), Demographic Analysis (Glencoe, Ill.: The Free Press, 1956), pp. 34-43. All reference hereafter will be to the former.

[5] Wendell W. Cleland, The Population Problem in Egypt (Lancaster, Penn.: Pennsylvania Printing Co., 1936), p. 6.

[6] Issawi, op. cit., p. 99.

[7] Ibid.

[8]W. Cleland, op.cit., p. 7 and M. A. El-Badry, "Some Demographic Measurements for Egypt Based on the Stability of Census Age Distribution," Milbank Memorial Fund Quarterly, XXXIII (July, 1955), 3.

[9]According to the calculations of J. I. Craig, former Controller of the Egyptian Department of Statistics in 1917.

[10]United Nations, Department of Economic and Social Affairs, Demographic Yearbook, 1963 (New York, 1963), p. 142.

[11]Ibid., pp. 124, 132.

[12]Ibid., pp. 123, 124, 134.

[13]Ibid., p. 527.

[14]Frank W. Notestein, "The Population of the World in the Year 2000," in J. J. Spengler and O. D. Duncan (eds.), Demographic Analysis (Glencoe, Ill.: The Free Press, 1956), pp. 34-43.

[15]Central Committee for Statistics, Collection of Basic Statistics, (Cairo: S.O.P. Press, 1962), pp. 208-209.

[16]United Nations, Department of Economic and Social Affairs, Provisional Report on World Population Prospects as Assessed in 1963 (New York, 1964) pp. 220-21.

[17]Joseph J. Spengler, "The Economics of Population Growth," in Stuart Mudd (ed.), The Population Crisis and the Use of World Resources, (Bloomington: Indiana University Press, 1964), p. 89.

[18]Ibid.

[19]Spengler, op. cit.

[20]United Nations, Department of Social Affairs,

Population Division, The Determinants and Consequences of Population Trends (New York, 1953), p. 94.

[21]Spengler, op. cit., p. 89.

[22]Ibid.

[23]The rates for India and the world are for the period 1958-62. See United Nations, Department of Economic and Social Affairs, Demographic Yearbook,1963 (New York, 1963), pp. 142-45.

[24]Kingsley Davis, "Institutional Patterns Favoring High Fertility in Underdeveloped Areas," in Lyle W. Shannon, Underdeveloped Areas (New York: Harper and Brothers, 1957), pp. 88-95.

[25]Ibid. Similar factors are advanced by Skinner in his analysis of the role of cultural values, social structure in fertility trends in Asia; see G. William Skinner, "Cultural Values, Social Structure, and Population Growth," in United Nations, Department of Economic and Social Affairs, Population Bulletin of the United States, No. 5 (New York, 1956), pp. 5-12.

[26]Central Committee for Statistics, Collection of Basic Statistics (Cairo: S.O.P. Press, 1962), p. 168.

[27]It should be noted that the female role is changing now considerably. See Aziza Hussein, "The Status of Women in Family Law in the United Arab Republic," a paper presented in a seminar on Status of Women in Family Law, United Nations Commission on the Status of Women, Lome, Togo, August-September, 1964.

[28]Ibid., pp. 208-209.

[29]S. Swaroop, "Growth of Population and Health Programmes in Asia and the Far East," United Nations, Department of Economic and Social Affairs, Population Bulletin of the United Nations, No. 5 (New York, 1956), p. 27.

[30]The next major religious group is the Christian (7 per cent). Republic of Egypt, Ministry of Finance and Economy, Statistical Department, Statistical Pocket Yearbook, 1954 (Cairo: Government Press, 1955) p. 9.

[31]A. M. Zikry, "Fertility Differential of the U. A. R. Women," a paper contributed to the United Nations World Population Conference, Belgrade, Yugoslavia, September, 1965, (Mimeographed), p. 7.

[32]Ahmed El.Sharabasy, Religion and Family Planning (Ministry of Social Affairs, Public Relations Office: Cairo, 1966), in Arabic, pp. 50-51.

[33]Imam Abu-Hamid Ibn Mohammed El-Gazaly, Ihya Elome El-Din (Commercial Press, Cairo), Vol. 2, p. 48.

[34]M. A. El-Badry, "Trends in the Components of Population Growth in the Arab Countries of the Middle East: A Survey of Present Information." Demography, II (1965), 144.

[35]Hanna Rizk, "Population Growth and Its Effects on Economic and Social Goals in the United Arab Republic," in Stuart Mudd (ed.), The Population Crisis and the Use of World Resources (Bloomington: Indiana University Press, 1964), p. 169.

[36]For some comments on the reliability of vital statistics in underdeveloped areas see Magdi M. El-Kammash, "Stockwell's Infant Mortality Index for Measuring Economic Development: A Comment," Milbank Quarterly, XL, No. 2 (January, 1962), pp. 112-19.

[37]El-Badry, op. cit., pp. 144-45.

[38]Ibid.

[39]Robert C. Cook,"Egypt's Population Explodes," Population Bulletin, XII (July, 1956), 57.

[40]Larry A. Sjaastad, "The Costs and Returns of

Human Migration," Journal of Political Economy, Supplement, LXX (October, 1962), 83-87.

[41]Larry A. Sjaastad, "Income and Migration in the United States" (unpublished Ph.D. dissertation, University of Chicago, 1961) and James G. Maddox, "Private and Social Costs of the Movement of the People out of Agriculture," American Economic Review, Papers and Proceedings, L (May, 1960), 392-402.

[42]El-Badry, op. cit., p. 160.

[43]Population density is still high in these governorates. Population per square mile reached 2,654 in Sohag, 2,217 in Asyut, 1,933 in Kena, and 1,129 in Aswan.

[44]Kingsley Davis and Hilda Hertz Golden, "Urbanization and the Development of Pre-industrial Areas," Economic Development and Cultural Change, III (October, 1954), 18.

[45]Ibid., p. 16.

[46]Philip M. Hauser (ed.), Urbanization in Asia and the Far East, Proceedings of the Joint UN/UNESCO Seminar on urbanization in the ECAFE Region (Calcuta: UNESCO Research Center on the Social Implications of Industrialization in Southern Asia, 1957), pp. 6-7, especially pp. 9 seq.

[47]In some studies the number of inhabitants is taken to exceed 100,000. See M. H. Buntle, "L'Hypertrophic Urbaine," Bulletin De L'Institut International De Statistique, Actes De La 32 Session De Statistique, XXXVIII (Tokyo, 1960), 521-28.

[48]For a discussion on the several criteria for determining the degree or urbanization see, C. Rosier, L'Urbanisme ou La Science de L'Agglomeration (Paris: Dunod, 1953), Ch. II, and Davis and Golden, op. cit., p. 7.

[49] Bert F. Hoselitz, "The City, Factory and Economic Growth," American Economic Review, Papers and Proceedings, XLV (May, 1955), 171 and 166.

[50] Abu-Lughod, op. cit., pp. 313-343 and Davis and Golden, op. cit., pp. 16-24.

[51] Calculated from Collection of Basic Statistics, op. cit., pp. 30-32.

[52] Hauser, op. cit., p. 3.

[53] Calculated from data in Abu-Lughod, op. cit., pp. 334-335.

[54] For a discussion of some of the sociological problems of urbanization, especially for Cairo, see, Janet J. Abu-Laghod, "Migrant Adjustment to City Life: The Egyptian Case," American Journal of Sociology, LXVII (July, 1961), 22-32.

[55] Hoselitz, op. cit., pp. 180-83.

[56] Ibid., p. 180.

[57] Stephen Enke, Economics for Development (Ennglewood Cliffs, N. J.: Prentice-Hall, 1963), pp. 136-38.

CHAPTER 5 INVESTMENT IN HUMAN RESOURCE

The ultimate goal of economic activity is the satisfaction of individual needs and the improvement in the population's welfare. However, we find that population plays two roles. While the welfare of population is the ultimate goal of economic activity, population--which is subject to change--is the source of the factor of production labor. In turn, this variability affects the process by which needs are satisfied. In other words, population affects the demand for goods and services, while at the same time, it is the source of the supply of a production factor. The quality of this factor depends on investment in education, specialized training, or improved health conditions that lead to a furthering of life expectancy and productivity.

This two-sided characteristic of population, a supply factor in addition to the source of demand, represents a basic problem in underdeveloped countries, which, as is generally known, are in most cases overpopulated. An increase in population is sometimes considered advantageous, for it provides an abundant supply of labor on one hand, while it may create purchasing power on the other hand. Yet, this is not usually the case. The increase in income and output that could be created by using the larger supply of labor is limited by disproportionalities in other factors of production, in addition to the low quality of human resources due to the lack of education and the deficiency in training and health facilities. Then, it is not only the quantity of the factor of production labor, but rather the quality as reflected in the level of training, education, and dexterity. As a statistical study of the UNESCO concludes, "a high rate of illiteracy or a large number of illiterates in the adult population, is certainly one of the handicaps of an underdeveloped or even moderately developed country."[1]

DEVELOPMENT OF HUMAN RESOURCES

It is agreed that the now developing countries should benefit from the scientific and technological knowledge of the highly developed ones. In this process of transferring technology, it is "...the human being and not the technique as such, that has become the centre of great enterprise."[2] Thus the development of human resources is considered by many the cornerstone of economic development. Human resources may be developed in many ways, but the most obvious are formal education from primary or first level education to higher education, and technical and administrative training, whether "on the job" or in institutions. Investment in education and training programs certainly contributes to economic development, but also economic development makes it possible for nations to invest in educational development. Education, therefore, "is both the seed and the flower of economic development."[3]

The importance of education to the development of human resources conducive to economic development has been recognized by many economists. Even generations ago, Smith, Mill, and Marshall saw the relevance of education to economic progress. While Smith considered the cost of education and apprenticeship as a part of the fixed capital, the improvement of which repays the cost,[4] Mill emphasized the "improvement in education" as an element in determining the productiveness of labor.[5] Marshall, not overlooking the role of technical education, considers education a national investment.[6]

The difficulty in measuring human capital deterred the modern economists from devoting much attention to the role of human resources in development. The shift in study has recently been brought into focus by Schultz and others.[7]

Three aspects of investment in the development of human resources could be distinguished. In the first we find that a high degree of correlation is observed between the level of per capita income and the degree of education. In a study of 41 countries by the UNESCO on the relationship between adult illiteracy rates and per capita income in 1950, the following distribution was found:[8]

Degree of illiteracy	Per capita income less than $300	Per capita income more than $300
High	12	0
Medium	12	2
Low	0	16

A high degree of illiteracy means that 50 per cent or more of the adults are illiterate, medium 20-49 per cent and, low, less than 20 per cent. The degree of illiteracy is higher in 24 countries with per capita income less than $300 while it is considerably lower in countries with per capita income more than $300. The analysis of time series data for the United States also confirms these results. The illiteracy rate declined from 20 per cent in 1870 to 3.2 per cent in 1950 while per capita gross national product (in 1929 dollars) increased from $268 in the period around 1870 to $1,093 in 1950.[9] This is confirmed by the results Harbison and Myers obtained in their studies on manpower, education, and economic growth. In these studies of several countries the analysis shows especially that "there is a close association between enrollment ratios and all levels of education and GNP per capita."[10] Other studies by Harbison and Myers report a very high positive correlation between an index of human resource development and GNP per capita (.888).[11]

The second aspect is that, while income increases as a consequence of the development of human
resources, education and training, in turn, will be
enhanced further by the increase in income.   With the
increase in the level of income, the economy could
afford increased expenditure on education.   Countries
with 50 per cent or more of their adult population illiterate spend on education less than 3 per cent of
their national income.[12] In countries with a low level
of illiteracy, the per cent of national income devoted
to public expenditure on education is over 5 per cent
as we can see from Russia (7.1), Finland (6.3), Japan
(5.7), Belgium (5.6), and the Netherlands (5.2).[13]

Finally, we should note that, when the level
of income is low, the nation simply cannot afford to
have most of its young people in the age of 15-19 in
full-time education.   Education of this group will
result in withholding it from gainful employment.
Thus, the lack of education and training due to low
income leads to low productivity and low income which
in turn does not permit much expenditure on education,
and a vicious circle is formed.

In the light of this analytical framework, we
propose to examine the development of human resources
in the Egyptian economy.   First, the level of education, degree of skill, the training and dexterity of
the working population, area, sex, and related religious differentials will be discussed and checked
against changes in income. Second, the life expectancy
of the population is a determinant of the productive
life span i.e., the period during which labor can
contribute to production as an active agent.[14]

INCOME AND INVESTMENT IN HUMAN RESOURCES

During the first part of the twentieth century
there was little improvement in income in Egypt. Beginning in 1937 we find that per capita income, stated
in 1953 prices, increased from $82 to $88 by 1947 and
jumped to 101 by 1950. This reflects an improvement

in education that took place mainly during the war and postwar period. With little invested in education, the percentage of total population 15 years and over that is illiterate amounted to 92.8 per cent according to the 1907 census data, and 86.6 per cent in the 1927 and 1937 censuses.[15] The improvement in the educational level in the postwar period came about as a result of contact with other people, and consequently, increased demand for education. For example in 1944, the government passed a law requiring all companies employing thirty or more people to provide elementary education to their employees.[16] At the same time, the increase in income during the war period permitted still further expenditure on education.   In 1947, the percentage of illiterates dropped to 80.1 and in 1950 it was estimated to be between 75 and 80 per cent.[17] With the development that took place during the 1950's, the percentage of illiterate population, 15 years and over, declined to 72.4 per cent by 1960.[18]

Regional and Sex Differentials. Geographical and sex differentials found in the degree of illiteracy reflect largely the income factor. These differentials are more than apparent in urban areas where income is higher than in rural areas.   In the Egyptian economy, moreover, men earn more than women. Table 21 shows the percentage distribution of literacy by sex for rural and urban areas.   Children less than five years of age are excluded for the period 1927-60. Literacy is defined here as the ability to read and write.

Table 21 illustrates the marked sex and regional differentials. In a society where females do not participate in production, there has not been much reason to urge their education. As recent as 1927, only 5 per cent of the women knew how to read or write, as opposed to more than 20 per cent of males. There has been a steady increase in the degree of literacy of females. By 1960, the percentage of literate females became 16.4, or about four times its level in 1927.   At the same time, the degree of literacy continues to increase among males. By 1960 a little less

Table 21.   Per cent of Total Population Literate,
by Sex, for Urban and Rural Areas,
Census Years, 1927-60[a]

Year	Sex	Urban areas	Rural areas	Total
1927	Males	42.9	16.6	22.9
	Females	17.4	1.1	4.7
1937	Males	48.8	20.7	27.6
	Females	23.0	6.9	10.7
1947	Males	49.5	23.7	31.6
	Females	24.4	7.0	12.1
1957	Males	58.7	28.8	n.a.
	Females	31.1	7.7	n.a.
1960	Males	n.a.	n.a.	44.8
	Females	n.a.	n.a.	16.4

[a]Children below five years of age were not included up
to 1957. In 1960, children below 10 years of age were
not included.

Source: Central Committee for Statistics, Collection
of Basic Statistics (Cairo: S.O.P. Press,
1962), pp. 86-198.

than one half the males could read and write. This
progress is the result of the efforts directed in the
last two decades towards general education. By then
compulsory elementary education had been introduced.
Education up to the university level has been demanded
for all. Moreover, during this development period efforts were also directed toward increasing vocational
schools.

Almost all of the female population, 98.9 per
cent, found, in 1927, in rural areas were illiterate.
In the urban areas, literate females amounted to 17.4
per cent. We also find that more than 40.0 per cent
of urban males were literate as compared with 16.6 per
cent in rural areas. This difference occurs largely
because the level of income is considerably lower in
rural areas and schools are fewer than they are in the
cities. These variables go together. Moreover, villages in rural areas are scattered and roads are lacking, a fact that makes it difficult to attend school
in an area where a school may be located. This combination of circumstances naturally discourages going to
school. Finally, farmers need the help of their
children on their highly labor-intensive farms and
they cannot afford the income foregone by sending
their children to school.

As stated above, there has been a considerable
improvement in the degree of literacy among males and
females in both rural and urban areas. To expand upon
this proposition, we find a marked increase in the
percentage of literate females in both of these regions. In 1927, from 17.4 per cent in urban areas, it
became 31.1 in 1957, and from 1.1 in the same year in
rural areas it increased to 7.7 per cent by 1957. The
corresponding increase in literate males was from 42.9
to 58.7 for urban areas and from 16.6 to 28.8 in rural
areas for the same period. The rise in the degree of
literacy among males and females in urban areas and
males in rural areas is expected to continue, as a result of the concentrated efforts to provide free education and because of the demand of the newly created

industries for trained educated workers and a consequently greater participation of women in economic activities. A factor that enhanced such a movement was the recognition of the woman as a citizen, thus opening the door to her for full participation in public life. Women were granted the right to vote and be elected in the General Assembly--which is the legislative body in Egypt--in 1956. For some years to come the education of females in rural areas may lag behind the rate for the nation because of traditions, and in fact, until the new industrial society changes the existing pattern and provides for the opportunities for females in the labor market, especially in the rural areas.

This pattern is characteristic of many underdeveloped countries. Generally, we find a marked difference among developed and underdeveloped countries as to the level of education, the degree of skill, and training of population. All of these factors affect the labor input. In underdeveloped countries, several indicators set forth the low level of education and training. For example, a comparison of the percentages of illiterate population shows that the percentage reaches 89 per cent among underdeveloped countries while it does not as a rule exceed 4 per cent in the case of developed ones. In fact, some developed countries, Sweden, in particular, have managed to eliminate illiteracy.[19]

It could be argued that the degree of illiteracy--or any other similar indicator--reflects the results of the past trends rather than projecting the future. Nevertheless other variables describing the present situation in underdeveloped countries support the difference. Consider furthermore, the total enrollment in school--primary, secondary, technical, and higher. The percentage of total population enrolled in school for New Zealand, the United States, Finland, and the Netherlands averaged about 23 per cent in 1958 as compared with 11.9 per cent for Egypt and 9.5 per cent for India.[20]

Not only is the level of enrollment in school

generally low, the composition of that enrollment has often been incompatible with the development process. The structure of the educational system should help in development by providing the needed skills. In industrial development, the role of technical schools is very important. In this area of training we find a major difference between developed and underdeveloped countries. Table 22 shows the enrollment in technical schools as a percentage of total enrollment in school. In seven countries of the underdeveloped group, less than 1 per cent of the students are enrolled in technical schools. These figures are already far lower than those for developed countries. In such an industrialized country as Germany, the percentage so enrolled was 25.8 in 1958 by comparison with Egypt's 2.8 per cent.

Harbison and Myers developed an index for measuring human resource development which takes into consideration both the stock of human capital and the additions to it as well as some indicators of higher education. This index consists of two sets of indicators. The first set which is a partial measure of the stock of human resources includes three indications: number of teachers, number of engineers and scientists, and the number of physicians and dentists per 10,000 of population. The second set of four indicators consists of enrollment ratios to population at various levels of education. To this, they added two other indicators of higher education. The first is the percentage of students enrolled in scientific and technical faculties in recent years. The second is the percentage of students in faculties of humanities, fine arts, and law in the same year.[21]

This composite index used on 75 countries results in the following four levels of human resource development:[22]

Level I, Underdeveloped (17 countries)

Level II, Partially developed (21 countries)

Table 22.   Enrollment in Technical Schools,
as Percentage of Total Enrollment (1958)

Country	Per cent	Country	Per cent
Germany (West)	25.8	Switzerland	3.7
United Kingdom	20.5	El Salvador	3.4
Austria	17.5	Australia	2.7
Sweden	12.1	Egypt	2.8
Belgium	11.2	Korea (South)	2.6
Denmark	9.3	Turkey	2.4
Netherlands	8.7	Philippines	2.1
Luxembourg	8.5	Malaya	0.9
Norway	7.5	Guatemala	0.8
Finland	5.5	India	0.6
Colombia	4.3	Mauritius	0.3
Japan	4.0	Nigeria	0.2
Honduras	3.9	Pakistan	0.2
France	3.8	Ceylon	0.1

Source: Compiled and calculated from United Nations
Department of Economic and Social Affairs,
Statistical Yearbook, 1959 (New York, 1959),
pp. 552-69 and 1960, pp. 574-93, and 1961,
pp. 612-29.

Level III, Semiadvanced (21 countries)

Level IV, Advanced (16 countries)

They found significant degrees of correlation between
the composite index and measures of economic development such as per capita income, the percentage of active population in agricultural occupations, public expenditures on education as a percentage of national
income and the percentage of total population in the
age group 5 to 14, inclusive. According to this index

Egypt is classified as a semiadvanced country with respect to its level of development of human resources. Since most of the data used in the construction of the index relate to the latter part of the 1950's, such a level is expected. Egypt has embarked since 1952 on a program to develop its human resources as we are going to see in the next section.

THE EDUCATIONAL PATTERN IN EGYPT, 1953-60

Listing the basic problems which must be faced in any realistic program of the Egyptian economy, Harbison and Ibrahim write, "...the fifth area is the expansion of schools, universities, and health and welfare activities. This will be necessary in order to eradicate disease, eliminate illiteracy, and generally to improve the deplorable conditions of masses."[23] This is exactly what the Egyptian government tried to accomplish during the 1950's. At the beginning of the development era, it was realized that a sound educational policy is a prerequisite to the planned economic development. Such a policy should be shaped in the light of the development schemes in industry, agriculture, construction, trade, and all other activities. The planned projects in these fields needed leaders, experts, technicians and skilled workers, in addition to those who will be responsible for training and education, in order to ensure a prompt flow of skills needed for the execution of development projects.

It is true that education was compulsory for the first stage, even before the reform of 1952. However, we find that the per cent of compulsory school age population (6-12) in school was only 45 per cent in 1951-52.[24] Since investment in education is considered one of the social overheads and an asset for development, the educational system was reformulated during the years following 1952 in order to make it compatible with the development drive. The new system enables the country to increase the percentage of compulsory school age population to 60 per cent.[25] These basic schooling stages were provided:[26]

(1) The primary stage which consists of 6 years of compulsory education. The 1956 constitution guaranteed free (and compulsory) education for the age group 6-12.

(2) The preparatory stage covering three years instead of four in the old system. Eligibility for preparatory education is based on merit proved in a competitive examination in order to give equal opportunity to the students entering this stage.

(3) The secondary stage covering three years. In this stage, in addition to general secondary education, emphasis is placed on technical agriculture, industrial and commercial education. This stressing of particular forms of education is one of the major changes which was introduced to divert the students from always seeking a college education of the white-collar type which is far removed from the requirement for development. It also helps to create a supervisory class lacking in Egyptian industries, which is being encouraged by the expansion of the number of technical schools which increased from 104 in 1951-52 to 247 in 1960-61.[27] This was enhanced by the ineffectiveness of the 1944 law to promote the education of the working class. That law required employers of 30 workers or more to provide them with free elementary education.

The change in the educational pattern can best be seen from the data presented in Table 23. It shows enrollment in schools by type of education for the two periods 1953-54 and 1960-61. Total enrollment in all types of education increased from two million in 1953-54 to over three million by 1960-61. Generally, there has been a numerical increase in all stages of education except preparatory. However, the expansion in technical education can be seen from the percentage share of each stage in total enrollment. While enrollment in technical school in 1961-62 became five times its 1953-54 level, its share in total enrollment increased from 1.1 to 3.5 per cent. It should be noted also that the educational scale has shifted toward

Table 23. Enrollment in School by Type of Education in Egypt, 1953-54 and 1960-61

Type of education	1953-54		1960-61	
	Number (1,000 students)	Per cent of total	Number (1,000 students)	Per cent of total
Nursery	--	--	8.2	0.2
Primary	1401.6	68.9	2616.4	78.1
Preparatory	351.6	17.3	255.8	7.6
General Secondary	92.1	4.5	132.2	4.0
Technical				
Industrial	11.1	0.5	42.2	1.3
Commercial	4.6	0.2	41.8	1.2
Agricultural	3.3	0.2	19.3	0.6
Multiple Purpose[a]	3.1	0.2	11.4	0.4
Higher Education	167.4	8.2	220.7	6.6
Total Enrollment	2034.8	100.0	3348.0	100.0

[a]Includes home economics and domestic.

Source: Compiled and computed from Ministry of Education, Department of Statistics, Comparative Statistics on Education (Cairo: S.O.P. Press, 1961), pp.10-93.

the earlier stages. In other words, instead of a small group attending higher education, more people are being educated at the first stage. Such expansion was made possible by increasing expenditure on education over time.

Expenditures on public education in Egypt were insignificant during the last quarter of the nineteenth century as evidenced from the following figures.[28]

Year	Expenditures on education as a percentage of total budget
1882	1.02
1890	0.87
1900	1.03
1910	3.40
1920-21	3.93
1930-31	10.90
1940-41	11.77
1945-46	11.67

Up to 1900, only about 1 per cent of the total budget went for education. With the turn of the century it increased to 3 per cent. However, as Matthew and Arkawi point out, "The real turning point in the Egyptian educational policy came after the termination of British occupation and the adoption of the Egyptian constitution in 1873 when actual control of education passed into Egyptian hands."[29] Government policy with respect to universal compulsory elementary education resulted in increasing the share of expenditure on education to 11.67 per cent of the annual national budget by 1945-46. In 1953-54, the budget allocation to the Ministry of Education and the universities amounted to $68.8 million, an amount that was roughly 15 per cent of the national budget of $454.3 in 1953-54. By 1960-61, the allocation to education more than doubled to reach $163.5 million, while its share of the national budget became 19.2 per cent. The increase in income from $1,902 to $3,052 million permitted this outlay.

Another notable change is observed in the fields of specialization of graduates of the universities and institutes of higher education. Table 24 presents data on the distribution of graduates of universities and higher institutes of learning by field of specialization for the two biennia 1953-54 and 1960-61. Too many students were enrolled in law, teaching, and social sciences, and too few in science, engineering, and business. During the early 1950's most of the graduates were from the schools of law and education who looked toward a guaranteed job with the government. This distortion was a result of the influence of French education and the fact that most statesmen earned a degree in law, as a matter of abiding by tradition.

Coordinated planning as developed in Egypt resulted in correcting the structural imbalance between supply and demand for university graduates. The three universities which existed before 1952 were Cairo University, Alexandria University, and Ein-Shams University. Al-Azhar University, which is a divinity school, did not play a significant role in education since its function was limited to training "ulemas" in religious matters. It was not until 1961 that it was reorganized. Besides keeping its functions as a divinity school, it came to embody all the faculties similar to the other universities in Egypt. The fifth one is Asyut University, which, although established in 1950, did not operate until 1957. In addition, several institutes of higher learning were established in many places which are far from the university centers. In 1960-61, aside from the increase in the number of universities from three to five and a corresponding increase in the number of graduates to 16,189 as compared to 9,158 in 1953-54, the fields of specialization changed considerably. The graduates of law schools dropped both in number and in their share of total graduates. Graduates of the schools of education, although their share in the total declined, increased in number to meet the significant expansion in education. There is a notable increase in the number

Table 24. The Distribution of Graduates of
University and Higher Institutes of
Learning by Field of Specialization
in Egypt, 1953-54 and 1960-61

Field of specialization	1953-54		1960-61	
	Number	Per cent	Number	Per cent
Art	98	1.0	328	2.1
Home economics	281	3.1	266	1.6
Science	302	3.3	473	2.9
Agriculture[a]	400	4.4	972	6.0
Engineering	515	5.6	1017	6.3
Medicine[b]	603	6.6	1059	6.6
Social sciences	666	7.3	2435	15.0
Commerce and economics	1069	11.7	2213	13.7
Law	1296	14.1	1122	6.9
Education	3928	42.9	6304	38.9
Total	9158	100.0	16189	100.0

[a]Includes veterinary medicine.

[b]Includes pharmacy and dentistry.

Source: Compiled and calculated from: Ministry of Education, Department of Statistics,Comparative
Statistics on Education (Cairo: S.O.P. Press,
1961), pp. 99-108.

and the shares of those specializing in commerce, economics, and social sciences. As to engineering, agriculture, sciences, and medicine, specializations crucial to development, the number of graduates increased,
but their share in the total increased only slightly.
Limitation upon students in this area is attributable
to equipment and laboratories shortages.

There has been an over-all change in education
toward a pattern compatible with the development
plans.

OCCUPATIONAL STRUCTURE OF THE LABOR FORCE

The lack of education and training is reflected in the size, occupational structure, and growth
of the labor force.   Despite the tremendous growth in
the population of Egypt, it did not result in a proportional increase in human resources.   Tables 25 and
26 bring out this fact.

These tables state the distribution of human
resources by economic activity in Egypt for the period, 1927-60.   While total population increased by
45.6 per cent during the same period, the labor force
(total occupied persons including the unemployed) increased only from 5,845,000 to 7,667,000, an increase
of less than one-third. In the same period the number
of unemployed persons almost doubled.

Looking now at the distribution of labor force
by economic activity, it can be seen that about one
half of the increase in labor force (1927-60) went into the agricultural sector. Agriculture on the numerous small farms is still carried on by long-estab-
lished and traditional methods with little training or
education. This contributes to much of the disguised
unemployment which prevails in the agricultural sector
of the Egyptian economy.   The labor force of manufacturing industries and construction has grown in number, becoming in 1960 more than double its 1927 level.
Yet the share of these two sectors in the total labor

Table 25. Distribution of Human Resources
by Economic Activity in Egypt, Census Years, 1927-60[a]

Economic activity	Thousand of persons			
	1927	1937	1947	1960
Agriculture[b]	3,526	4,284	4,215	4,379
Mining and quarrying	10	11	c	11
Manufacturing industries	608	476	707	747
Building and construction		118	112	157
Transportation and communication	131	138	201	257
Trade	408	458	617	637
Services of persons	284	255	391	
Public administration social services	283	317	508	1,362
Nonremunerative and others	596	1,318	1,567[d]	117
Total occupied persons	5,845	7,375	8,318	7,667
Unoccupied persons	6,301	6,391	8,064	11,411
Total	12,147	13,766	16,382	19,078

[a]Children 5 years old and less are excluded, but married women are included.

[b]Including fishing and hunting.

[c]Not available separately, included in nonremunerative and others.

[d]Includes those occupied in mining and quarrying.

Sources: Department of Statistics and Census, Population Census of Egypt, 1947, General Tables (Cairo: Government Press, 1952); Central Committee for Statistics, Collection of Basic Statistics (Cairo: S.O.P. Press, 1962), pp. 42-45; Egyptian Federation of Industries, Yearbook 1955-56 (Cairo: S.O.P. Press, 1956), p. 306.

Table 26.   Percentage Distribution of Occupied Persons
     by Economic Activity, Census Years, 1927-60[a]

Economic activity	Per cent of occupied persons			
	1927	1937	1947	1960
Agriculture[b]	60.3	58.1	50.7	57.1
Mining and quarrying	0.2	0.1	c	0.1
Manufacturing industries	10.4	6.4	8.5	9.7
Building and construction		1.6	1.4	2.1
Transportation and communication	2.2	1.9	2.4	3.4
Trade	7.0	6.2	7.4	8.3
Services of persons	4.9	3.5	4.7	
Public administration and social services	4.8	4.3	6.1	17.8
Nonremunerative and others	10.2	17.9	18.8[d]	1.5
Total occupied persons	100.0	100.0	100.0	100.0

[a]Children 5 years old and less are excluded, but married women are included.

[b]Including fishing and hunting.

[c]Not available separately, included in nonremunerative and others.

[d]Includes those occupied in mining and quarrying.

Sources: Department of Statistics and Census, Popula-
           tion Census of Egypt, 1947, General Tables
           (Cairo: Government Press, 1952);   Central
           Committee for Statistics, Collection of Basic
           Statistics (Cairo: S.O.P. Press, 1962), pp.
           42-45; Egyptian Federation of Industries,
           Yearbook 1955-56 (Cairo: S.O.P. Press, 1956),
           p. 306.

force has not shown an appreciable increase. From a percentage of 10.4 in 1927, the proportion became 11.8 per cent by 1960. Concurrently, the decrease in the share of the agricultural sector in the labor force was not significant. As compared to 60.3 per cent in 1927, agriculture still absorbs more than half of the labor force, or 57.7 per cent in 1960.

The sectors which did not show a marked increase in their share in total labor force are transportation, communication, and trade. It is true that the number of workers engaged in this sector increased from 539,000 in 1927 to 894,000 by 1960. Yet its share in total labor force grew only from 9.2 per cent to 11.7 per cent for this period. The two sectors which gained both in number and their proportion in the total labor force are services of persons and public administration and social services. Their ratios rose from 9.7 per cent in 1927 to 17.8 per cent in 1960.

From these figures, it can be concluded that labor force in Egypt is considerably concentrated in two sectors. These are the agricultural sector and the services of persons and public administration and social services. Together they account for three-fourths of the labor force. The sector of public administration and social services does not have a high level of productivity since it evidences many of the features of an unyielding bureaucracy. Except for the few high administrative jobs that require high levels of education, most jobs in government require a minimum of training or skills. Trade and transportation, which needs to expand as the process of development ensues, still absorbs small portions of the total labor force. The sectors embracing manufacturing industries and building and construction are in a similar state.

The definition of labor force, which includes children between the ages of five and fourteen, is quite broad and tends to distort the picture of the labor market. In 1961, a sample survey of the labor force was undertaken by the Central Committee for Statistics.[30] In this survey, labor force has been redefined as all population 12 years old and over who participate in the production of goods and services, as well as those who are able to work and seeking work, but are unemployed. However, human resources is still defined as that part of total population that could be engaged in any economic activity, excluding children under 6 years of age and people over 65 so long as they do not participate in economic activities as well as those who are permanently physically handicapped. The number of those outside the labor force is stated as the difference between human resources and the labor force. It includes people who are able to work but do not work either because they do not want to, or need to, or for some reason or other cannot enter the labor force. In this category we find housewives, students, and people on pensions. This survey resulted in the following age distribution of labor force:[31]

Age group	Per cent of population in total labor force
12-15	10.3
16-19	7.3
20-29	20.0
30-39	23.3
40-49	18.8
50-64	17.1
64 and over	3.2
All groups	100.0

From these figures we see that there is still employment of children of school age. The proportion of people in the age group, 12-19, is 17.6 per cent, a little over one sixth of the labor force. Furthermore, one fifth of the labor force is drawn from people 50 years old and over. This leaves 62.1 per cent of total labor force as comprising the usually productive age group, 20-49. Naturally, a lack of educational

facilities tends to force many into the labor force at
an early age.

In Chapter 4, we discussed the improvements
in public health programs and their effect in reducing
mortality; the population pressure in Egypt is therefore inflated. However, such improvements are still
beneficial for they increase worker productivity. In
a study on population growth and public health programs in Asia and the Far East, Swaroop concluded that
although health programs save an increasing number of
lives, thus adding to the pressure of population, they
also reduced the level of sickness, "...which in turn
promises to raise the health level and productivity of
the people inhabiting Asia and the Far East." [32] When
life expectancy increases, it will have some effect on
the productive life span of the individual, that is
the period in which he is able to participate in production. It depends on two factors: (1) the period
spent in education and (2) life expectancy. If life
expectancy is not relatively high, the productive period may obviously be very short. This problem, in addition to increasing the social cost of education, also
represents a large loss to the economy. In fact, we
find all these factors operating in the economies of
underdeveloped countries. Table 27 provides a comparison of the life expectancy at birth in selected developed and underdeveloped countries for certain years.
There is a marked difference in the figures for the
two groups. With the exception of Ceylon, the life
expectancy at birth of the underdeveloped group is
generally less than 60 per cent of that for the developed ones, Egypt is no exception. Apart from the short
life expectancy for the entire population, we find important sex differentials. These may be seen from the
following figures on life expectancy in Egypt: [33]

Period	Males	Females
1936-38	35.7	42.1
1946-48	41.4	47.0
1959-61	51.6	53.8

Table 27. Life Expectancy for Selected Countries

| Country | Year | Life expectancy in years at birth | |
		Males	Females
Norway	1951–55	71.1	74.7
Netherlands	1953–55	71.0	73.9
Sweden	1951–55	70.5	73.4
Denmark	1951–55	69.9	72.6
United Kingdom[a]	1956–58	67.2	72.3
Switzerland	1948–53	66.4	70.9
Canada	1950–52	66.3	70.8
United States	1957	66.3	72.5
Ceylon	1954	60.3	59.4
Egypt	1959–61	51.6	53.8
El Salvador	1949–51	49.9	52.4
Mauritius	1951–53	49.8	52.3
Philippines	1946–49	48.8	53.4
Korea	1938	47.2	50.6
Guatemala	1949–51	43.8	43.5
India	1941–59	32.5	31.7

[a]Average of England and Wales, Ireland, and Scotland.

Source: United Nations Department of Economic and Social Affairs, Demographic Yearbook 1959 (New
York, 1959), pp. 638–645.

Life expectancy for males is below that for females.
Since the rate of illiteracy is higher among females,
they do not participate much in economic activity.
Thus, we learn that the group of population not participating in production survives those upon whom the
economy depends.

AGE STRUCTURE AND PARTICIPATION RATES

Life expectancy can better be seen in the age structure of population. As mentioned before, Egypt has a young population with high fertility and a considerably high, but decreasing mortality. This variation causes a change in the percentage distribution of the total population by age groups. Note the developments as may be seen in the period 1927-60 (Table 28). The share of young people in total population (less than 15 years old) increased from 38.6 per cent in 1927 to 42.8 in 1960. This large increase is primarily attributable to the improvement in health conditions and child care. At the same time, the share of the productive group in population (15-59), roughly over one-half of the population, shows some decline. From the high of 54.3 per cent in 1927, it sinks to 51.2 in 1960. The share then of aging population, 60 and over, also declines slightly. Again, the economy encounters a loss. A great number of the young people who receive education or training do not survive to the years in which they return to the economy that part invested in them.

Let us now obtain the participation rates by age groups constituted as a percentage of population of each age group in the total labor force. We find that in 1960 participation rates were as follows:

Age group	Participation rates
20-29	35.9
30-39	45.9
40-49	51.7
50-64	53.6
64 and over	23.9

Participation rates are thus somewhat less for the first two age groups. This trend is due to the fact that intensive programs for education and training have been undertaken and the age of labor force entry is thus delayed. The highest participation rates are for the age groups 40-49 and 50-64, both of which are

Table 28. Percentage Distribution of the
Population of Egypt by Age Groups (1927-60)

Age groups	1927	1937	1947	1960
Less than 5	14.3	13.3	13.7	15.9
5-9	13.3	13.9	12.6	14.6
10-14	11.2	12.0	11.7	12.3
15-19	9.2	8.4	10.0	8.3
20-29	15.8	15.2	15.1	14.3
30-39	14.2	14.6	13.8	13.0
40-49	9.4	10.1	10.4	9.3
50-59	5.7	5.9	6.4	6.3
60 and over	6.6	6.4	6.0	6.0
Not stated	0.3	0.2	0.3	-
Total	100.0	100.0	100.0	100.0

Sources: Calculated from Department of Statistics and
Census, Population Census of Egypt, 1947,
General Tables (Cairo: Government Press,
1952), pp. 2-3; Central Committee for Statistics, Collection of Basic Statistics
(Cairo: S.O.P. Press, 1962), pp. 32-39; Department of Statistics and Census, Ten Years
of Revolution Statistical Atlas (Cairo: S.
O.P. Press, 1962), Table 3.

over 50 per cent. In general, these rates are low,
probably due to the low level of participation of women in production of goods and services.

FUTURE POPULATION GROWTH

Let us now recapitulate on Egypt's problem of

population growth and development of human resources. The population of Egypt has been growing at considerably high rates, which now approach 3 per cent annually. Such high rates result from a young population with high fertility and high, but decreasing mortality, an after-effect of the improvements in sanitation and health conditions. Birth rates did not experience any appreciable reduction. Thus the population gap is widening. With little out-migration, this condition contributes to an increasing population pressure on land and natural resources. Although there exists some deficiency in vital statistics, especially from areas without health departments, the adjusted rates do not differ considerably from the reported.

With respect to future population growth, there is some evidence that it is not likely to be checked under the new economic development and a consequent increase in income, as is contended in the "classical" theory. On the contrary, Egyptian population may increase during the course of economic development, to lend support to Malthus on population growth. In his article on population as a factor in economic development, Spengler introduces the concept of population elasticity, "to represent any small relative change in a population's size consequential upon a small relative change in that population's national income or net national product."[34] Recognizing the limitation of this concept in the use of empirical analysis and predictive models, Spengler discusses several cases. He argues that improvement in income and associated circumstances tends to yield different reactions of demographic behaviour in different types of societies. One of the models Spengler developed is that in a society with intermediate per capita income, income increases will affect natality far more than mortality. Natality tends to rise among income receivers situated at various levels who find themselves indisposed to increase their personal consumption as incomes rise. This is the demographic transition we believe Egypt is now experiencing.

If we take the annual rate of population

growth and the annual rate of growth of real income, we find that population elasticity in Egypt was 0.31 in 1952-53 and became 0.33 and 0.32 in 1958-59 and 1959-60. This coefficient of population elasticity is less than one, and is expected to rise. The effect of the increase in family income on fertility may be expected to take place at a later stage of development. The dependency on agriculture, the social structure of rural areas, as well as the reduced cost of rearing children, are the main factors that will contribute to the relative increase in population during the early stages of development.

Although Egypt has not experienced any sizable external migration into or from the country, internal migration, which started during the Second World War, is continuing.   This has resulted in the postwar urbanization of some Egyptian cities. Actually it was found that the two largest cities, Cairo and Alexandria, are overurbanized considering the country's stage of economic development. Although urbanization is not undesirable in itself, overurbanization creates several sociological and economic problems. The main problem is the drain on other areas for human and other resources which tend to move toward urban areas in order to benefit from the internal and external economies created by that phenomenon.

Another problem facing Egypt is the underdevelopment of its human resources due to the lack of education and training. Low levels of income have prohibited any appreciable investment in education. This lowered the level of manpower productivity and in turn contributed to lower levels of income. Thus the educational structure was not conducive to industrial or economic development.

In other words, three major problems faced the new regime in 1952: first, the increasing population pressure; second, the poor quality of human resources; and third, the overurbanization of some cities. The last two problems are somewhat easier to discuss than the first, and we will take them first.

As to education, the government realized that a sound educational policy is the prerequisite to a planned economic development. Reformation of the educational system took place after 1952. The system consists of three stages: primary, preparatory, and secondary with emphasis on technical education in the last stage. Higher education expanded with the expansion of universities and the creation of higher institutes of education, separate from the university and located in the remote areas of the country. All this was made possible by a sizable increase in expenditure for these purposes. Expenditure on public education, as a percentage of the national budget, increased from 15 per cent in 1953-54 to 19.2 per cent in 1960-61, as compared to a little over 3 per cent in the beginning of the century. As we have seen from the increase in number of graduates of technical schools, science, engineering, and business, all this effort made the pattern of education compatible with economic development. As a result, Egypt is now classified as semideveloped with respect to its level of development of human resources.

The problem of overurbanization is not expected to last. The distribution of new industries and new higher educational institutions all over the country is expected to solve this problem through a redistribution of population, thus releasing the pressure on Cairo and Alexandria. In addition to creating new industrial projects, the government takes part in creating in these areas new houses and other facilities that will attract people to them.

The population problem is of a somewhat different nature. With the change in the regime in 1952, President Nasser found that one of the major problems facing him was population control. The prodigious fertility of the Egyptian woman was eating up the fruits of the development programs, and the high rate of population growth continued to nullify whatever economic gains were made in Egypt's stride for industrialization. Even with the completion of the Aswan Dam and the consequent increase in the cultivable land area,

Egypt's present population of thirty million is expected to double by 1980, only fourteen years away.
Thus, the new administration became aware of the size
of the population problem confronting it and its effects on the course of development. In a report describing the relationship between population and the
economic resources of the country, Ali El-Greitly
looks upon the problem in terms of agriculture and industry.[35] He considers the rapid growth in population
an obstacle to economic development and the spread of
public services in Egypt. The report concludes that

> A wide gap existed between the economic re-
> sources and population in the course of the
> past 30 years, and that though, as ex-
> pected, the new projects of agricultural and
> industrial expansion will lead to an in-
> crease in the national income far superior
> to that obtained in the recent past when in-
> vestment in new industries had nearly come
> to a standstill, population growth at its
> present rate with the coming 10 years will
> cancel the effect of the increase in nation-
> al income and will impede the hoped for rise
> of the yearly per capita real income.[36]

Then an intensive birth control campaign was
launched in Egypt. Large amounts of money were allocated to initiate an extensive family planning program. Because of the importance of these programs in
the future development, we will devote to it this final section in these two chapters dealing with human
resources.

FAMILY PLANNING IN EGYPT

Although there were individual and group efforts to bring the importance of family planning to
public awareness, the Egyptian Government had generally ignored the population problem until the 1952 Revolution. The Permanent Council for Public Services was
established in 1953 for the purpose of changing the

social structure of the farm people by building
schools and providing clinics and welfare and recreation
services.   An important arm of the Council was the
National Committee for Population Problems--the first
official recognition of the population problem.   Committee members included the Ministers of Social Affairs, Agriculture, Education, Health, Finance (Deputy
Minister), and professors of related fields.   In 1957
the National Committee for Population Problems became
part of the new National Planning Commission, which
developed from a merger of the Permanent Council for
Public Services and that for National Production, established in 1952.   The National Commission for Population Problems changed its name and became the Egyptian Association for Population Studies, a nongovern-
mental organization with government financing.

The Beginning of Family Planning Efforts. Government efforts in the area of family planning began
on an experimental basis in 1955.   Family Planning
Clinics were established in that year by the Committee.   The first eight were in the two largest cities,
Cairo and Alexandria, followed by others in smaller
towns, villages, and rural areas. The number of clinics
opened each year in the rural and urban areas is shown
in Table 29. These clinics, when opened, were attached
to societies and organizations of public interest,
such as hospitals, which furnish only the accommoda-
tions. The Association supplies all other services
and needs such as personnel, material, and equipment.

The clinics were designed not only to provide
birth control services, but to supply data and carry
out experimentation in the field.   Sterilization was
requested by one-third of the new visitors to the
clinics. Use of contraceptives has fallen slightly in
spite of the increase in the number of clinics because
of difficulty of importation. However, attempts at
local manufacture have been made recently.   In 1964,
the Charter of the country recognized the use of contraceptives as wise and healthy; thus, a great increase occurred in the first nine months of 1964 in
demand for contraceptives.

Table 29. Number of Family Planning Clinics
Functioning in Urban and Rural Areas in Egypt
1955-64

| Year | Number of clinics | | Total |
	Urban	Rural	
1955	8	--	8
1956	12	--	12
1957	12	6	18
1958	12	12	24
1959	13	12	25
1960	13	13	26
1961	14	13	27
1962	14	14	28
1963	20	14	34
1964	24	14	38

Source: Hasan M. Hussein, "Evaluation of Progress in
Fertility Control in U.A.R.," United Nations
World Population Conference (Belgrade, Yugo-
slavia, 1965), p. 5.

Contraceptive services are free, but devices
are sold at full or partial cost or given free according to economic situations or needs.   To be eligible
for birth control services, one must first obtain the
medical and husband's approval and have at least three
children alive.

In February, 1966, a massive family planning
campaign was launched by President Nasser.   Added to
the existing program is a network of Combined Service
Units (CSU) which covers the entire country. There
are 2,000 CSU's--one for every two or three villages
and in reach of every peasant.   Each unit includes a
social center and a clinic. The clinic functions as a
birth control center each afternoon. Interuterine devices are given free, but the pills are sold. A budget
of 1.5 million pounds ($3.45 million) has been al-
located in addition to a Ford Foundation grant of

$440,000 for staff training and adapting international birth control methods to Egypt.   A further Ford grant of $478,000 is under consideration.[37] The Population Council of New York is assisting local manufacture of interuterine devices.

As a recognition of the importance of the population problem, the Cabinet established a Higher Council for Family Planning with a permanent executive staff headed by the Prime Minister.   The Council's secretariat consists of the Ministers of Health, Guidance, and Social Affairs.   The main function of the Council is the programming and budgeting of family planning projects in all areas of the country.   In each of the 25 governorates of Egypt, the Council set up a committee headed by the Governor for the purpose of supervising and implementing its projects on the local level.   The Council started with a budget of one million Egyptian pounds ($2.3 million).

Effectiveness of Family Planning Methods.   It is difficult to assess the effect of family planning efforts on actual population growth, since the latter is a result of a multitude of factors.   Despite all the efforts made since 1955, for example, the rates of population growth do not appear to have changed considerably.   An obvious explanation is the enormous size of the Egyptian population in relation to the number of clinics available and cases treated.   With respect to the massive campaign started in February, 1966, it is still too soon, at this writing, to give any accurate evaluation of its effects on birth control.

A few statistics, however, may be of interest: In his study of the progress of fertility control in Egypt, Dr. Hussein shows the number of new birth control cases treated annually in the urban clinics since 1955 as compared with the number of clinics.   This is shown in Table 30 in addition to the annual rate of population growth. Apart from the increase in the number of cases treated from 1956 to 1957, which could be due to the fact that many people were curious about new contraceptive devices, there has been some decline

Table 30. The Number of New Cases Treated
in the Urban Clinics for Birth Control,
Number of Clinics, and the Annual Rate
of Population Growth

Year	Number of cases	Number of clinics	Annual rate of population growth (per cent)
1956	4811	12	2.54
1957	5929	12	2.07
1958	4150	12	2.28
1959	3421	13	2.67
1960	3704	13	2.07
1961	3506	14	2.82
1962	4997	14	2.46
1963	4880	20	2.40
1964	8946[a]	24	2.47

[a] January-September.

Sources: For the number of cases and clinics, Hassan
M. Hussein, "Evaluation of Progress in Fertility Control in U.A.R.," United Nations
World Population Conference (Belgrade, Yugoslavia, 1965), pp. 5-6. For the annual rate
of population growth, Table 11, p. 63, Chapter 4.

in the number of cases up to 1961. This took place
while the number of clinics increased from 8 in 1955
to 14 by 1961. During the three years that followed,
the number of clinics increased by a little over 70
per cent. This may have caused an increase in the number of cases treated, which more than doubled by 1964.
It should be noted that the uprise in the number of
cases treated in the first 9 months in 1964 could be
due to the recognition by the Charter of the use of
contraceptives as wise and healthy.[38] Of course, the
figures in the table do not represent all those prac-
ticing birth control because there were some other

Table 31. The Degree of Success and Acceptability of
the Birth Control Methods in Association's Clinics

Method used	Usage (per cent)	Acceptability (per cent)	Success (per cent)
VD & J	20	90	90
VFT	30	90	85
PJ or DC	15	85	80
OCP	20	80	98
IUCD	15	95	98
Total	100		

Source: Hassan M. Hussein, "Evaluation of Progress in
Fertility Control in U.A.R.," United Nations
World Population Conference (Belgrade, Yugo-
slavia, 1965), p. 6.

individual efforts. In addition, physicians all over
the country are giving advice and treatment in birth
control to all those who ask for it or need it.

In his evaluation of the success of birth control in Egypt, Dr. Hussein gave a summary of the experience in the Association's clinics with respect to
the use of the five methods of birth control in
Egypt. These methods are: Vaginal Diaphram and Jelly
(VD & J), Vaginal Foaming Tablets (VFT), Preceptive
Jelly and Delfin Cream with Applicator (PJ & DC), Oral
Contraceptive Pills (OCP), and Interuterine Contraceptive Devices (IUCD). Table 31 shows the percentage
distribution of users of these five methods, the degree of acceptability and the degree of success from
the experience in the Association's clinics at the
present. Although the experiment is on a small scale

it is met with a high degree of acceptability and success.

Given the agrarian nature of the economy, the conservative religious beliefs, the high illiteracy rate, etc., the birth control campaigns so far conducted have barely scratched the surface, and a great deal more remains to be done. A successful birth control program seems, therefore, impossible to achievement without a simultaneous attack on the socio-economic-religio-problems.

Notes to Chapter 5

[1]UNESCO, World Illiteracy at Mid-Century (Paris: UNESCO, 1957), p. 192.

[2]United Nations, Science and Technology for Development, Vol. VI, Education and Training (New York: United Nations, 1963), pp. 20-21.

[3]Frederick Harbison and Charles A. Myers, Manpower and Education (New York: McGraw Hill, 1965), pp. X-XI.

[4]Smith writes that "the improved dexterity of a workman may be considered in the same light as a machine or instrument of trade which facilitates and abridges labor, and which, though it costs a certain experience, repays that experience with a profit." Adam Smith, An Inquiry into the Nature and Causes of the Wealth of Nations, Cannan's edition (New York: Random House, 1937), pp. 265-266.

[5]"The intelligence of the workman is a most important element in the productiveness of labour." John Stuart Mill, Principles of Political Economy, 5th London edition (New York: D. Appleton and Company, 1872), I, p. 241.

[6]Marshall included both public and private expenditure on education as the most valuable of all

capital invested in education. He emphasized technical education since it, "...can save much natural artistic genius from running to waste..." Alfred Marshall, Principles of Economics, 8th edition (New York: The Macmillan Co., 1948), pp. 215-216.

[7]Frederick Harbison and Charles A. Myers, Education, Manpower and Economic Growth (New York: McGraw Hill, 1964), pp. 3-5. Several studies have been done on the return on education in the United States, see Investment in Human Beings, a supplement to the Journal of Political Economy, LXX (October, 1962).

[8]World Illiteracy at Mid-Century, op. cit., pp. 171-173.

[9]United States Bureau of the Census, Historical Statistics of the United States, 1789-1945 (Washington, D. C.: Government Printing Office, 1949), p. 15 and United States Bureau of the Census, Statistical Abstracts of the United States, 1955 (Washington, D.C.: U. S. Government Printing Office, 1955), p. 287.

[10]Harbison and Myers, Manpower and Education, op. cit., p. xi.

[11]Harbison and Myers, Education, Manpower, and Economic Growth, op. cit., p. 40.

[12]World Illiteracy at Mid-Century, op. cit., p. 176.

[13]Harbison and Myers, Education, Manpower, and Economic Growth, op. cit., p. 172. It should be noted that these figures do not include private funds.

[14]This is a consequence of the improvement in health conditions. Actually, Mushkin considers that "health and education are joint investments made in the same individuals." Selma J. Mushkin, "Health as an Investment," Journal of Political Economy, Supplement, LXX (October, 1962), 130.

[15] *World Illiteracy at Mid-Century*, op. cit., p. 52.

[16] This law did not produce the expected results; see Frederick Harbison and Ibrahim A. Ibrahim, *Human Resources for Egyptian Enterprise* (New York: McGraw-Hill, 1958), pp. 112-113.

[17] *World Illiteracy at Mid-Century*, op. cit., pp. 38 and 52.

[18] *Collection of Basic Statistics*, op. cit., p. 198.

[19] United Nations, Department of Economic and Social Affairs, *Report on World Social Situation* (New York, 1957); UNESCO, *Basic Facts and Figures 1959* (Paris: UNESCO, 1960).

[20] United Nations, Department of Economic and Social Affairs, *Statistical Yearbook, 1961* (New York, 1961), pp. 612-28.

[21] Harbison and Myers, *Education, Manpower, and Economic Growth*, op. cit., Ch. III, especially pp. 26-31.

[22] *Ibid.*, p. 32.

[23] Harbison and Ibrahim, op. cit., p. 32.

[24] *Collection of Basic Statistics*, op. cit., p. 188.

[25] *Ibid.*

[26] This system was adopted by other Arab countries with the implementation of the Arab Cultural Unitary Agreement concluded in 1957 between Egypt, Jordan, and Syria.

[27] *Ibid.*, pp. 189-191.

[28]Roderic D. Matthew and Matta Arkawi, Education in Arab Countries of the Near East (Washington, D. C., The American Council on Education, 1949), p. 16.

[29]Ibid.

[30]Collection of Basic Statistics, op. cit., pp. 6-8.

[31]Ibid., p. 56.

[32]S. Swaroop, "Growth of Population and Public Health Programmes in Asia and the Far East," Population Bulletin of the United Nations, No. 5 (New York, 1956), p. 27.

[33]A. G. Abdel Rahman, The Egyptian Normal Life Table No. 2 (Cairo: Government Press, 1958), R. Makar, The Egyptian Life Table No. 3 for 1947 (Cairo: Government Press, 1957), Central Committee for Statistics, Population Trends in the United Arab Republic (Cairo, 1962).

[34]Joseph J. Spengler, "Population as a Factor in Economic Development," in Philip M. Hauser (ed.) Population and World Politics, (Glencoe, Ill.: The Free Press, 1958), p. 164.

[35]Permanent Council for Public Services, National Population Commission, The Population Problem in Egypt (Cairo: 1955) reprinted in part in Robert C. Cook, "Egypt's Population Explodes," Population Bulletin, XII (July, 1956), 64-67.

[36]Ibid., p. 67.

[37]Patrick Seal and Irene Beeson, "Babies Along the Nile," The New Republic, Vol. 154, No. 9 (Washington, D. C., May 1966), pp. 10-11.

[38]Hassan M. Hussein, "Evaluation of Progress in Fertility Control in U.A.R.," United Nations World Population Conference (Belgrade, Yugoslavia, 1965), p. 6.

CHAPTER **6** INCOME AND
ECONOMIC GROWTH

Although the methods of census taking and collection of vital statistics in Egypt are well advanced, data on national income and its composition
are scanty. One reason for this is that income tax was
not instituted until 1950. However, estimates of national income have been made since World War I. In
1913 national income was estimated at $345 million
(150 million Egyptian pounds).[1] By 1935, national
income was estimated at $425 million.[2] An estimate of
gross national product in 1939 gave a figure of about
$460 million.[3] Another estimate of national income for
1945 was undertaken by one of the professional societies.[4] This estimate gave a figure of $1,334 mil-
lion.[5]

Fairly reliable estimates start with Anis's
study of the national income of Egypt for the period
1937-45.[6] Thereafter, the Department of Statistics and
Census has been undertaking the task of estimating the
national income of Egypt.

CHANGES IN NATIONAL INCOME

In order to have a time series on the national
income of Egypt, we have tried to reconcile the frag-
mentary data available from the different sources. The
main sources we relied upon are Anis's study, the
estimates of the Department of Statistics and Census,
and the Central Committee for Statistics.

Table 32 shows national income in current prices and in millions of U. S. dollars for 1937-65 as well as the annual rate of growth of national income. National income, which amounted to only $380 million in 1937, grew to eight times this level by 1960 when it increased to $3,052 million. It should be noted, however, that most of this increase took place during the period following 1937, that is, during the Second World War. Between 1937 and 1939 there was no appreciable increase. However, by 1940, the first of the war years, national income jumped to $439 million as compared with $386 million in 1939, and $1,155 million by 1945. Thereafter national income showed an increase with the exception of the period 1951-52 when it decreased by $366 million or about 16 per cent of its level in 1951. However, the percentage rate of increase was also declining. The annual percentage rate of growth reached its peak during the war period with a maximum of 39.9 per cent during 1941-42. Then, there was a decline in the rate of growth following the war period until national income decreased at a rate of 6.1 per cent during 1951-52. Following this, the annual rate of increase began to rise but never reached prior levels. From a rate of 2.6 per cent in 1952-53, it increased to 8.5 per cent in 1959-60.

DEFLATION OF INCOME FIGURES

The apparent high rates of growth of national income do not really represent a similar increase in production and output as reflected in the goods and services available in the economy. A good portion of the apparent increase in national income was due to a change in the price level which showed a tremendous increase during this period. The index of the cost of living increased from 100 in 1939 to 328 by 1951, while the index number for wholesale prices increased from 100 to 386 during the same period.[7]

It is appropriate to use the cost-of-living index number in deflating income figures at current prices in order to obtain real national income. In

Table 32. Egypt's National Income at
Current   Prices and the Annual Rates
of Growth During the Period 1937-65

Year	National income (millions of dollars)	Annual rate of growth (per cent)[a]
1937	380	
1938	382	0.6
1939	386	1.2
1940	439	13.7
1941	536	22.0
1942	750	39.9
1943	897	19.6
1944	1,067	19.0
1945	1,155	9.2
1946	1,290	11.8
1947	1,442	11.8
1948	1,610	11.6
1949	1,799	11.7
1950	2,008	11.6
1951	2,220	10.5
1952	1,854	-6.1
1953	1,902	2.6
1954	2,033	6.9
1955	2,169	6.7
1956	2,337	7.7
1957	2,523	8.0
1958	2,627	4.1
1959	2,813	7.1
1960	3,052	8.5
1961	3,192	4.6

(continued)

Table 32 (continued)

Year	National income (millions of dollars)	Annual rate of growth (per cent)[a]
1962	3,387	6.1
1963	3,667	8.3
1964	3,976	8.4
1965	4,142	4.2

[a]Percentage increase on the previous year.

[b]An estimate based on the first half of 1965.

Sources: 1937-45: Mahmoud A. Anis, A Study of the National Income of Egypt, a special issue of Égypt Contemporaine, Nos. 261-62, November-December 1950 (Le Caire: Societé Orientale De Publicite, 1950), pp. 675-682; 1946-49: Estimated by using the average annual rate of growth of national income between the years 1945-50 for which data were available. The calculated annual rate of growth (average) used is 11.7 per cent; 1950-51: Central Committee for Statistics,Collection of Basic Statistics (Cairo: S.O.P. Press, 1962), pp. 239-240; 1952-60: Ten Years of Revolution, Statistical Atlas (Cairo: S.O.P. Press, 1962), Table 9. Estimates were given for this period for fiscal years. Adjustments were made to bring the figures to calendar years. This was done by dividing the figures given for the fiscal years (July-June) into two equal parts: one for the second half of the year mentioned first and the other for the first half of the year mentioned second, then adding the appropriate parts to get the figures for the calendar years.

this way we are able to get an indication of the purchasing power of money incomes and, consequently, the
amount of goods and services available in the economy.
However, the aggregation involved in constructing
index numbers raises problems about the validity of
such indexes and sometimes limits its applicability.
Therefore, before deciding on the index to be used in
deflating income figures, let us examine the construction of the two indexes available in Egypt for such
purpose, i.e., the cost-of-living index number and the
wholesale-price index number.

     Cost-of-Living Index Number.[8] The index of
the cost of living in Egypt is constructed with a base
period June-August 1939 (= 100). It is computed as a
weighted arithmetic average with fixed base. The index
consists of five groups of items: food, rent, fuel
and soap, clothing, and miscellaneous.   The weights
given to these groups of items correspond to the base
year (1939).   These weights represent a pattern of
family expenditure derived from a family expenditure
survey of lower middle income families with a monthly
income of $28-41. This typical family consists of an
average of 6.3 consumption units. The number of items
and percentage weights used in the computation of the
index are as follows:[9]

Group	Number of items	Percentage weights
Food	28	41.5
Rent	1	16.0
Fuel and soap	4	3.5
Clothing	32	16.7
Miscellaneous	6	22.3
Total	71	100.0

Price data on these items are collected in Cairo.
Food prices are collected on Thursday of each week and
prices of other items once a month by agents or by
mail from about 25 retail stores and other market out-
lets in Cairo. Rent and prices of other services are

quoted according to governmental laws and regulations; rent includes direct and general taxes on premises.

Wholesale-Price Index. Although the wholesale-price index has the same base as the cost-of-living price index (June–August = 1939), the computation is different. The wholesale-price index is computed as a geometric average of price relatives. An indirect weighting system is used whereby the number of price quotations for each item is proportional to its importance in the wholesale trade. The commodities selected comprise the chief staple items and include raw material, semifinished goods and finished goods as we can see from the following list:[10]

Items	Number of items	Number of price quotations
Foodstuffs		
Cereals and pulses	8	49
Dairy products	3	14
Edible oils	1	12
Meat and fish	3	17
Sugar, tea, and coffee	3	13
Others	13	41
Industrial products and materials		
Fuel	4	13
Coal and chemicals	7	30
Paper	1	9
Building materials	8	94
Fertilizers	3	4
Metals	7	19
Textiles	2	140
Hides and tanning materials	1	20

Price quotations on these items are collected weekly

by representatives of the Statistical Department of
the Ministry of Finance and Economy directly from the
markets and by mail from approximately 300 merchants.

From this explanation, we can see the difference between the two indexes with respect to the
method of construction and aggregation. The index numbers of the cost of living and wholesale prices for
Egypt during the period 1939-60 are shown in Figure 8.
The two indexes show virtually the same trend. The
fluctuations in both indexes otherwise correspond,
with the exception of the year 1956 when the wholesale
index number dropped sharply because of the depressed
economic conditions, while the cost-of-living index
number showed a small increase. The distance between
the two indexes remained fairly constant, until the
latter part of the 1950's, when the gap began to widen
somewhat.

The cost-of-living index number is generally
the appropriate one to use in deflating income at current prices to obtain real national income. However,
several drawbacks in the case of the Egyptian index
suggest the use of the wholesale index number. Before
pointing out the advantages of using the wholesale
index number, let us first look at the drawbacks of
the cost-of-living index number of Egypt.

In the first place, the weights used in construction of the index are based on a pattern of
family expenditure that refers to a year that is no
longer representative, i.e., the year 1939. Several
items of consumption are now widely used which cannot
be included in this index because of its rigidity.
For example, rent now constitutes a percentage larger
than the 16 per cent used in the index. Second, the
average number of consumption units in the typical
family (6.3) is somewhat higher than the average size
of the family which has not exceeded 5.0 since 1947.[11]
Third, the typical family included in the survey of
expenditure is that of a middle class family with a
monthly income of $28-$41. In Egypt, with an extremely
skewed distribution of income, the middle class income

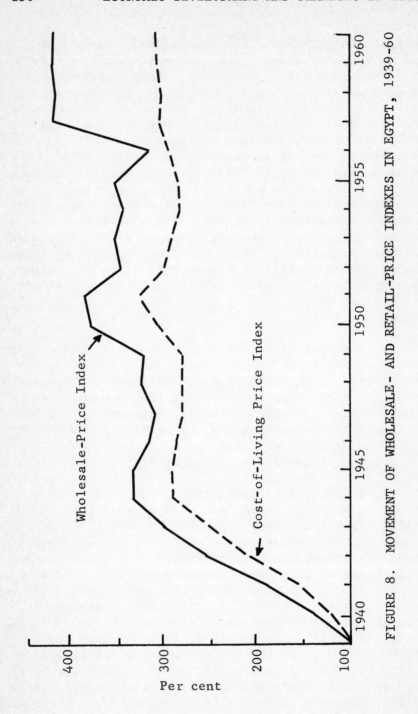

FIGURE 8.   MOVEMENT OF WHOLESALE- AND RETAIL-PRICE INDEXES IN EGYPT, 1939-60

is not representative of the whole country.   Take for
example the average income of farmers, a group which
constitutes a large part of the Egyptian population.
The average monthly income per owner from agriculture
amounted to $22 while that of the tenant was less than
$5 in 1946-47.[12]   Fourth, the cost-of-living index
number reflects prices controlled in large part by the
government. For instance, the government always tries
to stabilize the prices of food items demanded by the
majority of low income groups,and sometimes resorts to
rationing. This results in the spread   of black
market which cannot be surveyed by government agents
in the process of collecting data on prices. Finally,
price data on the items used in this index are collected mainly in Cairo, a matter that limits the use
of the indexes as representative of the whole country.

        For all these reasons, the Egyptian cost-of-
living price index is not the most appropriate deflator
of national income data. Let us turn now to the wholesale-price index.   Although this index includes some
intermediate goods, it also consists of many items of
consumer goods such as foodstuffs, soap, fuel, and
cloth. Also, it is superior to the cost-of-living
index both in the method of construction and aggregation. Thus,we believe that in this case the wholesale-
price-index, though not perfect, is a better deflator
for income data than the cost-of-living price index.

        The year 1953 marks the beginning of the
development period in the Egyptian economy.   Therefore
an index number that is based on 1953 = 100 is taken
here in order to be able to compare this period with
the preceding one. Table 33 shows the wholesale price
index for the period 1937-60, taking the year 1953 as
a base period.

        Correcting the data of Table 32, which show
national income at current prices, for the changes in
the price level as represented in Table 33, we get the
first column in Table 34 which shows national income
at constant prices of 1953.   Instead of the apparent
increase in national income at current prices during

Table 33.   Wholesale-Price Index, 1937-50

Year	Price index (1953 = 100)	Year	Price index (1953 = 100)
1937	29	1952	105
1938	29	1953	100
1939	30	1954	97
1940	37	1955	99
1941	46	1956	110
1942	59	1957	119
1943	75	1958	118
1944	88	1959	117
1945	93	1960	118
1946	91	1961	120
1947	86	1962	119
1948	93	1963	118
1949	88	1964	123
1950	97	1965	133
1951	108		

Source: United Nations, Department of Economic and
         Social Affairs, Statistical Yearbook, 1956
         (New York, 1956), p. 450; 1958, p. 408; 1961,
         p. 479.

the war period, we find that real national income declined from $1,288 million in 1939 to $1,165 million
in 1941. The real increase took place at the end of
the war period in 1946 when it became $1,418 million.
From there on real national income at 1953 prices
showed a steady increase with the exception of the two
years prior to the revolution, 1951 and 1952.   Also,
it declined during the Suez Crisis in 1956.   During
the whole period (1937-65), we find that real national
income a little more than doubled as compared with an
elevenfold increase in national income at current
prices.

Table 34.   National and Per Capita Income of Egypt
at Constant (1953) Prices for the Period 1937-65

Year	National income (billion dollars)	Per capita income (dollars)
1937	1.31	82
1938	1.32	81
1939	1.29	78
1940	1.19	70
1941	1.16	68
1942	1.27	73
1943	1.20	67
1944	1.21	67
1945	1.25	67
1946	1.42	76
1947	1.68	88
1948	1.73	89
1949	2.04	103
1950	2.07	101
1951	2.06	99
1952	1.77	82
1953	1.90	86 ←
1954	2.10	93
1955	2.19	95
1956	2.12	89
1957	2.12	87
1958	2.23	90
1959	2.41	94
1960	2.59	99
1961	2.66	100
1962	2.85	105
1963	3.11	111
1964	3.23	113
1965	3.11	---

Source: Computed from Tables 32 and 33.

In analyzing national income, still another equally important factor should be taken into consideration--population growth--because in the final analysis our concern is with the amount of goods and services that reach the individual in the economy. Egypt experienced a tremendous growth in population during the first half of the twentieth century and up to 1964. Let us adjust the data of Table 34, national income at 1953 prices, for the growth of population as represented by the data in Table 11 (Chapter 4). This is shown in the second column of Table 34 which shows per capita income at 1953 prices or real per capita income. This gives a true picture of the individual's share of the goods and services produced in the economy. In 1964, national income at current prices became ten times its level in 1937, while real national income a little more than doubled for the same period. With respect to real per capita income for the same period, we find that the increase only amounted to 38 per cent as a result of the increase in population. Even with such an increase, real per capita income is still low.

To sum up we chart the three variants of income in Figure 9. This comparative figure shows that the steady, and quite large, increase in income at current prices was due mainly to increase in prices. Real national income increased but to a lesser degree. Changes in real per capita income followed more closely the changes in real national income due to the steady growth in population.

After real national income declined during the years 1952 and 1953, aggregate national income showed some increase during the period 1953-65. This is due to the structural change that took place in the economy and the development program the government initiated during this period. Some of the components of national income have undergone a considerable change. Aggregate national income and its movement tells little about the transformation that took place in the structure of the economy. This is apparent in the distribution of national income by industrial origin.

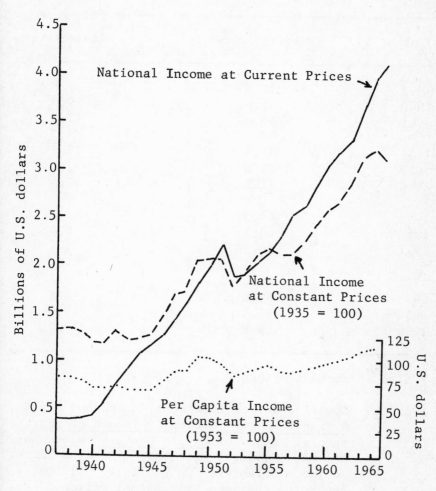

FIGURE 9.   NATIONAL INCOME, REAL INCOME,
AND REAL PER CAPITA INCOME (1937-65)

Table 35. Percentage Share of Agriculture
and Manufacturing Industries in National
Income[a]   (Selected Years, 1939-60)

Year	Agriculture	Manufacturing
1939	48.8	7.8
1940	43.6	9.0
1941	40.5	11.5
1942	41.4	11.8
1943	41.0	12.0
1944	41.3	12.6
1945	44.5	11.1
1950	44.7	8.4
1951	40.3	8.3
1952	36.0	8.7
1953	35.0	9.8
1954	35.8	10.8
1960	29.9	19.8

[a]Value at current prices.

Sources: Compiled and calculated from Mahmoud A.Anis,
A Study of the National Income of Egypt,
special issue of Égypte Contemporaine, Nos.
261-62, November-December, 1950 (Le Caire:
Societé Orientale De Publicite, 1950), p.
684;United Nations Statistical Office, Yearbook of National Accounts Statistics (New
York, 1962).

We are concerned here mainly with the changes that
took place in the comparative shares of two sectors,
agriculture and industry. Table 35 shows the percentage share of agriculture and manufacturing industries
in national income for selected years during the

period 1939-60.   During the period 1937-45   and up to
1950, the agricultural sector   provided   more   than 40
per cent of national income.   Manufacturing industries
contributed a portion that did not   exceed 10 per cent
by 1940; that is less than one-fourth as much as agriculture.   At best their   contribution was 12 per cent
in 1944, and had declined to around 8 per cent   during
the early fifties.

        The percentage   share of manufacturing   indus-
tries, which had previously   accounted for   only 8 per
cent of national income,   became one-fifth of national
income by 1960.   The share of agriculture, which   increased in absolute   terms   with the   increase   in national income, declined from   44.7 per cent in 1950 to
29.9 per cent by 1960.   In other words, there was some
shift toward industry and at the same   time an attempt
to maintain agricultural growth. Taking 1952 as a base
year for comparison (= 100),   we find   that   the index
number for   manufacturing   more than   doubled by 1960,
rising up to 208. All these could be attributed to the
investment strategy of the 1950's.

                        RATES OF GROWTH

        In order   to give   an over-all picture   of the
changing economy of Egypt in the period   1937-60,   the
annual average compounded rates of change were computed
for the two   variants of income,   national   income and
real per capita income (at 1953 prices).

        Table 36 shows the annual   average   compounded
rate of growth   of real   national   income for   any two
years during the period 1937-60.   In the first   place
we find that   whether we take 1937,   1938,   or 1939 as
the initial   year,   the   rates of   growth   up to   1945
showed a decrease.   It is true that the magnitudes   of
these negative   rates were   declining.   The   positive
change took place starting in 1946 and   continued from
there on.   However, the rates showed a downward trend
during the postwar   period and especially   starting in
1949.

Table 36.   Average Annual Rates of Growth of National Income at Constant Prices (1953 = 100)a

Terminal Year	Initial Year																						
	1937	1938	1939	1940	1941	1942	1943	1944	1945	1946	1947	1948	1949	1950	1951	1952	1953	1954	1955	1956	1957	1958	1959
1938	0.60																						
39	-0.79	-2.17																					
1940	-3.19	-5.04	-7.82																				
41	-2.87	-4.00	-4.99	-1.88																			
42	-0.59	-0.88	-0.49	3.46	9.08																		
43	-1.49	-1.90	-1.84	0.24	1.32	-5.88																	
44	-1.08	-1.36	-1.20	0.53	1.35	-2.31	1.40																
1945	-0.66	-0.83	-0.61	0.90	1.60	-0.77	1.89	2.37															
46	0.89	0.93	1.38	3.00	4.01	2.78	5.84	8.13	14.21														
47	2.51	2.73	3.35	3.06	6.26	5.70	8.82	11.41	16.22	18.26													
48	2.58	2.78	3.34	4.83	5.82	5.29	7.68	9.31	11.72	10.50	3.24												
49	3.78	4.08	4.73	6.22	7.28	7.02	9.34	11.00	13.27	12.96	10.40	18.05											
1950	3.59	3.84	4.41	5.72	6.60	6.29	8.15	9.32	10.76	9.92	7.27	9.35	1.28										
51	3.28	3.48	3.97	5.11	5.84	5.84	7.00	7.83	8.76	7.70	5.21	5.88	0.28	-0.72									
52	2.02	2.12	2.46	3.36	3.85	3.34	4.42	4.81	5.16	3.72	1.03	0.49	-4.76	-7.65	-14.09								
53	2.36	2.48	2.82	3.69	4.17	3.73	4.75	5.13	5.48	4.29	2.12	1.90	-1.78	-2.78	-3.79	7.74							
54	2.81	2.95	3.30	4.14	4.62	4.26	5.23	5.62	5.99	5.00	3.23	3.23	0.50	0.30	0.65	8.94	10.16						
1955	2.90	3.04	3.38	4.17	4.61	4.28	5.17	5.52	5.84	4.95	3.40	3.42	1.16	1.14	1.61	7.46	7.32	4.56					
56	2.70	2.82	3.12	3.84	4.23	3.90	4.69	4.97	5.21	4.35	2.91	2.87	0.87	0.79	1.10	5.30	4.49	1.77	-0.93				
57	2.44	2.53	2.81	3.47	3.81	3.47	4.17	4.39	4.56	3.72	2.37	2.28	0.46	0.34	0.52	3.73	2.75	0.39	-1.62	-2.31			
58	2.56	2.66	2.92	3.55	3.88	3.57	4.23	4.43	4.59	3.83	2.61	2.55	0.95	0.91	1.15	3.94	3.19	1.52	0.53	1.27	4.99		
59	2.80	2.91	3.17	3.78	4.11	3.82	4.46	4.67	4.83	4.15	3.05	3.03	1.64	1.68	1.98	4.51	3.98	2.79	2.35	3.47	6.49	8.01	
1960	3.01	3.12	3.38	3.97	4.29	4.03	4.64	4.85	5.01	4.39	3.39	3.40	2.16	2.25	2.59	4.89	4.49	3.57	3.38	4.48	6.85	7.80	7.59

a. Figures in this table show the average annual compounded rates of change between any two years in the period from 1937 to 1960. To obtain the annual rate of change between any two years, find the column for the initial year at the top of the table and read the figures in the row of that column opposite the terminal year shown at the left.

Source: Computed from data in Table 29.

Let us now compare the average annual compounded rates of growth starting in 1937 with the two years 1950 (line 13 in the table) and 1960 (the last line in the table).[13] It is worth noting that the magnitudes of the rates for the former are in general higher than those for the latter because of the low level of real national income in 1950. For the five years 1943-48, they are almost double. In other words, whatever we take for an initial year from 1937 up to 1950, the rates of growth are considerably high. But moving up to 1960, the rates of growth become smaller compared with those which prevailed up to 1950.

The average annual compounded rates of growth of real per capita income are shown in Table 37. Here we notice again the negative rates of growth up to 1946 taking as the initial year any year between 1937 and 1945. Also, there are marked negative rates up to 1959 taking for the initial year any year between 1949 and 1955. Actually, the highest rates of growth attained were during the period 1945-46 and the years 1945-47, 1945-49, and 1946-47. In fact, the average compounded rates of growth (taking for initial year 1937) which were negative up to 1946 did not reach 1 per cent for any year during the period 1952-60. In general the rates for the real per capita income were far below that of the total real national income. This could be attributed to the population pressure.

Let us now look at both Tables 36 and 37 to compare the trend of growth rates, taking as initial years 1939, 1946, and 1951; the last one is the year before the Revolution which marks the development period. Taking 1939 as initial year and going up to 1960, the rates of growth of real national income and real per capita income showed the same trend. The negative trend which prevailed during the period following 1939 turned into a positive one at the end of the war period and the rates began to increase up to 1950. During the development period (1952-60), both rates showed a downward trend but began to increase at the end of the period. It should be noted that the rates of growth of per capita real income lagged in

Table 37. Average Annual Rates of Growth of Per Capita Income at Constant Prices (1953 = 100)a

Initial Year

Terminal Year	1937	1938	1939	1940	1941	1942	1943	1944	1945	1946	1947	1948	1949	1950	1951	1952	1953	1954	1955	1956	1957	1958	1959
1938	-1.72																						
39	-2.81	-3.89																					
1940	-5.07	-6.71	-9.45																				
41	-4.71	-5.70	-6.58	-3.61																			
42	-2.45	-2.63	-2.21	1.63	7.16																		
43	-3.32	-3.63	-3.57	-1.53	-0.47	-7.55																	
44	-2.90	-3.10	-2.94	-1.24	-0.44	-4.03	-0.39																
1945	-2.48	-2.59	-2.37	-0.89	-0.19	-2.53	0.08	0.55															
46	-0.95	-0.85	-0.41	1.18	2.17	0.96	3.97	6.21	12.19														
47	0.73	1.01	1.64	3.33	4.53	4.01	7.12	9.75	14.66	17.18													
48	0.70	0.95	1.50	2.96	3.94	3.41	5.75	9.71	9.71	8.49	0.45												
49	1.88	2.21	2.84	4.31	5.34	5.09	7.35	8.97	11.18	10.85	7.82	15.72											
1950	1.64	1.92	2.47	3.74	4.59	4.28	6.08	7.20	8.58	7.70	4.71	6.91	-1.23										
51	1.30	1.53	1.20		3.81	3.44	4.90	5.68	6.56	5.47	3.50	3.50	-2.12	3.00									
52	-0.03	0.09	0.40	1.27	1.73	1.20	2.22	2.55	2.84	1.36	-1.54	-2.03	-7.33	-10.23	-16.92								
53	0.29	0.42	0.74	1.57	2.01	1.56	2.51	2.84	3.13	1.90	-0.45	-0.63	-4.34	-5.36	-6.51	5.21							
54	0.69	0.85	1.17	1.98	2.42	2.03	2.95	3.29	3.60	2.58	0.64	0.68	-2.09	-2.30	-2.07	6.32	7.45						
1955	0.78	0.93	1.24	2.00	2.41	2.05	2.90	3.20	3.47	2.54	0.85	0.90	-1.38	-2.09	-1.00	4.95	4.83	2.27					
56	0.44	0.57	0.83	1.51	1.87	1.50	2.23	2.45	2.63	1.71	0.13	0.09	-1.97	-1.96	-1.91	2.25	1.29	-1.66	-5.44				
57	0.31	0.42	0.66	1.39	1.61	1.25	1.90	2.08	2.21	1.35	-0.11	-0.17	-1.20	-2.11	-1.96	1.34	0.40	-1.85	-3.84	-2.23			
58	0.42	0.53	0.77	1.37	1.67	1.33	1.95	2.17	2.25	1.46	0.14	0.11	-1.49	-1.53	-1.31	1.56	0.85	-0.74	-1.72	0.18	2.65		
59	0.63	0.75	0.98	1.56	1.86	1.58	2.16	2.33	2.45	1.74	0.55	0.52	-0.84	-0.80	-0.52	2.07	1.56	0.42	-0.03	1.83	3.93	5.21	
1960	0.82	0.94	1.17	1.73	2.02	1.75	2.32	2.49	2.62	1.97	0.89	0.92	-0.32	-0.23	0.08	2.43	2.04	1.17	0.95	2.62	4.28	5.11	5.00

a. Figures in this table show the average annual compounded rates of change between any two years in the period from 1937 to 1960. To obtain the annual rate of change between any two years, find the column for the initial year at the top of the table and read the figures in the row of that column opposite the terminal year shown at the left.

Source: Computed from data in Table 29.

their movement one year behind those of real national income. When the rates of the latter became positive in 1946, those of the former did the same in 1947.

Taking 1946 for the initial year, the rates of growth of real national and per capita income were almost equal, and continued to have the same magnitudes during the period 1947-51 with a downward trend. In fact, the rates for 1946-47 were the highest during the whole period 1937-60. The rate of growth of real national income was 18.05 per cent while that of real per capita income reached 17.18 per cent in 1946-47. After 1951 the gap began to widen between the two rates with those of real national income becoming about double the rates of real per capita income. However, they showed the same downward trend at the beginning of the development period with some increase at the end of that period.

Finally, to examine the development period, let us take for the initial year 1951. Here we find a marked difference between the rates of growth of real national and per capita income, both in size and magnitude. Though real national income showed a negative, and considerably high, rate of change during 1951-52 and 1951-53, it became positive by 1954 and began to increase slightly, reaching an average of 2.59 per cent for 1951-60. The rates of growth for per capita real income were negative from 1951 to 1960 due to the increase in population, although the rate of decline slackened. From a rate of -16.92 per cent in 1951-52, it averaged 0.08 per cent from the period 1951-60. To sum up, the rates of growth of real national and per capita income were low during the development period as compared with those prevailing during the Second World War period. However, an upward positive trend began at the end of the development period.

INCOME INEQUALITY AND THE FUNCTIONAL
DISTRIBUTION OF INCOME

The pattern of income distribution affects the

economic growth of a country, especially if it is characterized by a low level of per capita income. In his presidential address to the American Economic Association in 1954,[14] Kuznets discussed the effects of the inequality in the distribution of income changes (increase or decrease) on the course of a country's economic growth.[15] Considering the case of underdeveloped countries, Kuznets based his analysis on family income data available for India in 1949-50, for Ceylon in 1950, and for Puerto Rico in 1948.[16] Taking into consideration the wide margin of error in the data, he concludes that, "the data show that income distribution of these countries is somewhat more unequal than in the developed countries during the period after the Second World War."[17] Thus, in conclusion, he assumed that, "the secular income structure is somewhat more unequal in underdeveloped countries than in the more advanced..."[18] This conclusion lead Kuznets to three important implications. First, "in underdeveloped countries savings could be realized only at the very peak of the income pyramid, say, by the top 5 or 3 per cent."[19] Second, the unequal income distribution coexisted with a low rate of growth of income per capita.[20] Finally, Kuznets contended that it is quite possible that income inequality has not narrowed in the underdeveloped countries within recent decades.

In spite of the meagerness of reliable information, Kuznets' speculations are typical of underdeveloped countries. This is actually the case of Egypt. In spite of the considerable effort to estimate income and output, Egypt does not have any data on the personal distribution of income. In view of this deficiency we are going to try to draw some inferences about income distribution from the limited information available on income by distributive shares for the period 1937-45.

Table 38 shows the percentage distribution of national income by major shares: rent of land and buildings, profit and interest from agricultural and

Table 38. Percentage Distribution of National Income by Distributive Shares for the Period 1937-45

Year	Rent		Profit and Interest		Salaries and Wages	Government Income
	Land	Building	Agr.	Nonagr.		
1937	21.0	7.8	13.8	22.8	31.1	3.6
1938	20.7	7.7	13.6	23.1	31.3	3.6
1939	20.6	7.6	13.5	23.5	31.2	3.6
1940	20.0	6.7	11.8	25.6	32.3	3.6
1941	15.9	5.9	13.8	24.7	35.5	4.2
1942	13.9	4.4	17.7	26.0	34.8	3.2
1943	15.9	3.8	14.6	25.9	37.0	2.8
1944	15.4	3.4	16.0	26.3	36.2	2.7
1945	17.4	3.1	15.3	26.3	35.8	2.1

Source: Computed from Mahmoud A. Anis, The National Income Output and Expenditure of Egypt for the Years 1937-45 (Cairo: Nile Printing House, 1950), p. 11.

nonagricultural sources, salaries and wages, and government income, for the period 1937-45. The share of salaries and wages in national income was about one-third during the whole period, while that of rent, profit, and interest did not go below 60 per cent of national income. In a predominantly agrarian economy like Egypt, a minority of landlords own the larger part of the agricultural land. Before the agricultural reform of 1952, there were the total of 1.2 million acres in the hands of only 2,136 landlords, while more than 2 million small farmers (2.18 million) shared 777,000 acres. At the same time, most of the landlords in that minority are owners of capital. So, this group draws the major part of the income represented by rent, profit, and interest, while the laboring class, who constitute the majority of the population, shares only one-third of the national income. This pattern of functional distribution of income results in some degree of inequality. However, before we show that, let us compare this pattern with other countries.

The share of labor (wages and salaries) in national income in Egypt is low as compared with the return to labor in other countries. Compensation of employees as a percentage of national income amounts to 60.9 in Finland (1948), 54.0 per cent in Australia (1948), 58.8 per cent in Canada (1949), 48.9 per cent in Southern Rhodesia (1949), 46.0 per cent in Chile (1948), and 42.2 per cent in Peru (1947).[21] In his study of the functional distribution of income in the United States since the early days of development, Johnson found that compensation of employees was about 50 per cent during the period 1870-1900.[22] When he adds to this the share of entrepreneurial income, the total share of labor income becomes about 75 per cent for the same period. At the beginning of the twentieth century (1900-1904), compensation of employees amounted to 58 per cent of national income, while total labor received 69 per cent of national income.[23] For later decades, the percentage increased to 64 for compensation of employees and to 75 for total labor share.[24]

Thus, compared with countries in the early
days of development, the labor share of income in
Egypt is still small. This in itself enhances the
inequality of income distribution. In other words,
the pattern of the functional distribution of income
in Egypt contributes to inequality. In the first
place, the share of labor is low. With little industrialization during the period 1937-45 and a large
number of farm workers sharing such a low percentage,
we can see the low level of per capita income of the
working class. On the other hand, the distribution of
ownership of agricultural land was very skewed during
that period as we saw earlier (Tables 5 and 6, Chapter
2). This results in an inequality of distribution of
property income from agriculture. Property income
from agriculture (land, profit, and interest) did not
decrease over time, and amounts to about one-third of
national income. If we add to this the share of wages
and salaries, we find that the major part of national
income (two-thirds) is unequally distributed. The
rest, which is the return to property in nonagricultural activities, amounts to about one-fourth of national income. The last part, even if it were equally
distributed, could not correct the inequality caused
by the other components, especially since it is in
itself a property income that tends to cause more
inequality.

Although a degree of inequality in the distribution of income is sometimes desirable as a means of
stimulating capital formation, in a state where the
level of national income is low it may produce adverse
effects on the economy. Strassmann showed that economic growth depends, among other things, on a growing
income equality.[25]

Although production can increase regardless of
growing income inequality, the increase may be less
than the possible maximum. In a model where a pattern
of income distribution shifts workers into more efficient industries, Strassmann concludes that "income
distribution can accelerate economic growth."[26]
Actually the inverse relationship between growth and

income inequality is implied in Nurkse's doctrine of balanced growth in which he states that, "People working with more and better tools in a number of complementary projects become each others customers."[27] Thus, if "the bulk of the output of the complementary industries is to be consumed by workers in these industries, the workers must also receive the bulk of the new purchasing power."[28] In an economy with an unequal distribution of income such as Egypt, landowners have been in the habit of spending the bulk of their incomes on imported luxuries in addition to investing their saving in foreign countries. Thus the distribution of income also affects the aggregate rate of consumption. All these factors tend to depress income level and productivity.

ECONOMIC GROWTH AND OCCUPATIONAL STRUCTURE

Colin Clark considers the movement of working population from agriculture to manufacture and from manufacture to commerce as "the most important concomitant"[29] of economic growth. From statistical investigation and analysis of data from several countries, he shows that, "The different levels of economic advancement are very closely associated with the proportions in which the working population is distributed."[30] This resulted in his thesis that economic progress is characterized by the redistribution of the gainfully occupied population out of primary production and fabrication into the production of services and tertiary industries in "distribution, transport, public administration and all other activities producing a non-material output."[31] This he based on the a priori assumption of superior consumer's preference for material things. Clark's thesis can be seen from the following statement:

> Studying economic progress in relation to
> the economic structure of different countries, we find a very firmly established
> generalization that a high average level of
> real income per head is always associated

with a high proportion of the working population engaged in tertiary industries...low
income per head is always associated with a
low proportion of the working population
engaged in tertiary production and a high
percentage in primary production, culminating
in China, where 75-80 per cent of the population are primary producers...as income
rises...the demand for such (tertiary) services increases and being non-transportable
they must be supplied by workers within the
country concerned.[32]

Bauer and Yamey disputed the empirical and
analytical basis of the widely accepted Clark thesis
with their finding from West Africa.[33] They found that
in West Africa, as in other emerging economies, "the
indispensable task of commodity distribution is expen-
sive relative to available resources; of the available
resources, capital is scarce and unskilled labor is
abundant."[34] This results in the mass use of unskilled
labor instead of capital in the performance of the
task of distribution.   The argument advanced by Bauer
and Yamey rests mainly on the following grounds:[35]

First, a substantial proportion of tertiary
products are not luxuries with a relatively high income elasticity of demand.

Second, there may be large scale substitution
of capital for labor in tertiary production in the
course of economic progress.

Third, problems are raised by aggregation in
applying the concept of the income elasticity of demand to a whole economy.

Looking back at Table 24 (Chapter 4), we can
now examine the hypothesis of whether economic progress causes a redistribution of workers from primary
and secondary into tertiary industries. The following
figures give the percentage distribution of occupied
persons by economic activity in the Egyptian economy:

	1927	1937	1947	1960
Primary	60	58	51	57
Secondary	11	8	10	12
Tertiary	29	34	39	31

These figures point out two distinct periods: The first from 1927 to 1947 and the second from 1947 to 1960. The first period witnessed a decline in the percentage share of workers in primary production and a considerable increase in the share of those engaged in tertiary production. Since income data are not available for 1927, let us concern ourselves with the period 1937-47. During this period, real per capita income in 1953 prices increased at an annual rate of 0.73 per cent, while the rate increased to 0.89 per cent during the period 1947-60. In the latter period we find a reversal from the first one with respect to the share of occupied persons in primary and tertiary production. These results tend to confirm Bauer and Yamey's thesis rather than Clark's. In other words, there had been a decrease in the share of working population in tertiary production during the development of the 1950's. It should be noted also that the rise in the percentage share of occupied persons in tertiary production during 1937-47 was due mainly to the increase in the production of services needed for the armed forces stationed in Egypt during the Second World War. Actually two conclusions could be derived from the Egyptian experience of development. First, the percentage share of working population in the production of tertiary services is considerably higher for the underdeveloped Egyptian economy. The percentage share of this type of production is about one-third, which is relatively higher than that existed in the early days of development of the now advanced countries.[36] Second, with the development that took place during the 1950's, the percentage share of working population in primary production increased while that of tertiary production decreased. This may be explained by the increase in population during the

early stages of development and the consequent increase in demand on foodstuffs.

THE BALANCE AMONG SECTORS

We have noticed the dominance of the agriculture in the Egyptian economy. At the same time, the
manufacturing sector has a minor share in national
income. Up to 1954, the share of manufacturing in
national income amounted to only about 10 per cent.
This raises the question: Is such imbalance among
sectors a unique characteristic of the Egyptian economy, or is it shared by other underdeveloped countries?
On the other hand, is the characteristic displayed in
the Egyptian economy, i.e., the imbalance among sectors, different from the pattern prevailing in developed countries?

The concept of "balanced development" (balanced growth) is closely associated with Professor
Ragnar Nurkse who devoted a good part of his book on
capital formation in underdeveloped countries to this
question.[37] Starting from a modern variant of Adam
Smith's dictum that "the division of labor is limited
by the size of the market," Nurkse states his first
proposition: "The inducement to invest is limited by
the size of the market." This is also a variant of
Young's proposition: "The division of labor depends
upon the extent of the market, but the extent of the
market depends upon the division of labor."[38] In the
poorer countries Nurkse states, "the use of capital
equipment in the production of goods and services for
domestic market is inhibited by the small size of that
market, by the lack of domestic purchasing power, not
in monetary but in real terms."[39] To these factors we
might add the low level of wages. However, as Young
wrote in his article, the crucial determinant of the
size of the market is productivity, which is largely
dependent upon the degree to which capital is employed
in production. Then he points out two factors operating in underdeveloped countries which keep them in a

vicious circle.   These are the "technical discontinu-
ities" which may call for sizable jumps in the rate of
output and the smallness and inelasticity of demand in
low income groups which render these jumps risky.
Hence the need for "balanced growth," or rather
balanced development, a notion inherent in Say's Law
of the Markets.

Balanced development   creates economies by
raising the marginal productivity of capital in the
various industries as a result of rendering large-
scale production feasible.   The absence of such a
scheme limits any attempt to develop and may even
dampen its effects.   Since there is no ideal framework
with which to compare the structure of underdeveloped
economies, our frame of reference will be the pattern
prevailing in developed countries. A comparative analysis of the sectoral structure of some developed and
underdeveloped countries may help illustrate this point.

Assuming that gross domestic product gives a
good indication of the output in the different sectors
of the economy, we can draw a comparison between the
sectoral structures of Egypt with some developed countries.   The developed group selected consists of:
Austria, Canada, Denmark, Japan, Norway, the United
Kingdom, and the United States.

Table 39 shows the percentage distribution of
gross domestic product by industrial origin (eight
sectors) for the seven countries and for Egypt in
1955. A glance at this table shows the marked difference in the share of agriculture in gross domestic
product between Egypt and the other countries. While
it ranges from 5 to 22 per cent for the seven developed countries, it amounts to a little over one-third
in the case of Egypt. On the other hand, the share of
manufacturing ranges between 24 and 41 per cent for
the seven developed countries, as compared with 11 per
cent in the case of Egypt.   In other words, the percentage shares of agriculture and manufacturing in
gross domestic product are almost reversed between
Egypt and the seven developed countries.   This would

Table 39. Percentage Distribution of Gross Domestic Product by Industrial Origin for Egypt and Seven Countries, 1955

Country	Agriculture[a]	Mining	Manufacturing	Construction	Transportation[b]	Trade and commerce	Public administration[c]	All others[d]
Austria[e]	14	3	41	7	8	10	7	10
Canada	10	4	29	7	11	13	7	19
Denmark	19	-[f]	29	7	11	14	9	11
Japan[g]	22	2	24	5	9	16	7	15
Norway	14	2	27	8	18	12	4	15
United Kingdom	5	3	39	6	11	12	7	17
United States	5	2	32	5	8	17	12	19
Average	13	2	32	6	11	13	8	15
Egypt	34	-[f]	11	4	7	6	16	22

(continued)

Table 39 (continued)

aIncluding forestry and fishery.

bIncludes communication.

cIncluding defense.

dComprises banking, insurance and real estate, ownership of dwellings, and personal and other services.

eMining and manufacturing were not available separately for Austria, the total percentages were divided according to the ratio for the remaining six countries.

fMagnitudes less than half a unit (nil or negligible).

gPublic administration and all others were not available separately for Japan. The same procedure in (e) above was applied.

Sources: All except Egypt, computed from United Nations Department of Economic and Social Affairs, Statistical Yearbook, 1958 (New York, 1958), pp. 432-36, Statistical Yearbook, 1957, (New York, 1957), pp. 450-54, and Statistical Yearbook, 1960, (New York, 1960), pp. 460-65. For Egypt the percentage distribution is computed from data collected and consolidated from United Arab Republic, Central Committee for Statistics, Collection of Basic Statistics (Cairo: S.O.P. Press, 1962), pp. 239-240.

not represent a problem if agriculture in an underdeveloped economy such as Egypt was efficient enough
to provide high per capita production. This is not
the case in Egypt where more than half of the labor
force produces only one-third of gross domestic product. Hans Singer considers that for underdeveloped
countries, the output per employed person in agriculture is two-thirds of the output per employed person
in the economy as a whole.[40] That this represents the
situation in most underdeveloped countries we can see
from a study of the Food and Agriculture Organization
of the United Nations per capita income in agriculture, forestry and fisheries as a percentage of per
capita income in all other occupations for developed
and underdeveloped countries. This study shows that
while the ratio never exceeded 60 per cent in the case
of underdeveloped countries, per capita income derived
from this sector in developed countries is almost the
same as, and sometimes more than, that from other occupations.[41]

In other words, in developed industrial economies, agriculture is more productive than in those
countries where agriculture furnishes a larger share
of income and output. In an underdeveloped economy
such as Egypt, where agriculture is the dominant industry and the major occupation, it is not the most
productive economic activity.

Moving horizontally across the table we notice
that the percentage share of the two sectors, transportation and communication and trade and commerce, is
greatly lower than it is in the developed countries
and sometimes amounts to less than half its level in
those countries. This is part of the infrastructure
which plays a major role in initiating development.
Looking at the last two columns in the table which
represent public administration and defense and the
other sector of services which comprises banking insurance, real estate, ownership of dwellings, personal
and other services, we find that it is higher in Egypt
than it is in all other countries. This does not mean
that this branch of economic activity is "progressing"

more in Egypt, but rather it takes a larger proportion
of services in Egypt than it does in a developed country to produce a comparatively lower level of income
and output.

Although government services and other services which comprise the noncommodity sector are integral parts of the economy, they are largely oriented
toward local demand. Moreover, they are in a sense
"intermediary" with respect to the other branches of
economic activity. They are self-contained considering their relationship to the other sectors. In other
words, as Chenery and Watanabe have shown, their backward and forward linkage effects are small. In their
study of the structure of production for Italy, Japan
and the United States, they found that transport, services, and trade have the lowest backward and forward
linkage effects.[42] As a result, these sectors fail to
generate as much employment as do the other branches
of economic activity. The fact that the share of
these noncommodity sectors is considerably higher in
Egypt is a partial explanation of the low-level equilibrium. The growth of these sectors does not produce
the far-reaching effects in the economy which generate
further growth.

In order to see the picture more clearly, we
take for the seven developed countries an average of
the percentage shares of each of the eight sectors in
gross domestic product as representing the pattern in
a developed economy. This is reasonable since the
range of the percentages for the seven countries is
narrow. This is shown in row 8 in Table 39. Comparing these averages with the corresponding figures for
the Egyptian economy, we notice a strong negative correlation between the two sets of percentages. This
can be seen more clearly from Figure 10 in which the
averages for the seven developed countries are plotted
against the distribution of gross domestic product by
industrial origin for Egypt.

To conclude, the situation in Egypt was characterized by a slow rate of growth of national income.

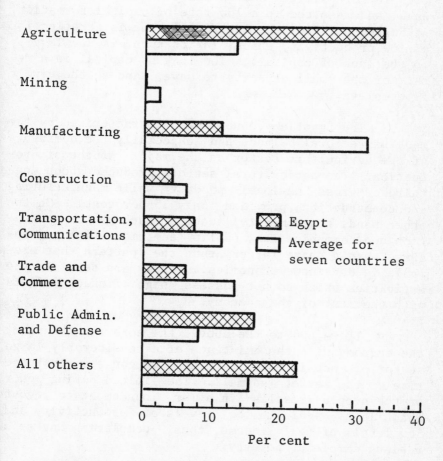

FIGURE 10.   PERCENTAGE DISTRIBUTION OF GROSS
DOMESTIC PRODUCT BY INDUSTRIAL ORIGIN FOR EGYPT
AND AN AVERAGE FOR SEVEN COUNTRIES, 1955

____ough there has been some increase in national income at current prices, real national income did not show a considerable increase. The tremendous population growth absorbed these small increments in income resulting in a low level of real per capita income. This in turn limited the ability and unwillingness to save, and resulted in a low rate of capital formation. As Nurkse put it, "the low real income is a reflection of low productivity which, in its turn, is due largely to the lack of capital. The lack of capital is a result of the small capacity to save, and so the circle is complete."[43]

The Egyptian economy was characterized by the lack of sectoral balance and especially the dominance of the agriculture sector as the major source of production. The agricultural sector produced about one-third of gross national product while manufacturing and construction provided only 15 per cent. On the other hand, noncommodity sectors such as transportation and communication, public administration and defense, had a share larger than the pattern that prevails in developed economies. These are service-type activities which do not possess high linkage effects with the rest of the economy.

If we add to the above the agrarian nature of the economy with the existence of a considerably large sector of subsistence farming, we can see that the size of the market is small. The limited buying power of the people results in a low inducement to invest which leads again to low levels of productivity and low levels of real income, thus, completing Nurkse's vicious circle of poverty.

Notes to Chapter 6

[1]The Egyptian pound is equivalent to $2.30. Although it was equivalent to $2.8 until 1961, all data in this study were converted to U. S. dollars at the rate of $2.30 per Egyptian pound in order to allow comparisons over time in terms of U. S.

dollars. In other words it is an accounting equivalent.

[2]Galal Faheem, in the Magazine of Social Affairs, (Cairo: Government Press, 1942).

[3]Richard Adler,"Les Linges Principales du Problème de la Population D'Egypte,et Leur Coordination," Egypte Contemporaine, XXXIV (March, 1943), pp. 184-86 and, Charles Issawi, Egypt: An Economic and Social Analysis (London: Oxford University Press:1947),p.52.

[4]This was called the Fouad 1st Society of Economics, Statistics, and Legislation.

[5]Egyptian Embassy, Washington, D.C.,Egypt News Bulletin (April, 1950). Available in the Library of Congress.

[6]Mahmoud A. Anis, A Study of the National Income of Egypt, a special issue of Egypte Contemporaine, Nos. 261-62, November-December, 1950 (Le Caire: Societe Orientale De Publicite, 1950).

[7]National Bank of Egypt, Economic Bulletin, Vol. VI, No. 3 (Cairo, 1953), pp. 242-243.

[8]The source of information on the construction of the cost-of-living and wholesale-price indexes is the Monthly Bulletin of Statistics of the United Nations, especially in 1963. See United Nations, Monthly Bulletin of Statistics,XVII (September-December 1963), 193 and 225-226. This index is called recently by the United Nations publications, "The Consumer's Price Index."

[9]Ibid., p. 225.

[10]Ibid., p. 193.

[11]Collection of Basic Statistics, op. cit., p. 27.

[12]Mohamed Ahmed El-Shafie, "Population Pressure on Land and the Problem of Capital Accumulation in Egypt," Ph.D. Thesis, University of Wisconsin, 1951, p. 294. Data are converted from Egyptian pounds to U. S. dollars and from annual to monthly averages.

[13]That is, comparing the rates of the years 1937-50, 1938-50, ... 1949-50 with those for the years 1937-60, 1938-60, ... 1959-60.

[14]Delivered at the Sixty-Seventh Annual Meetings of the American Economic Association.

[15]Simon Kuznets, "Economic Growth and Income Inequality," American Economic Review XLV (March 1955), 1-28.

[16]Ibid., p. 20.

[17]Ibid.

[18]Ibid., p. 23.

[19]In more advanced countries savings are possible in the fourth quintile. Ibid.

[20]Ibid.

[21]United Nations, Statistical Office, National Income and its Distribution in Underdeveloped Countries, Statistical papers series E, No. 3 (New York, 1951), p. 17.

[22]According to W. King's estimate of national income. See, D. Gale Johnson, "The Functional Distribution of Income in the United States," Review of Economics and Statistics, XXXVI (May, 1954), 178-79.

[23]Ibid., p. 178.

[24]Ibid.

[25]Paul Strassmann, "Economic Growth and Income

Distribution," Quarterly Journal of Economics, LXX (August, 1956), 425-40.

[26]Ibid., p. 427.

[27]Ragnar Nurkse, "Some International Aspects of the Problem of Economic Development," American Economic Review, XLII (May, 1952), 527.

[28]Strassmann, op. cit., p. 426.

[29]Colin Clark, The Conditions of Economic Progress (London: Macmillan and Co., 1940), p. 176, especially Chapter V.

[30]Ibid., p. 177.

[31]Colin Clark defined production as three types : primary, secondary and tertiary.   Under primary he included "agricultural and pastoral production, fishing, forestry, and hunting." Mining is included with secondary which covers manufacture, building construction and public works, gas and electricity supply.   Ibid., p. 182.

[32]Ibid., pp. 6-7.

[33]P. T. Bauer and B. S. Yamey, "Economic Progress and Occupational Distribution," Economic Journal, LXI (December, 1951), 741-55. Also see their "Economic Progress, Occupational Distribution, and Institutional Wage Rigidities: A Comment," Review of Economics and Statistics, XXXV (November, 1954),   461-62 which is a reply on a comment by S. Rottenberg.   "A Note on Economic Progress and Occupational Distribution," Review of Economics and Statistics, XXXVI (May, 1953), 168-70.

[34]Ibid., p. 746-47.

[35]Ibid., p. 748.

[36]See Colin Clark for figures, op. cit., Ch. V.

[37]Ragnar Nurkse, Problems of Capital Formation in Underdeveloped Countries (Oxford: Basil Blackwell, 1953).

[38]Allyn A. Young, "Increasing Returns and Economic Progress," Economic Journal, XXXVIII (December, 1928), 539.

[39]Nurkse, op. cit., p. 6.

[40]He states that "...for a surprising number of countries, figures come remarkably close to a constant relation of the form: A = 2/3 N where A is output per employed person in agriculture and N is output per employed person in the economy as a whole." Hans Singer, "The Concept of Balanced Growth in Economic Development: Theory and Practice," in E. Nelson (ed.), Economic Growth (Austin: University of Texas Press, 1960), p. 74.

[41]United Nations, Agriculture in the World Economy (Rome: November, 1955), p. 54.

[42]H. B. Chenery and T. Watanabe, "International Comparisons of the Structure of Production," Econometrica, XXVI (October, 1958), 70.

[43]Nurkse, op. cit., p. 5.

CHAPTER 7 INDUSTRY

During the nineteenth century and the first part of the twentieth century, the Egyptian economy experienced several attempts at industrialization. Most of these attempts met with little success. Despite the failure of their attempts, however, a few industries continued to process some agricultural raw materials and to meet the local demand.

A REVIEW OF INDUSTRIAL DEVELOPMENT

Industrialization in Egypt was enhanced by the First World War, especially with the establishment of Bank Misr and its affiliated industries. The Egyptian Federation of Industries, established in 1922, helped prepare for and push the industrialization movement.[1] The Federation was influential in establishing a government agency, the Economic Council, in the Department of Statistics and Census. This council was concerned with studying some problems of industry, such as improvement in means of transportation, railway fares, and customs. One of the major accomplishments of the Federation was a study of the customs system which resulted in the 1930 reform. The Federation was also instrumental in the establishment of two government agencies, the Department of Industry and Commerce and the Department of Labor.

Although the Second World War helped create and expand some industries, the majority of these did

not survive after the war. Thus, while European industries which were destroyed during the war began to re-
cover in the postwar period, the Egyptian industries
which flourished during the war began to decline. Several factors contributed to this situation. In the
first place, prices were artificially high during the
war period, a fact which rendered most industries profitable.   The wholesale-price index tripled between
1939 and 1946.   After the war ended, however, high
prices could not be maintained and most industries
created or expanded during the war could not continue
profitably. An exception to that was the textile industry which was already established in the economy before the war. This industry depends mostly on domestic
inputs and it has a wide domestic market.

Competition from the European markets increased after the war as indicated by the figures on
imports and exports. Figures presented in Table 40 on
the Egyptian foreign trade for selected years during
the period 1800-1954 indicate that Egypt had hardly
any foreign trade at the beginning of the nineteenth
century.   This was before the introduction of cotton
cultivation which later became the major export commodity, especially after the American Civil War. Figures in Table 40 show the increase in the value of
imports and exports toward the end of the century. However, the great leap in the value of imports and exports took place after World War I, when the value of
exports and imports in 1925 amounted to a little over
three times the 1900 level.   Up to 1925, the balance
of trade showed a surplus. The excess of exports over
imports during the latter part of the nineteenth century and the early part of the twentieth century was
used to pay the interest on the heavy public debts
that had been run up in the previous period of building canals and railway systems.[2] Following the 1930
depression, Egypt began to experience a deficit in its
balance of trade with the exception of the year 1939.
That deficit reached its highest in 1952 amounting to
$180.3 million.

The rising deficit in the balance of trade

Table 40.   Egyptian Foreign Trade, Selected Years,
1800-1954

(Millions of dollars)

Year	Imports	Exports	Balance of trade
1800	0.6	0.7	+ 0.1
1880	20.0	30.4	+ 10.4
1900	41.9	45.8	+ 3.9
1925	135.2	139.1	+ 3.9
1930	109.3	75.7	− 33.6
1938	84.8	69.2	− 15.6
1939	78.4	80.0	+ 1.6
1940	72.2	65.1	− 7.1
1945	139.2	104.0	− 35.2
1947	235.5	206.5	− 29.0
1949	408.7	317.4	− 91.3
1951	557.3	467.1	− 90.2
1952	514.0	333.7	−180.3
1953	408.9	315.8	− 93.1
1954	371.2	318.1	− 53.1

Sources: Compiled from Department of Statistics and
Census, Annuaire Statistique 1959 (Cairo:
Government Press, 1960), pp. 362-63; Insti-
tut National De La Statistique Et Des Études
Économiques, Mémento Économique L'Égypte
(Paris: Presses Universitaies De France,
1950), p. 141; National Bank of Egypt, Eco-
nomic Bulletin, Vol. II, No. 4 (Cairo, 1949),
p. 271; Vol. III, No. 1, p. 65 and Vol. XIII,
Nos. 3 and 4, p. 361.

resulted from the increase of imports at a rate higher than that of exports. During the period 1940-52, the value of exports increased from $65 to $334 million while that of imports from $72 to $514.   It should be noted that the increase in the value of exports and imports was not all monetary. An index of the quantity of imports and exports shows that, taking 1939 = 100, while the quantity of exports increased to 117 by 1950, that of imports increased to 188.[3]   The increase in exports was due mainly to the increase in the proceeds from cotton exports which constituted about 87 per cent of the total value of exports in 1950 and 80 per cent in 1951. Actually the value of cotton exports almost doubled during the period 1947-52, increasing from $157 million to $291 million.   However, this was not due to the increase in the quantity exported but rather to the increase in prices. The quantity of cotton exported in 1952 amounted to 80 per cent of its level in 1947.[4] The value of rice exported--rice also became an export commodity during the Second World War--amounted to less than one million dollars in 1939, increased to $14 million by 1947, and to $37 million by 1948.[5]

The increase in exports was outpaced by the increase in imports.   From $72 million in 1940, the value of imports increased to $514 million by 1952. The goods imported were not of the type needed for development, but were mainly consumer goods.   This can be seen from the following figures which show the relative value of some major imports in Egypt.[6]

Group of commodities	Per cent of total value of imports	
	1938	1951
Cereals and milled products	0.7	16.9
Sugar and confectionary	1.9	0.3
Tea, coffee, and cocoa	3.2	4.1
Wood, cork, and articles thereof	4.7	5.3
Cotton price goods	7.7	1.6

Group of commodities	Per cent of total value of imports	
	1938	1951
Silk, rayon, and woolen cloth	3.5	3.6
Transport equipment (mainly automobiles)	5.5	3.8
Total	26.2	35.6

It can be seen that Egypt, an agricultural country, became an importer of cereals, mainly wheat. In 1952, the value of imports of wheat, flour, tea, coffee, tobacco, wool, and automobiles amounted to $143.8 million, or over one-fourth of the total value of imports. In other words, the Egyptian economy depended on the export of agricultural products, mainly cotton, while imports consisted mainly of consumption goods. Such a trade pattern is not compatible with the development of industry. It was not until 1953 that efforts were directed toward reducing the balance of trade deficit and changing the pattern of trade to aid in industrialization. In 1954 the deficit in the balance of trade decreased to $53 million as compared with $180 in 1952 as shown in Table 40. The large deficit in the balance of payments which amounted to $123 million in 1952 declined to $18 million by 1953 and was wiped out completely in 1954, the balance of payments for that year showing a surplus of five million dollars.[7]

On the other hand, most profits realized during the war period were not reinvested in industry. Since these profits were a windfall type due to the circumstances of the war and were not expected to continue, they were invested in agricultural land, residential building, or they were hoarded. This was because of the lack of entrepreneurial ability and the tendency of capitalists to put capital in safe, though not high-yielding, investments. It is also due to the structure of a society and its way of thinking which

gives high prestige to landowners. In agrarian societies, social status and economic security are closely
associated with land ownership. Hence, the preference
for investment in land with the end result that small
amounts of capital are made available to industrial
development.

According to Schackle's numerical subjective
probability, the investor in land finds that nonland
investments bear a high degree of risk and uncertainty, a belief based on his experience in farming and
nonexperience in nonfarming.[8] In addition, the landowners attach a high degree of liquidity to land, a
matter that makes it a more preferable form of wealth
as Keynes pointed out.[9]

An equally important obstacle to the industrialization movement was the minimum value set by law
for ownership in corporations.   The minimum value for
shares issued by corporations was set at $9.20 (4
Egyptian pounds).   Thus we find most of the shares issued in values of $23 (10 Egyptian pounds) or $57.50
(25 Egyptian pounds), which is beyond the means of the
small investor.   The result was a concentration of
shares in the hands of the few who could afford it.
This trend continued up to 1956.   For example, during
the period 1954-56, seven to ten people owned forty-
two corporations, or 77.8 per cent of all the corporations established during the period.   This accounted
for 50.3 per cent of the total capital invested in
corporations.[10]   In 1954 the minimum value of share
was reduced to $4.60 (2 Egyptian pounds). Another re-
duction to $2.30 (1 Egyptian pound) was effected   in
1956.

The decline of industry can be seen from the
yearly decline in the number of industrial corporations.   In 1948, only 15 corporations were established
with a capital of only $5 million, and 15 corporations
in 1949 with a capital of $6.4 million.   In 1950, 16
corporations were established with a capital of $2.7
million. This compares unfavorably with the record
for 1946 and 1947 when 62 and 37 corporations were

established with a capital of $39 million and $9.3 million, respectively.[11]

An attempt to remedy the situation did not meet with success. In 1946, a five-year project was approved to spend $81.9 million in an effort to develop the economy. The plan was to spend this on water supply, railway transportation, roads, and participation of the government in the capital of the Industrial Bank.[12] During the years 1946-47 and 1947-48, only about one-third of the amount allocated for the projects was actually spent. The same ratio holds for the total allocation of all projects planned. In fact, by the end of the five years only one or two projects were completed out of more than ten projects planned.[13]

It was not until 1952 that a systematic drive for development with emphasis on the industrial sector was launched by the new administration. Government machinery was set up for planning and erecting development projects. In 1952, the Permanent Council for National Production was established to study the feasibility of projects related to development. The National Planning Commission was established in 1955 to draw up a general plan for economic and social development. A Ministry of Industry was established in 1956. In the meantime, the Industrial Bank expanded its loan operations and the promotion of industries in addition to studying the industrial structure.

The idea of establishing an Industrial Bank goes back to 1940. However, the bank was not established until 1948 and did not start operating until October, 1949. The bank was limited in its operations in the first three years and, as a result, followed a conservative policy. In 1953, the bank was reorganized with the object of playing a larger role in the development of the country. It assumed the function of an industrial development bank and undertook the task of studying the industrial sector in order to use such study as a guide for their lending policy. The expansion of its operation can be seen from the following figures on total loans granted by the bank:[14]

ans ($1,000)	Year	Loans ($1,000)
667	1956	1,656
787	1957	5,957
2,392	1958	3,349
4,243	1959	3,756

The two leading industries on the basis of the amount of loans granted were the mechanical and metal industries and cotton ginning, spinning, and weaving. It should be noted, too, that there had been a tendency toward long-term loans (5 years or more). By 1955, 61.5 per cent of loans were long term.

The Industrial Bank started another policy of promoting and participating in new corporations. During the period 1954-56, the bank participated in the formation of 12 corporations with a capital of $54.4 million. The bank's share was $5.8 or 10.7 per cent of total capital of these corporations.

Early in 1957, the state decided to speed up industrialization by adopting a five-year plan, and the first steps in its execution were taken in July, 1957. In the meantime it was decided to develop the economy according to a general plan. Therefore, the industrial five-year plan was shortened to three years, and beginning in 1960 the industrial sector was incorporated in the ten-year general plan for social and economic development.

Undoubtedly, the Suez crisis in 1956 affected Egypt's economic development. It became difficult to import goods needed for industrialization, and in addition it was difficult to export goods, especially cotton. Cotton exports fell to $227 million in 1956 as compared with $247 million in 1955. The number of bales exported fell from 1.06 million in 1953 to 709 thousand in 1957. However, the bilateral trade agreements between Egypt and some of the socialist countries helped the situation during this period, since 60 per cent of the trade was done under such agreements.

INVESTMENT IN INDUSTRY AND PRODUCTIVITY

Data on total investment and especially investment by industry are very scanty, particularly for the period before 1952. However, an analysis of investment in the industrial sector can be made with the limited information available from the census of corporations (with the main office in Egypt) and the census of production.

Before the beginning of the Second World War, little capital was directed to industrial investment. Capital formation was low due to the low level of income. Moreover, there is a sentimental attachment to land especially for the prestige it bestows on land-owners. The lack of incentive to invest in industry is observed by Myrdal as a characteristic of all under-developed countries. Myrdal writes, "Profits tend to be invested in land, or else hoarded or transferred abroad...There is a low propensity to save and to invest productively in new enterprises."[15] Commercial activities were also attractive, because they yield a fast return and the capital in such investments can be recovered in a short period. This is illustrated by Myrdal in his statement: "It is...highly characteristic of all underdeveloped countries that business classes are bent upon earning quick profits not by promoting long-term real investment and production but by buying and selling, money lending, and other easier ways of making money, which also often escape taxation."[16] This can be seen from Table 41, which shows capital investments for all corporations and for industrial corporations where main offices are in Egypt along with the ratio of industrial to total capital during the period 1937-41. Total capital of all corporations amounted to $131 million in 1937. By 1941, it had increased to only $142 million, that is by only 8.6 per cent. The capital of industrial corporations, which amounted to only 13.5 per cent of capital of all corporations, increased from $17.7 million to $22.9 million in 1941, a rise of 29.8 per cent. This raised its share in total capital of all corporations to 16.2 per cent.

Table 41. Capital of all Corporations
and Capital of Industrial
Corporations Operating in
Egypt, 1937-41

Year	Capital of all corporations (millions of dollars)	Capital of industrial corporations	Share of industry in total capital of corporations (per cent)
1937	131	18	14
1938	134	19	14
1939	135	20	15
1940	139	22	16
1941	142	23	16

Source: Department de la Statistique Generale, Annuaire Statistique de Poche 1942 (Le Caire:
Imprimerie National, 1943), pp. 248-253.

During the period 1946-50, the capitalization of industrial corporations rose by $65 million
which represented 59 per cent of the increase in capitalization of all corporations.[17] It is also estimated
that, "the capitalization of industrial concerns,
which had risen by 75 per cent between 1938 and 1945,
doubled during the period 1945 to 1950."[18] Most of
the increase went into the textile industry (40 per
cent of total), with the electrical, metal, engineering, and chemical industries following in that order.
It should be noted that capital invested in the textile industry in 1950 became 170 per cent of its level
in 1945.[19]

With the beginning of the second half of the
twentieth century, there was a further increase in the

Table 42. Capital Invested in Industrial
Establishments, 1951-55

(1,000 dollars)

Year	New capital	Increase in capital	Decrease in capital	Total
1951	2,454	3,082	612	4,924
1952	2,854	2,852	741	4,965
1953	4,308	2,951	4,586	2,673
1954	6,383	3,080	1,159	8,304
1955	16,942	7,599	2,151	22,390

Source: Compiled from Egyptian Federation of Industries, Yearbook 1955-56 (Cairo: S.O.P. Press,
1956), p. 391.

capital invested in industrial establishments. Industrial establishments are defined to include corporations and all forms of partnerships, but not sole
proprietorships.   Data available on investment in industrial establishments for the period 1951-55 are
shown in Table 42.   There was a tremendous increase in
new capital during that period.   Rising from $2.4 mil-
lion in 1951, it increased to $16.9 million by 1955.
In addition the capital of some establishments more
than doubled during this period. Even with the reduction in capital of some establishments immediately
following the Revolution, the total capital invested
in industrial establishments increased from $4.9 mil-
lion in 1951 to $22.4 million in 1955, more than a
fivefold increase.

The only available data on the total capital
invested in the various industries are for 1947. These

are somewhat reliable data derived from the 1947 census of industrial production. Table 43 shows the total
number of establishments, the number of persons engaged, capital, and value added by industry in 1947.
The total number of establishments was 26,743.   They
employed 367,336 persons representing a capital investment of $160.8 million. On the average the amount
of capital per person engaged in all industries was
$438 per man-year.   However, there is considerable
variation among industries in the number of establishments, as well as their size, employment, and capital.
Two major industries, whose capital is about 60 per
cent of total capital invested in industry, employed
more than 70 per cent of all persons engaged in industry.   These are the manufacturing of food and kindred
products and the textile industry. The textile industry is by far the largest in the Egyptian economy.[20]
There are 12,284 establishments in this industry or
46.7 per cent of all establishments in industry. The
share of this industry in total capital is 29.2 per
cent, and it employs about one-half of all persons engaged in industrial production (45.2 per cent).   In
1947, there were 6,321 establishments in the food and
kindred products industry, employing 26.7 per cent of
all persons engaged in industry. Capital invested in
this industry amounted to $45.2 million which is more
than one-fourth of total capital invested in industry
(28.1 per cent).   The share of basic industries such
as chemicals, petroleum and coal, metals, and machinery in employment or capital invested is rather small.

From the data in Table 43, we computed the la-
bor/output, capital/output, and capital/labor ratios
for the Egyptian industries in 1947. This is shown in
Table 44.   The labor/output ratio is rather high for
most industries such as mining and quarrying, textiles, clothing, lumber and furniture, paper, metallics, and machinery. Using data from the Italian
economy and Southern Italy in order to study the role
of industrialization in development programs, Chenery
estimated the capital and labor coefficients for
domestic production.[21] The results of his study show

that the labor/output coefficient for all the industries is lower than that computed for Egyptian industries. According to his results the labor/output coefficient for textiles is 0.50, clothing 1.00, food
.15, petroleum .15, chemicals .35, mining .45, and met-
allurgy .50.[22] In other words, the existing number of
workers per unit of output in the Egyptian industries
is higher than that compatible with industrial development. This explains the underemployment or disguised
unemployment that exists in many industries in Egypt.
On the other hand, we find that, with the exception of
the mechanical and metallurgic industries, the capi-
tal/output coefficient for Egyptian industries is lower than that computed by Chenery.[23]

The last column of Table 44 shows the capital/
labor ratio, or the amount of capital per person
engaged in industry. The textile industry has a relatively low level of capital per person engaged, i.e.,
$283 per man-year. The same is true with respect to
the manufacturing of food and kindred products. The
industries with highest capital/labor ratios are the
basic industries. This includes chemicals with a ratio of $975, petroleum and coal with $734, metal and
metal products with $732, and machinery, except elec-
trical, with $761.

The above characteristics of the Egyptian industries, that is the low capital coefficient and the
intensity of labor, resulted in a low level of output
per person employed. The following figures show the
value of net output per person employed (in 1939
prices) in Egypt (1944), United Kingdom (1935), and
United States (1937), in United States dollars.[24]

Industry	Egypt	United Kingdom	United States
Chemicals	25	220	409
Textiles	14	57	114
Clothing	22	60	127
Leather	16	85	149
Quarrying	10	85	210

Table 43. Total Number of Industrial Establishments, Number of Persons Engaged, Capital and Value Added by Industry in 1947[a]

	Number of industrial establishments	Number of persons engaged	Capital (1,000 dollars)	Value added (1,000 dollars)
Mining and quarrying	30	4,445	2,111	2,666
Food and kindred products[b]	6,321	97,979	45,246	221,718
Textiles[c]	12,284	165,982	47,021	146,388
Apparel and footwear	1,998	8,746	3,231	7,273
Lumber, furniture, and fixtures	1,713	8,538	1,594	4,681
Paper and paper products	161	4,879	1,424	3,641
Printing and publishing	382	6,442	3,418	5,736
Leather and leather products	408	3,789	2,226	5,837
Rubber products	7	883	265	920
Chemicals and allied products	310	16,646	16,236	25,456
Petroleum and coal products[d]	3	5,528	4,055	16,857
Nonmetallic products[e]	963	15,636	7,737	9,515
Metal and metal products	1,512	17,895	13,105	11,189
Machinery except electrical	6	109	83	74

Transportation equipment	49	2,434	1,557	890
Utilities and public services[f]	43	5,362	10,371	12,735
Miscellaneous	353	2,043	1,109	4,600
Total	26,743	367,336	160,789	480,176

[a]Results of the 1949 Census of Industrial Production.

[b]Includes beverages and tobacco.

[c]Includes cotton ginning and pressing.

[d]Includes the petroleum industry.

[e]Includes cement, stone, and glass.

[f]Includes the production and distribution of electricity, gas and water.

Source: Department of Statistics and Census, Statistical Pocket Yearbook 1952(Cairo: Government Press, 1953), pp. 142-49.

Table 44.　Labor/Output, Capital/Output, and Capital/Labor Ratios
for Egyptian Industries, 1947

Industry	Labor/ output ratio[a]	Capital/ output ratio	Capital/ labor ratio[b]
Mining and Quarrying	1.67	.79	475
Food and kindred products[c]	.44	.20	462
Textiles[d]	1.13	.32	283
Apparel and footwear	1.20	.44	369
Lumber, furniture, and fixtures	1.82	.34	187
Paper and paper products	1.34	.39	292
Printing and publishing	1.12	.60	531
Leather and leather products	.65	.38	587
Rubber products	.96	.29	300
Chemicals and allied products	.65	.64	975
Petroleum and coal	.33	.24	734
Nonmetallic products[e]	1.64	.81	495
Metal and metal products	1.60	1.17	732
Machinery except electrical	1.47	1.12	761

Transportation equipment	2.73	1.75	640
Utilities and public services[f]	.42	.81	1,934
Miscellaneous	.44	.24	543
All industries	.77	.33	438

[a]Number of employees per $1,000 of output.

[b]Dollars of output per man-year.

[c]Includes beverages and tobacco.

[d]Includes cotton ginning and pressing.

[e]Includes cement, stone, and glass.

[f]Includes the production and distribution of electricity, gas, and water.

Source: Computed from data in Table 43.

Industry	Egypt	United Kingdom	United States
Paper and paper products	24	119	310
Food processing	29	174	271
All industries	20	94	213

For all industries, we find that the output per worker in the United Kingdom is about five times and in the United States more than ten times that of the Egyptian workers. Moreover, great differences exist in the major industries of Egypt such as textiles, clothing, and food processing.

In these industries, the productivity of workers was far below rates in the United Kingdom or the United States during the thirties. It should be noted that the figures for Egypt are during the war period in which some industries flourished. Actually, great differences exist in output per worker in industries which expanded during the Second World War and are considered the major industries in Egypt today such as textiles, clothing, and food processing. This low level of productivity of workers in the Egyptian industries reflects the deficiency in capital and technical skills and the lack of entrepreneurial ability. As has been pointed out, most investments were directed toward agriculture before the development period in 1952. It was only in 1952 that considerable efforts were directed toward industrialization. In 1952-53 investment in industry amounted to $68 million.[25] By 1960-61 investment in industry more than doubled, become $154 million.

THE SCALE OF INDUSTRY

As already noted, data on investment in industry and capital of firms are very scanty. The same applies to data on size of firms in the various industrial activities. Therefore, in this section we propose to examine the firms by their size of employment

and the value added in the various industries, in
order to throw some light on the change in the industrial structure in Egypt.

Table 45 shows the distribution of industrial
establishments which employ ten or more workers by
size of employment for selected years during the period 1952-60. It should be observed that there has been
a slight decrease in the total number of industrial
establishments: From 3,445 in 1952 the total number
declined to 3,368 establishments in 1960, although
there was a slight increase to 3,554 in 1957. Since,
according to the 1947 census of industrial production,
there were 26,743 industrial establishments, it is obvious that the firms with fewer than ten employees
dominate Egyptian industry. They dominate only in
terms of numbers, not economic importance. Actually,
within the industrial firms with ten employees and
more, the dominant size is the firm which employs 10-
49 workers. In 1952, industrial establishments of
that size amounted to 79 per cent of total industrial
establishments with ten employees or more. Although
this percentage decreased by 1960, it is still considerably high (77 per cent). There was a slight increase in the percentage of establishments with 50-499
workers during the period 1952-60. In 1960, they
amounted to one-fifth of the total. Also, there has
been an increase in the large establishments (500 are
more workers). While their number increased from 78
to 109 during the period 1952-60, their share increased from 2 to 3 per cent of the total.

Although industrial establishments which employ
10-49 workers constitute about four-fifths of the establishments with 10 workers and more, their share in
total employment of these establishments amounted to
less than one-fifth in 1960.[26] Moreover, during the
period 1952-60 the value added of these establishments
declined from 12 to 10 per cent of total value added
of all industrial establishments employing ten workers
and more.[27] For these reasons, and due to the unavailability of data on establishments with 10-49 workers,

Table 45. Distribution of Industrial Establishments which Employ Ten or More Workers by Size of Employment, Selected Years, 1952-60

Year	10-49		50-499		500 and more		Total	
	Number	Per cent	Number	Per cent	Number	Per cent	Number	Per cent
1952	2,734	79	633	19	78	2	3,445	100
1956	2,838	81	608	17	68	2	3,514	100
1957	2,841	80	634	18	79	2	3,554	100
1958	2,533	79	617	19	74	2	3,224	100
1960	2,583	77	676	20	109	3	3,368	100

Sources: For 1952, 1956, 1960: Central Committee for Statistics, Collection of Basic Statistics (Cairo: S.O.P. Press, 1962), p. 102. For 1957 and 1958: Department of Statistics and Census, Annuaire Statistique 1959 (Cairo: Government Press, 1960), pp. 262-66.

we propose to examine in detail establishments with 50
or more workers during the period 1952-61.

Tables 46 and 47 show the number of establishments, number of persons employed, total value added,
and value added per worker by industry for establishments with 50 or more workers for the years 1952 and
1961. In 1952, more than one-half of the establishments are concentrated in two industries: textiles
and food and kindred products. Chemicals, nonmetallic
products, and the metal products group constitute
about 20 per cent of total establishments, while there
was only one establishment in petroleum. By 1961,
although the number of establishments increased to
797, which is a 12 per cent increase of its level in
1952, there is a considerable structural change, i.e.,
a change in the share of each industry. Textile manufacturing still occupies first place with about one-
third of the total number of establishments. However,
while food and kindred products still occupies second
place, their percentage share in total number of establishments dropped from 18 per cent to 7 per cent in
1961. At the same time, we find a corresponding increase in the share of the metal and machinery groups.
Machinery (except electrical) and electrical machinery
with seven establishments in 1952 constituted less
than 1 per cent of total establishments in 1952 and
went up to 5 per cent in 1961. The number of establishments working in the field of petroleum and coal
increased from one to three.

With respect to employment in establishments
with 50 or more workers, textiles is in first place
employing about one-half the total persons engaged,
while food and kindred products ranks second, both in
1952 and 1961. It should be noticed that between 1952
and 1961 there was a considerable increase in the number of workers in the following industries: mining
and quarrying, apparel and footwear, paper and paper
products, chemical, metal and metal products, and machinery. Most of these groups experienced an expansion in the number of establishments. However, while
the increase in the number of establishments between

Table 46. Number of Industrial Establishments with Fifty or More Workers, Number of Persons Engaged and Value Added by Industry in 1952

	Number of industrial establishments	Number of persons engaged	Total value added (1,000 dollars)	Value added per worker[a] (dollars)
Mining and quarrying	7	4,207	2,613	621
Food and kindred products[b]	130	42,039	41,156	979
Textiles[c]	235	108,697	54,931	505
Apparel and footwear	19	2,784	1,989	714
Lumber, furniture, and fixtures	40	3,550	1,495	446
Paper and paper products	20	4,750	1,794	378
Printing and publishing	31	4,925	3,537	718
Leather and leather products	11	1,075	655	609
Rubber products	4	809	630	779
Chemicals and allied products	41	9,690	11,613	1,198
Petroleum and coal products	1	4,576	14,623	3,195
Nonmetallic products[d]	52	10,859	5,886	542

Metal and metal products	42	7,456	4,402	590
Machinery except electrical	3	280	301	1,075
Electrical machinery	4	946	690	563
Transportation equipment	46	7,543	4,759	631
Utilities and public services[e]	10	3,928	7,158	1,822
Miscellaneous	15	1,608	952	592
Total	711	219,722	159,184	724

[a]Dollars per worker per year.

[b]Includes beverages and tobacco.

[c]Includes cotton ginning and pressing.

[d]Includes cement, stone, and glass.

[e]Includes the production and distribution of electricity, gas, and water.

Source: Compiled from Central Committee for Statistics, Collection of Basic Statistics (Cairo: S.O.P. Press, 1962), pp. 108-109.

Table 47. Number of Industrial Establishments with Fifty or More Workers, Number of Persons Engaged and Value Added by Industry in 1961

	Number of industrial establishments	Number of persons engaged	Total value added (1,000 dollars)	Value added per worker[a] (dollars)
Mining and quarrying	24	12,573	41,451	3,297
Food and kindred products[b]	146	44,672	87,837	5,605
Textiles[c]	277	140,292	156,825	1,118
Apparel and footwear	11	5,727	5,203	909
Lumber, furniture, and fixtures	33	4,880	3,991	818
Paper and paper products	23	7,931	6,502	820
Printing and publishing	32	6,801	8,758	1,288
Leather and leather products	11	1,202	1,028	855
Rubber products	6	2,278	7,197	3,159
Chemicals and allied products	46	16,869	49,209	2,917
Petroleum and coal products	3	3,693	8,556	2,317
Nonmetallic products[d]	41	13,651	16,866	1,235

Metal and metal products	56	16,679	30,187	1,810
Machinery except electrical	25	4,400	3,988	906
Electrical machinery	13	2,987	6,808	2,279
Transportation equipment	37	6,073	5,536	911
Utilities and public services[e]	4	3,854	7,831	2,032
Miscellaneous	9	2,013	1,847	917
Total	797	296,575	449,620	1,516

[a]Dollars per worker per year.

[b]Includes beverages and tobacco.

[c]Includes cotton ginning and pressing.

[d]Includes cement, stone, and glass.

[e]Includes the production and distribution of electricity, gas, and water.

Source: Compiled from Central Committee for Statistics. Collection of Basic Statistics (Cairo: S.O.P. Press, 1962), pp. 110-111.

1952 and 1961 was 12 per cent, the increase in employment in these establishments was 35 per cent. This
means that there was an expansion in the average size
of these establishments.

Let us now look at column three in Tables 46
and 47 which is total value added. Here again we find
that textiles is the leading industry, and food and
kindred products is in second place. But, while the
share of textiles in total value added was about one-
fourth in 1952, it increased to a little over one-
third. This, of course, is due to the increase in
quantity and quality of labor. It is noticeable that
there has been a tremendous increase in the value
added in mining and quarrying that is not matched by a
similar increase in the number of establishments or
number of workers. During the period 1952-61, the
number of establishments in this industry increased
from 7 to 24, and its employment almost tripled from 4
to 12 thousand persons. At the same time, value added
increased from $2.6 to $41.5 billion, which is almost a
sixteenfold increase. This is due mainly to a new
law issued in 1953 for mining and quarrying to replace
the old restrictive one. The new law facilitates the
granting of licenses of research. It also made it
possible to renew the contract of exploitation which
was limited. In addition, several other regulations
with respect to royalties and transportation facilities
rendered investments in this field more profitable.
Rubber and rubber products witnessed a tremendous increase due to the introduction of manufacturing of
automobile tires. Other industries such as chemicals, metals, and machinery experienced a considerable
increase in value added.

The result of all these changes can be seen
from column four in Tables 46 and 47 where value added
per worker per year in dollars is calculated. There
has been a marked increase in value added per worker
in mining and quarrying, food and kindred products,
rubber and rubber products, chemicals, and electrical
machinery. The rest of the industries witnessed an
increase of less than 10 per cent, with the exception

of petroleum and coal and machinery (except electrical) where value added per worker declined. On the
average, value added per worker for all industries
more than doubled from $724 to $1,516 during the period 1952-61. This increase in productivity resulted
from the concentrated efforts on investment in the industrial sector during the period 1952-60. In particular, the exploitation of natural resources, the
building of social overhead, and the economies resulting from the interdependency among industries contributed to such an increase. However, we should not
forget that part of that increase is not real, but
rather is monetary, since the price index for industrial products increased from 432 in 1952 to 446 in
1961 (June-August, 1939 = 100). To sum up, there has
been a considerable change in the industrial pattern
since 1952. Investment in industry increased during
the development period of the 1950's, while there has
been a tendency toward the large size firm with 500
workers, with emphasis on the basic industries. This
led to some increase in the value added per worker.

THE EXPANSION OF INDUSTRY DURING THE 1950'S

The expansion in the industrial sector is due
to the large number of new industries introduced in
1955 and the following years, in addition to the expansion of the existing industries. Two major factors
are behind such expansion. First, the Suez crisis
created several shortages which caused the government
to encourage industrial production in order to ease
the supply difficulties. Thus, we find several industries introduced, such as the production of electric
bulbs, radios, cables and tubes, medical preparations,
automobile and industrial spare parts, railway cars,
rubber tires, and steel. Other industries expanded
such as the production of batteries, assembly of re-
frigerators, petroleum refining, textile manufacturing, the production of electricity, and superphos-
phates.[28] As an example of the industrial expansion,
a United Nations report states: "A steel mill with an

output capacity of 265,000 tons per annum started production in 1958, using iron ore mined near Aswan."[29]
The second factor that caused a major step forward in
the development of industry in Egypt was the approval
in January 1957 and the immediate implementation of
the Five-Year Industrialization Plan for the period
1957-61. This plan envisaged the expenditure of
$575 million on manufacturing industries, mining, pe-
troleum, and industrial training, in order to raise
income for the industrial sector from $230 million in
1947 to $423 million by 1961. Expected employment
created by this expenditure amounts to 120,000 workers. In 1959, the United Nations reported that, "the
five-year industrialization programme started in 1957
has been running ahead of schedule and the projects
are expected to be completed by 1960 with a total expenditure of some $690 million."[30] A new five-year
development program covering the period 1960-65 was
then in preparation.

During this period, we find an important development in the field of public control and financing of
industrial and other business activities. This is the
creation in 1957 of the Economic Organization to act
as a planning and administrative center and to act on
behalf of the state in the organization of and investment in new projects, and to supervise the management
of government shares and holdings in private enterprises. The organization purchased some of the firms
and foreign equity capital sequestrated during the
Suez crisis, and took charge of the public interest in
companies in which the government participated. In
addition, it established several companies to exploit
oil resources and other mineral resources, and participated in the capital of the pharmaceutical and ship-
ping industries. Among the industrial projects developed following the establishment of this organization
are the manufacturing of bicycles, sewing machines,
and radios. A petro-chemical industry was constructed
by an Italian firm. The Fiat Company built a plant
for assembling Fiat cars of which certain parts will
be manufactured in Egypt. Industrial motors of Belgrade completed the erection of a plant designed to

assemble tractors. The textile industry -- cotton, wool, artificial silk, and jute -- continued to remain the most important industry in the country. Other industries such as cement, manganese, paper and cardboard, beverages, and food processing continued to expand. As a result, industrial production experienced, in general, a substantial increase in the period from 1957 to 1960.[31]

Notes to Chapter 7

[1]The Federation was formerly called "The Egyptian Industries Society."

[2]A. E. Crouchly, "A Century of Economic Development, 1837-1937, A Study in Population and Production in Egypt," Egypte Contemporaine, XXX (February-March, 1939), 148.

[3]National Bank of Egypt, Economic Bulletin, Vol. X, No. 2 (Cairo, 1957), p. 210.

[4]Ibid., p. 211.

[5]Institut National De La Statistique Et Des Études Économiques, Mémento Economique, L'Égypte (Paris: Presses Universitaire De France, 1950), p. 144.

[6]United Nations, Department of Economic Affairs, Review of Economic Conditions in the Middle East -- 1951-52, Supplement to World Economic Report (New York, 1953), pp. 88-89.

[7]United Nations, Department of Economic and Social Affairs, Economic Developments in the Middle East 1956-1957, Supplement to World Economic Survey, 1957 (New York, 1958), pp. 14-15.

[8]G. L. S. Schackle, Expectations in Economics (Cambridge: Cambridge University Press, 1949).

[9]John Maynard Keynes, The General Theory of

Employment, Interest, and Money (New York: Harcourt, Brace and Co., 1938), p. 24.

[10]Industrial Bank, Quarterly Bulletin of the Industrial Bank, Vol. I, No. 1 (Cairo, 1957), pp. 40-46.

[11]Egyptian Federation of Industries, Yearbook 1950-51 (Cairo: S.O.P. Press, 1951), pp. 21-22.

[12]The government actually participated in the capital of the bank in the amount of $1,759,500. However, the bank's activities were limited until the expansion that took place after the Revolution.

[13]National Bank of Egypt, Economic Bulletin, Vol. II, No. 2 (Cairo, 1949), pp. 95-97.

[14]Department of Statistics and Census, Annuaire Statistique, 1959 (Cairo: Government Press, 1960), p. 355.

[15]Gunnar Myrdal, An International Economy (New York: Harper and Brothers, 1956), pp. 202-203.

[16]Ibid., underlining mine.

[17]National Bank of Egypt, Economic Bulletin, Vol. IV, No. 4 (Cairo, 1951), pp. 269-72.

[18]Review of Economic Conditions in the Middle East, 1951-52, op. cit., p. 49.

[19]National Bank of Egypt, Economic Bulletin, op. cit., p. 271.

[20]United Nations, Department of Economic and Social Affairs, A Study of Industrial Growth (New York, 1963), pp. 16-18.

[21]Hollis B. Chenery, "The Role of Industrialization in Development Programs," American Economic Review, papers and proceedings XLV (May, 1955), 40-57.

[22]Ibid., p. 46.

[23]Ibid.

[24]Review of Economic Conditions in the Middle East 1951-52, op. cit., p. 47.

[25]Department of Statistics and Census, Ten Years of Revolution: Statistical Atlas (Cairo: S.O.P. Press, 1957), Table 11.

[26]Collection of Basic Statistics, op. cit., p. 102.

[27]Ibid.

[28]United Nations, Department of Economic and Social Affairs, Economic Developments in the Middle East 1957-58, Supplement to World Economic Survey 1958 (New York, 1959), p. 16.

[29]Ibid.

[30]United Nations, Department of Economic and Social Affairs, Economic Developments in the Middle East 1958-1959, Supplement to World Economic Survey, 1959 (New York, 1960), p. 47.

[31]United Nations, Department of Economic and Social Affairs, Economic Developments in the Middle East 1959-1961, Supplement to World Economic Survey, 1961 (New York, 1962), pp. 41-42.

A United Nations study of the processes and problems of industrialization in underdeveloped countries singled out three factors as the principle immediate deterrents to the expansion of industry.[1] First, the unsuitability of basic economic facilities, or the deficiencies in the economy which tend to handicap production such as the lack of capital and transport facilities, and generally the deficiency in the infrastructure. Second, the disparities in the development of various sectors of the economy or what we called the lack of balance in development schemes. Third, the inadequacy of the domestic market. Low incomes are reflected in a pattern of expenditure unfavorable to the development of secondary industries since a higher proportion is spent on food.[2]

These three factors sum up what generally the economists agree upon as the obstacles to industrial development. In his early article on the problem of industrialization of "International Depressed Areas," Rosenstein-Rodan considers capital as the main component of the basic economic facilities.[3] Accordingly, he advocates international investment or capital lending on three grounds:[4]

(1) Development would proceed more quickly at a minimum sacrifice on consumption.

(2) It helps to get a system of diversification in industry which will give rise to two types of

218

economies. First are the strictly Marshallian economies external to a firm within a growing industry.
Second are the economies external to one industry due
to the growth of other industries.

(3) The normal multiplier effect will naturally lead to further industrialization if sufficient
capital (national and international) is available for
investment in "basic industries."

In a second treatment of the same subject, Rosenstein-Rodan restated his argument in terms of the
"three indivisibilities."[5] These three kinds of indivisibilities are: indivisibility in the production
function, especially in the supply of social overhead
capital, indivisibility (or complementarity) of demand, and the indivisibility (kink) in the supply of
saving.

Nurkse[6] concerned himself with capital formation. His variant of Smith's dictum, "the division
of labor is limited by the extent of the market" becomes "the inducement to invest is limited by the size
of the market."[7] However, the size of the market is
not only determined, but actually defined, by the volume of production. Hence the crucial determinant of
the size of the market is productivity. Nurkse states
that as follows, "the enlargement of the market
through the rise in productivity that would result
from increased capital intensity of production is inhibited by the initial smallness of the market."[8] To
sum up, Nurkse's analysis points out two major factors: the need for a frontal attack on a wide range of
different industries which calls for a program of balanced growth, and the importance of providing social
overhead capital or building the infrastructure.

In the light of these factors, we propose to
discuss the problem of industrialization of the Egyptian economy. In addition to an examination of the
resource-availability for development, emphases are
placed on analyzing the degree of interdependence in
the industrial structure.

THE HOME MARKET

An outlet for industrial products is the market in which industry disposes of its products. Such a market consists of two components, a home market and an outside market, i.e., an export market. Lecturing in Egypt on the aspects of industrialization, Arthur Lewis stated that "every inquiry into industrialization must begin with the market, since industry cannot survive unless it can dispose of its products."[9] With respect to Egypt, outside markets have been and are still limited to a considerable degree. Several factors have contributed to this. First, the quality of products of Egyptian industries could not compete with the well-established products from Europe which have long dominated the Egyptian market, let alone compete with European products in other markets, such as the Middle East or the Mediterranean countries. In the second place, frequent political disturbances among the Arab countries placed a limitation on trade in these countries which constitute the best market for products of Egyptian industries. To this we can add the lack of an efficient system of transportation and communication.

Indeed the main obstacle to industrialization in Egypt was the limited home market. In the first place, the home market was flooded with products from Europe and mainly from England. This represented a great obstacle because of the lack of confidence among the consumers in domestic products. Even if the price is lower than similar imported products, this in itself represents another obstacle since the consumer will think that is due to the lower quality of domestic products. In the second place, as a result of the wide differences in the levels of per capita income as we have seen in the last chapter, the higher income groups could afford the imported products and indeed they prefer them for the sake of prestige. The low income groups add to the narrowness of the home market because their limited income is devoted mostly to food, clothing, and lodging, and leaves practically

nothing to spend on manufactured products. Lewis considers this a characteristic of underdeveloped countries which represents an obstacle to industrialization. He states that: "As Mr. Clark has shown,
whereas rich countries spend 20 per cent or more of
their incomes on manufactured goods...the percentage
spent by the poorest countries on domestic plus imported manufactures ranges only between 5 and 10 per
cent."10

Thus the limited home market in the Egyptian
economy stood in the way of industrialization. And,
in fact, it patterned the industrial structure toward
the production of food and clothing. We have seen in
the last chapter that these were the two leading industries. Their contribution to industrial employment
and production amounted to about 50 per cent in 1952,
but there has been a declining trend since that time.
On the other hand, about a third of the population or
more than 50 per cent of labor force is engaged mainly
in the production of food.

NATURAL RESOURCES AND SOCIAL OVERHEAD

On the supply side some factors stand in the
way of industrialization, such as the deficiency and
shortages in some factors of production, especially the
basic ones; capital and entrepreneurship. And indeed
this was the case in Egypt until the beginning of the
development period when resources were mobilized and
external capital injected into the economy. However,
before that period, there was deficiency in the supply
of two factors necessary for development. These are
natural resources and social overhead.

Social Overhead. Investment in the social overhead structure is generally lumpy. In underdeveloped
countries, capital beyond the means of an individual
entrepreneur is required to build a hydroelectric
power plant, a dam for water reservation for irrigation, or an efficient highway system. Also, the gesta-
tion period is long and that renders the undertaking

of such investments risky. Considering the high cost, the return in the short run would not look promising, and in the long run the project seems to be too risky. Thus we find entrepreneurial motivation reluctant to undertake such investments.

In spite of its private unprofitability, social overhead investments are socially desirable in the long run. The risk and the high cost, coupled with the nature of the services of such facilities being diffused over large sectors of the economy, should not discourage the undertaking of such investments. Besides being socially desirable in the long run, these investments will render it possible to pay their cost and a justifiable return. We find a good example of that in the American experience of building an extensive transportation system during the first half of the nineteenth century. As Kemmerer and Jones pointed out in their study, American Economic History, when the state of New York started undertaking the construction of the Erie Canal, which was to cost seven million dollars, the project seemed rather impractical. However, "within a few years, and before it was completed...the Erie Canal began to pay for itself."[11]

If we accept the assumption that the process of development in underdeveloped countries will not take the Schumpeterian form of innovations and pioneering private entrepreneurs but rather the introduction and adaptation of already-established technology in the developed countries, we find that social overhead outlays are needed in order to precondition the economy for such an adaptation process. New and advanced techniques (and machinery) will not be imported from developed countries unless they have proved profitable in the original country. The structure of social overhead there, which is taken for granted, contributes toward lowering marginal cost. Where such a structure does not exist, adopting modern techniques will not be at all economical. Other factors in the process of adaptation, such as the difference in the climate, training of workers, and the need to substitute certain inputs, may raise the cost of production above

the levels prevailing in the developed countries. If
we add to this the high cost involved in providing the
social overhead, the margin of profit will be lowered,
a matter that renders such investments unattractive.

Generally, investment in social overhead structure in the early period of development is justified
on two grounds: first, social benefits accruing to
the economy. The cost-reducing effect of social overhead investments will encourage the undertaking of
other industries.   It makes expansion possible at a
relatively small additional cost.   Apart from being
basic to other industries, it has a high forward linkage effect. In Chenery and Watanabe's study of international comparisons, we find that the forward linkage
effects of petroleum and natural gas industries is
0.97, electric power 0.59, and transportation 0.26.[12]
From this we infer that these activities represent a
large part of cost to many industries.

Second, investment in social overhead has an
income-generating effect which is usually ignored. The
construction of projects to provide social overhead
services will result in the employment of workers and
the use of other factors of production. This, in turn,
will result in an increased income which will be reflected in an increased demand, a further inducement
effect for industrial expansion. So, investment in the
infra-structure becomes income-generating in addition
to promoting industry and stimulating development.

The social overhead hypothesis finds support
from several economists.   While Rostow considers such
investments as prerequisite for the take-off,[13] Nurkse maintains that, "it provides a skeleton structure
into which the economy must be encouraged to grow
through less lumpy and more widely diffused investments of capital, and, above all, through the endeav-
our and enterprise of individuals."[14]

Before 1952, the industrial sector of Egypt was
lacking many social overheads. Power is a vital physical element of the economic environment whose absence

or inadequacy may constitute a serious obstacle to industrialization.   In fact, the lack of electric power
is a characteristic of most underdeveloped countries.
Of all the installed capacity of electric power in the
world in 1952, only 8.5 per cent is found in underdeveloped countries.[15] Also, the share of underdeveloped countries in the production of electric power in
the world in 1952 amounted to only 6.8 per cent.[16]

     In Egypt, the production of electric energy, a
basic prerequisite for many industries, was too small
to stimulate any investment in industry. This is evident from the following figures on electric energy produced during the period 1951-62:[17]

Year	Energy (Million KW/H)	Year	Energy (Million KW/H)
1951	609	1957	1,712
1952	629	1958	1,905
1953	1,200	1959	2,125
1954	1,240	1960	2,638
1955	1,422	1961	3,760
1956	1,545	1962	4,400

In 1951, electric energy produced amounted only to 609
million KW/H. In 1953, it doubled, reaching 1,200 million KW/H. Due to the increase in demand for this
source of energy for the various industrial projects
initiated during the development period, especially
with the beginning of development planning, electric
energy produced amounted to 4,400 million KW/H by 1962.

     Transportation and communication are vital fac-
tors in the promotion of industry. They were and still
are lacking to a certain extent in the Egyptian economy. The total number of telephones, government and
private, which was 141,804 in 1953-54, increased only
to 210,882 by 1959-60.[18] If we consider population in
1960, this amounts to eight telephones per thousand
people.

     A United Nation's study notes that,"In many of

the less developed countries...transport difficulties
have been a major force tending to inhibit industrialization altogether."[19] Efficient means of transportation is frequently a decisive factor in the location
of industry and tends to reduce the cost for industries. It also widens the market. All this may be
lacking in the Egyptian economy. The railway system
is government operated except for three small private
companies which operate some minor lines. These are
the Delta Company, one in Lower Egypt, and another
operating in Upper Egypt. In 1951, there were only
3,495 miles of railroad track in Egypt, of which the
government owned and operated 2,633 miles. Government
owned tracks increased to 2,704 miles in 1960,but privately owned tracks decreased to 156 miles. In other
words, the railroads in total decreased from 3,495
miles in 1951 to 2,860 miles by 1960.

This deficiency in railroads was somewhat compensated for by the increase in rural and desert
roads. During the decade 1950-60, the length of rural
and desert roads increased from 10,238 miles to
13,103, about a one-third increase. However, most of
these are unpaved roads in the rural areas of Lower
and Upper Egypt. Rural roads, amounting to 8,770 miles
in 1950-51, increased to 10,299 miles by 1960-61. Desert roads which can be considered highways, amounted
only to 10 per cent of all roads in 1950-51. By 1960-
61 they doubled becoming 2,804 miles as compared with
1,468 miles in 1950-51. To sum up, we can say that
during the 1950's, there has been a concentration on
building the infrastructure. Yet there is more to be
built if development is to continue at a reasonable
rate.

Natural Resources. Egypt is not well endowed
with natural resources. Apart from agricultural land
which is limited by the water available from the
floods for irrigation, resources are extremely limited. Even the available resources were not fully ex-
plored until the development period.

Table 48. Production of Phosphate, Manganese, Salt,
and Iron Ore, 1953-61

(1,000 metric tons)

Year	Phosphate	Manganese	Salt	Iron ore
1953	443	277	128	---
1954	535	177	345	---
1955	626	220	402	36
1956	615	201	530	131
1957	n.a.	91	n.a.	264
1958	558	112	403	178
1959	629	128	383	246
1960	566	284	522	239
1961	626	278	415	422

Sources: Central Committee for Statistics, Collection
of Basic Statistics (Cairo: S.O.P. Press,
1962), pp. 98-99; Egyptian Federation of
Industries, Yearbook 1952-53, and Yearbook
1955-56 (Cairo: S.O.P. Press, 1956), p. 323;
Department of Statistics and Census, Ten
Years of Revolution: Statistical Atlas
(Cairo: S.O.P. Press, 1962), Tables 36 and
37.

Table 48 shows the production of the most important mineral resources in Egypt for the period
1953-61. These were phosphate, manganese, salt, and
iron ore.   The production of iron ore, which started
only in 1955, increased from 36,000 metric tons in
1955 to 422,000 metric tons in 1961, a twelve-fold increase in a period of five years.   Considerable increase took place also in the production of manganese,
a basic material for industry. From 60,000 metric tons
in 1948, it increased to 278,000 in 1961.[20]

The production of phosphate also doubled during the same period. With respect to salt, there has been a decline in its production since 1948. From a level of production of 364,000 metric tons in 1949, it declined to 128,000 in 1953. However, the government tried to reorganize the salt producing firms and to encourage its exports through specifying the quality for the export market. There has been some increase in the production of salt, and in 1961 it reached 415,000 metric tons as compared with 128,000 in 1953.

One of the prerequisites for industrialization is a source of power. Egypt does not have water falls to enable the generation of hydroelectric power. On the other hand, it is moderately endowed with alternative resources for power, such as oil. Table 49 shows the production of crude oil and the production and consumption of petroleum products, gasoline, kerosene, and heavy oils for the period 1953-61. It is true that Egypt is not rich in crude oil. Proven oil reserves as of January, 1962, were estimated at only 710 million barrels. This is small compared with other countries of the Middle East. Proven oil reserves are estimated at 35,000 million barrels in Iran, 26,500 in Iraq, and 52,000 in Saudi Arabia.[21] Yet, Egyptian reserves have not been fully exploited. Production was only 1,889,000 metric tons in 1948, but investment in the industry increased during the 1950's and the level of production more than tripled by 1961, reaching 4,145,000 metric tons.

With respect to petroleum production, we find that before the development period production always fell short of consumption, causing the importation of these products and imposing a limitation on industrialization. The production of gasoline which increased from 196,000 to 387,000 metric tons during the period 1946-61, only began to exceed consumption (which also increased) in 1959. There has been also some increase both in the production and consumption of kerosene and heavy oils. However, the consumption of these materials still exceeds production due to the intensive movement of automation and industrialization.

Table 49. Production and Consumption of Petroleum and Petroleum Products, 1953-61

(1,000 metric tons)

Year	Production of crude oil	Gasoline Prod.	Gasoline Cons.	Kerosene Prod.	Kerosene Cons.	Heavy oils[a] Prod.	Heavy oils[a] Cons.
1953[b]	2,351	188	254	207	717	1,807	1,319
1954	1,970	226	251	220	766	1,727	1,868
1955	1,808	258	288	275	784	1,923	2,193
1956	1,937	261	293	244	860	1,863	2,513
1957	2,362	289	n.a.[c]	258	n.a.[c]	2,294	n.a.[c]
1958	3,485	332	263	295	686	2,392	3,057
1959	3,401	341	261	291	712	2,495	3,166
1960	3,623	306	262	370	737	3,321	3,568
1961	4,154	387	252	455	756	3,369	3,328

[a]Consist of diesel and fuel oil.
[b]Does not include government consumption of these.
[c]Not available.

Sources: Department of Statistics and Census, Annuaire Statistique 1959 (Cairo: Government Press, 1960); Central Committee for Statistics, Collection of Basic Statistics (Cairo: S.O.P. Press, 1962), p. 100; Egyptian Federation of Industries, Yearbook 1955-56 (Cairo: S.O.P. Press, 1956), p. 322.

INTERDEPENDENCE OF THE INDUSTRIAL STRUCTURE

The industrial system is interdependent in the sense that the growth and expansion of one industry is enhanced (and limited) by the growth of other industries and the industrial complex as a whole. This interdependency among industries renders the success of an industry dependent not only on the environment of the industry, but the conditions prevailing in other industries and their reaction to its decisions as well. The imperfect situations prevailing in most underdeveloped countries in the industrial sector stand in the way of new projects. It makes it costly to enter an industry and thereby reduces the profitability of projects which might be socially desirable. The isolation of industries also tend to enlarge the element of risk.

Although the interdependency of the industrial complex runs in all directions, we can distinguish two main dimensions which lead to the creation of pecuniary external economies. These are the horizontal and vertical linkages.

However, before we examine each of these concepts, let us assume that we have three industries, A, B, and C. A is a basic industry (in the earlier stages of production), B is intermediate, while C is at the late stages of the line of production. Industry B uses A's output as an input and sells its output to industry C. In other words, though these three industries are producing different products, they are interdependent. Also, within each one we have several firms (A_1, A_2, ..., A_n, B_1, B_2, ..., B_m, C_1, C_2, ..., C_q), which produce the same commodity. Moreover, let us assume that the supply of labor in underdeveloped countries is somewhat elastic, while the internal supply of capital is fixed. Moreover, assume there is no inducement for foreign capital to flow to these areas because of the low levels of profitability of the projects as well as entry restrictions. Finally, we will be concerned only with those pecuniary external economies resulting from the growth of the industries and the industrial system. We shall exclude, for the time being, those that might result from the expansion of the market and a shift in demand curve.

Horizontal Linkages. Let us consider those industries at one stage of the same line of production--the A's (it could be the B's or C's). And let us assume that a firm will try to enter this industry or that one of the existing firms wants to expand. The immediate result of such an expansion will be an increase in the demand on the factors of production used by this industry. Although the supply of labor is assumed to be somewhat elastic, a firm may find it difficult to recruit its specific needs. Labor is by no means homogeneous, and the supply of labor in a particular industry is somewhat limited. As a result of the competition for that limited supply, new firms tend to try to start with trained workers. Training on the job takes a long time and involves the risk and expense of losing workers to other firms after being trained. Entering firms will attempt to draw their needs from existing firms, and thereby raise the level of wages for this type of labor in the whole industry. At the same time, an area with a fixed supply of capital allows the expansion of one firm only at the expense of contracting others. Such things create barriers around an industry which keep entrepreneurs from attempting to enter the industry.

Firms in the same line of production are linked horizontally because of the competition for factors of production and markets. In such a situation, external economies could be exploited and accrue to the firm as a result of the expansion of the other firms and the industry as a whole. To illustrate, let us relax the assumption that the supply of capital is fixed. This renders it feasible to initiate a large program of development to promote a number of industries simultaneously rather than concern ourselves with only one.

In the first place, the entry of new firms leads to the establishment of industrial centers which

provide facilities necessary for those working or involved in this industry. This means that the growth
of industry will render economies to all the firms.
The provision of services ranging from housing and
water supply to electricity and gas becomes more
feasible and less costly. These facilities will in
turn attract labor to these centers. This also will
relieve the firm from providing such facilities, a
matter that contributes toward reducing the cost. We
pointed out before that labor is immobile. However,
the increase in wages, the spread of knowledge, and the
improvement in transportation will all help break the
obstacles that impede mobility. In the second place,
we find that, with the growth of the size of the firm,
a supply of labor of the type needed by the industry
will be increased because the firm can afford to train
its workers. In addition, expansion of the firm makes
room for upward advancement of labor and makes room
for additional workers in lower ranks. Eventually,
this may create the class of "foreman" currently lacking in the industrial structure of underdeveloped
countries. All such efforts will result in increasing
productivity of labor, which will reduce the cost of
production for the firms in the industry, if wages do
not rise correspondingly.

Another source of economies to the firms in
the same line of production is the by-products and by-
services. Other industries could be constructed to
make use of the by-products of the original industry.
Unless there is a certain minimum of inputs to be used
to warrant its creation, the construction of such an-
cillary firms will not be economical or feasible,
apart from the question of capital supply. Sometimes
the growth of an industry leads to the creation of
units which provide the by-services needed for the industry more economically than the original firm can
produce internally and independently. As a case in
point, take the supply of electric power which in most
underdeveloped countries must be provided by the firm
itself. Sufficient expansion of industry in an area
could give rise to a firm producing this power at a
considerably lower cost. Another example is that the

expansion of industry will draw specialized units to provide computation, market research, advertising, and many other services adapted to the industry at a lower cost. In addition, there is a secondary effect, i.e., the industry's growth leads to the improvement in machinery and equipment used by the industry. This is because it can be produced on large scale and so lower the cost of input to the using firms.

Research in modern industry became an important factor in its growth. By research here we do not necessarily mean developing new materials and products, but the adaptations of new techniques and products to the environments of underdeveloped countries. Take as an example the underdeveloped country that starts an automobile industry of the American type where there are no highway systems or roads suitable. Several examples could be cited here from underdeveloped countries trying to copy exactly the western way of living as reflected in the modern consumer goods. This state of affairs results from the lack of research facilities.

Allyn Young states that, "The causal connections between the growth of industry and the progress of science run in both directions, but on which side the preponderant influence lies no one can say."[22] Arthur Lewis not only emphasizes the role of research in the profitability of possible new industries in attracting industrialists to start such industries, but also he considers that as a duty of the government.[23] In addition, "research into the market can be done by businessmen..."[24] In evaluating the role of education in economic development, Singer points out that the capacity to create wealth is "based upon the application of systematic research to the problems of production and of the best organization of the economic institutions of a country."[25] Small firms can hardly afford to devote capital to research. Consequently, in a world where continuous changes occur both in the input processes and products, few small firms can survive. The expansion of firms in industry will give rise to such research from which all firms can benefit with the end result of reducing the cost for the individual firm.

Vertical Linkages. Vertically, the industrial complex seems more closely linked and interdependent. Here we are considering the case of industries not in the same line of production but rather the interdependence between supplying industries (A or B) and using industries (B or C).

Let us suppose that industry B (or A) is producing steel rods. If there are plans for the construction of a new plant or the expansion of the existing one, the demand for the product of other industries such as A, which might be producing iron ore, will be increased. There will also be a greater demand for the products of other industries such as construction (secondary demand). In other words, there are interdependencies among several industries; in order for one of them to expand, the others have to increase their production to meet the expansion in the industry originally concerned and make that expansion feasible. Inputs are not perfect substitutes, and there must be a simultaneous expansion of many industries.

The interindustry relations exist for all industries in varying degrees. The degree of interdependence of economic sectors has been computed by Chenery and Watanabe for Italy, Japan, and the United States. They tried to show the extent to which any one industry depends on selling its output (forward linkage) and buying its input (backward linkage) from other sectors. According to the findings of this study, the intermediate primary production is characterized by a low ratio of interindustry purchases to value added (backward linkage), while, on the other hand, it has a high forward linkage as reflected in the sales to other sectors. The backward linkage for this group of industries ranges from 0.27 to 0.31, while the forward linkage from 0.59 to 0.72.[26] On the contrary, manufacturing both intermediate and final possesses a high backward linkage. For intermediate manufacturing, the backward linkage ranges between 0.49 and 0.66, while the forward linkages between 0.46 and 0.78. For final manufacturing, they range from 0.43 to 0.89 and from 0.12 to 0.42, respectively.[27] If underdeveloped countries efficiently develop their natural resources in industries such as fisheries, mining, agriculture and forestry, they will provide other industries on the same vertical line with relatively low-price inputs.

The expansion in other using or supplying industries might yield some economies to the original industry with a reciprocal effect for the former. On the one hand, the expansion of an industry enables it to use more efficient methods which yield the economies of large-scale production, if such exist. On the other hand, further growth will induce vertical disintegration with firms tending to become more specialized. A firm must integrate some processes in the same plant in order to make use of all its capacity. And in some cases, because certain services could not be provided by other firms or industries, this results in raising the unit cost of their final product. Expansion permits the introduction of large-scale production with specialization and the use of the most efficient equipment. This reduces costs and consequently the prices of inputs of other industries, if monopoly does not develop in the meantime.

Another source of economies that results from expansion is the economies of location. It is true that an industry (B) tends to be attached either to the sources of its inputs or its market, whichever leads to more economies. This is also true for industries in underdeveloped countries with limited sources of inputs or a narrow market for its products. In these areas, a newly created industry will have less choice in the matter of efficient location. The deficiency in the means of transportation and communications will be a limiting factor in choosing the location of the plant, and the disregard of other factors whose economies might overweight those of the location. With the growth of industry (B), the using industries and the supplying industries might promote

better means of communications and transportation, due
to the large volume of transactions. Thus the nearness
to the source of inputs or the markets is no longer a
limiting factor. In locating the industry, the advantages (and economies) or other cost-reducing factors
such as low prices of land, availability of facilities
for research, experimentation, weather, and many other
factors can be taken into consideration.

While in this analysis we were concerned mainly with the producer goods industries, we can say that
the argument holds for consumer goods industries in
their capacity as "using industries."

ESTIMATION OF LINKAGES FOR THE EGYPTIAN ECONOMY

Input-output tables represent the sales of one
producing sector to another and to final users, measured at current prices. Chenery and Watanabe note
that "the magnitudes of these flows depend on the
total amount and pattern of domestic demand, the composition of imports and exports, physical input-output
proportions, and relative prices."[28] However, for the
purpose of comparison of interindustry flows for
Japan, Italy, and the United States, the authors elimi-
nated the effect of variations in the pattern of domestic demand and trade. Following this model, we
shall try to estimate the interdependency among productive sectors of the Egyptian economy by the linkages concept. Chenery and Watanabe introduced the
method of studying the proportion of the ultimate production used to produce a given commodity which is
employed in the establishments producing that commodity.[29] For this purpose, they defined two types of
linkages: a "forward" linkage to denote the ratio of
intermediate to total demand and a "backward" linkage
measured by the ratio of purchased inputs to the value
of total production.[30] In other words, let

U_j = the value of purchased inputs,

X_j = the value of total production,

W_i = total intermediate demand, and

Z_i = total demand, then

the forward linkage (w_i) is given by $\dfrac{W_i}{Z_i}$, and

the backward linkage (u_j) is given by $\dfrac{U_i}{X_j}$.

The forward linkage shows the interdependence through sales to other sectors. The backward linkage gives the interdependence through purchases from other sectors.

Although there have been national income estimates of Egypt, especially since 1952, a national accounting system that permits the construction of input-output tables was only developed for the purpose of planning in 1959-60. An essential part of development-planning is the study of the flows of intermediate commodities among commodity producing sectors in order to estimate the interdependency among sectors. The outline of the ten-year plan includes two tables showing the flow of intermediate commodities among twelve commodity producing sectors for the years 1959-60 and 1964-65 at current user's prices of 1959-60.

In order to estimate the backward and forward linkages for the Egyptian economy, some consolidation was necessary. Data on total production and total demand were given by a different classification. Therefore, in order to construct a complete table showing the relationship of the flow of intermediate commodities to total supply and demand, we concentrate on eight commodity sectors and one for other industries. The three remaining sectors are consolidated with other industries because estimating their total supply and demand involves a large degree of error.

Table 50 shows the flow of intermediate commodities among nine commodity producing sectors of the Egyptian economy in 1959-60 at current prices in millions of dollars. The distribution of the intermediate use of commodities shows that the three major sectors in the economy are food processing, textile and clothing, and agriculture. The frequently empty cells in the table indicate that there is not much interdependence among sectors.

From the data in Table 50, the backward and forward linkages are estimated for the nine sectors of the Egyptian economy. This is shown in Table 51.

For the intermediate primary products group, we find agriculture has a high forward linkage effect (.99). This is quite high if compared with the results Chenery and Watanabe obtained from their study on Italy, Japan, and the United States where the coefficient was .72. The same difference is observed with respect to products of nonmetallic materials and the power and fuel sectors. The coefficients for Egypt are .88 and .65, respectively, compared with .52 and .59 in Chenery and Watanabe's study.[31] However, the backward linkages in this group are higher than those in Chenery and Watanabe's study, with the exception of agriculture.

The situation became different when we compared the linkage coefficients in intermediate manufacture. The forward linkages for industries in this group are lower than the corresponding average obtained by Chenery and Watanabe for Italy, Japan, and the United States, while the backward linkages are almost equal or higher. The final manufacture group in the Egyptian economy consists mainly of clothing and food processing industries, in addition to a few metallic and engineering products such as machinery and transportation equipment. Here we find that the coefficients of both the forward and backward linkages are somewhat higher for the Egyptian economy.

The differences in the coefficient on the linkages between the Egyptian economy and the pattern obtained by Chenery and Watanabe from the Italian, Japanese, and United States economies should not be taken seriously since the insufficiency of data on the intermediate flows did not permit a disaggregation

Table 50.   The Flow of Intermediate Commodities Among Nine Commodity Producing
Sectors in 1959-60 at Current Users Prices

(million U. S. dollars)

Sectors	(1)	(2)	(3)	(4)	(5)	(6)	(7)	(8)	(9)	T.I.D.
(1)	282.9	—	—	—	677.6	328.0	11.5	1.8	3.4	1,305.2
(2)	22.1	9.4	3.9	2.8	18.4	2.3	11.5	5.8	15.6	91.8
(3)	—	—	6.4	15.9	—	—	—	1.1	2.1	25.5
(4)	2.3	1.8	2.3	19.5	2.3	0.5	4.6	0.5	7.4	41.2
(5)	14.9	—	—	—	202.9	—	..	..	8.1	225.9
(6)	—	—	—	—	13.8	—	90.4	—	—	104.2
(7)	4.6	—	—	—	9.2	4.6	164.2	—	2.3	184.9
(8)	—	—	..	—	..	—	..	9.2	0.9	10.1
(9)	73.1	54.4	13.8	10.8	16.1	..	20.7	9.7	100.4	299.0
I.I.T.	399.9	65.6	26.4	49.0	940.3	335.4	302.9	28.1	140.2	2,287.8
Total output	1,319.7	141.7	43.8	94.2	1,118.0	344.3	435.2	49.0	290.5	3,836.4

.. Magnitude less than $50,000.

Key to Table 50:

(1) Agriculture

(2) Power and fuel, i.e., electricity, oil, and coal products

(3) Basic metallics

(4) Metallic and engineering, i.e., metallic products, electric and nonelectric machines, and means of transport

(5) Food processing

(6) Ginning and pressing

(7) Textile and clothing

(8) Nonmetallics

(9) Others and miscellaneous

T.I.D. - Total intermediate demand

I.I.T. - Interindustry total

Sources: Computed on the basis of data compiled and consolidated from: National Planning Committee for Southern Region, The Frame of the Five Year Plan for Economic and Social Development, July 1960-June 1965 (Cairo: General organization for Government Printing Offices, 1960), pp. 39-177.

Table 51. Types of Productive Sectors, a
Classification of the Forward and Backward
Linkage Coefficients for the Egyptian Economy
in 1959–60

Sector[a]	Forward linkage (w)	Backward linkage (u)
I. Intermediate Primary Products		
Agriculture	.99	.30
Products of non-metallic materials	.88	.50
Power and fuel[b]	.65	.46
II. Intermediate Manufacture		
Basic metallics	.59	.61
Ginning and pressing	.30	.97
Products of non-metallic industries	.21	.57
III. Final Manufactures		
Metallic and engineering	.43	.52
Food, beverages, and tobacco	.20	.84
Weaving, spinning, and clothes[c]	.42	.70

[a]The coefficients for the sector of "other industries and miscellaneous" are not included since it includes several heterogeneous industries.

[b]This could be included in II since part of it is intermediate manufacture.

[c]Spinning and weaving is intermediate manufacture but separate inputs are not available.

Source: Computed from Table 50.

comparable to that of Chenery and Watanabe. However, some observations could be made on the pattern prevailing in the Egyptian economy. It is noticeable that the coefficients are higher at both ends of the production process, the intermediate primary products and the final manufacture. Also, as we have observed, there were many empty cells in Table 46, an indication of the lack of interaction among the various sectors of the economy. With the exception of ginning and pressing, the intermediate manufacturing sector is small. Although ginning and pressing has a high backward linkage (.97), it is actually a part of the agricultural sector and does not tend to generate as much activity as might appear from its high backward linkage coefficient.

To sum up, the Egyptian economy is highly specialized in the production of primary products and in the processing of some consumer goods. It is lacking in the intermediate processes which, apart from generating income, could stimulate more production at the final manufacturing stage.

CONCLUDING REMARKS

One of the major factors in stimulating industrial development is then the economies resulting from the interdependence of the industrial structure. This lack of interdependence, in fact, could sum up the picture of both the development of industry in Egypt and the obstacles to this development before the 1952 Revolution.

We have pointed out the dominance of small size units in industry. Only a small number of large firms (with 50 workers and more) have contributed significantly to value added. In this state of affairs, we find that numerous small size firms scattered all over the country, even in the same industry, tend to prohibit the establishment of a nucleus of firms that could provide such efficiency of services as would improve the over-all productivity. At the same time,

these large-size firms have tended to become self sufficient and they seek to provide all the services
needed internally. It was only during the 1950's that
a firm was established to furnish the textile industry
with the accessories and spare parts for its machines
which frequently have to be rebuilt or changed. This
expansion, of course, helps to create the economies
resulting from the horizontal linkages. An example of
the vertical linkages is found in the textile industry. Until recently, a good portion of the products
of this industry was sent to Europe for dyeing and
finishing. After the expansion of these activities in
1953, the Industrial Bank helped establish some firms
for dyeing and finishing which are of high quality.

With the build-up of many social overheads and
the expansion of private investments, it would seem
that the goals of the development plan could be accomplished, provided the necessary capital can be made
available. The increase in the scope of the industrial
sector will require more and more roads and electric
energy, not to mention the training of workers for the
skills needed for industrial development.

Notes to Chapter 8

[1] United Nations, Department of Economic and
Social Affairs, Processes and Problems of Industrialization in Underdeveloped Countries (New York, 1955).

[2] Ibid., pp. 11-15.

[3] P. N. Rosenstein-Rodan, "Problems of Industrialization of Eastern and South-Eastern Europe,"
Economic Journal, LIII (June-September, 1943), 202-11.

[4] Ibid., pp. 203-8.

[5] P. N. Rosenstein-Rodan, "Notes on the Theory
of the Big Push," in Howard S. Ellis (ed.), Economic
Development for Latin America (New York: St. Martin's
Press, 1961), pp. 57-67.

[6]Ragnar Nurkse, Problems of Capital Formation in Underdeveloped Countries (Oxford: Basil Blackwell, 1953).

[7]Ibid., p. 6.

[8]Ibid., p. 10.

[9]William Arthur Lewis, Aspects of Industrialization, National Bank of Egypt Fiftieth Anniversary Commemoration Lectures (Cairo: N. B. E. Printing Press, 1953), p. 1.

[10]Ibid.

[11]Donald L. Kemmerer and C. Clyde Jones, American Economic History (New York: McGraw-Hill, 1959), pp. 179-80.

[12]Hollis B. Chenery and Tsunchiko Watanabe, "International Comparisons of the Structure of Production," Econometrica, XXVI (October, 1958),487-521.

[13]W. W. Rostow, The Stages of Economic Growth (Cambridge: Cambridge University Press, 1961), pp. 24-26.

[14]Nurkse, op. cit., p. 154.

[15]United Nations, Processes and Problems of Industrialization on Underdeveloped Countries, op. cit., p. 12.

[16]Ibid.

[17]Central Committee for Statistics, Collection of Basic Statistics (Cairo: S.O.P. Press, 1962), p. 101; Department of Statistics and Census, Ten Years of Revolution: Statistical Atlas (Cairo: S.O.P. Press, 1962), Table 52.

[18]Collection of Basic Statistics, op. cit., p. 176.

[19] United Nations, _Processes and Problems of Industrialization in Underdeveloped Countries_, op. cit., p. 12.

[20] See Table 4, p. 23 _supra_ for earlier years.

[21] United Nations, Department of Economic and Social Affairs, _Economic Development in the Middle East, 1959-1961_, Supplement to World Economic Survey, 1961 (New York, 1962), p. 130.

[22] Allyn A. Young, "Increasing Returns and Economic Progress," _Economic Journal_, XXXVIII (December, 1928), 535.

[23] W. Arthur Lewis, op. cit., p. 29.

[24] Ibid.

[25] H. W. Singer, _International Development_ (New York: McGraw-Hill, 1964), p. 66. He also notes that, "the history of post-war years has shown that given this underlying capacity and systematic application of research, economies can make up for gaps or destruction in their physical capital equipment in a surprisingly short time." Ibid.

[26] Hollis B. Chenery and Tsunehiko Watanabe, "International Comparisons of the Structure of Production," _Econometrica_, XXVI (October, 1958),492.

[27] Ibid., p. 493.

[28] Chenery and Watanabe, op. cit., p. 489.

[29] Ibid., p. 492.

[30] Ibid.

[31] Ibid., p. 493.

CHAPTER **9** AGRICULTURE

It has always been maintained that Egypt is a
gift of the River Nile and that by its nature it
should remain an agrarian economy. If the Egyptian
economy is an agrarian one, it should be comparatively
efficient in the field of agricultural production. In
addition, agricultural land should be able to absorb
and support the increasing population. However, this
was not the case in Egypt, as we have seen in Chapter
2: Cultivated area increased only by 25 per cent
during the period 1882-1960. With the increase in
population, density per square mile of cultivated area
rose from 870 to 2,755. Even if we take into consideration the development in agricultural techniques which
allows the cultivation of more than one crop a year,
we still find that the increase in crop area is lag-
ging far behind the growth in population. While crop
area more than doubled during the period 1882-1960,
population density per square mile of crop surface
increased from 869 to 1,564.

THE AGRARIAN ECONOMY

The Egyptian economy depended largely on the
production and export of a few major crops. Table 52
shows the production of major crops in Egypt during
the period 1952-60. Cotton, rice, and onions are
mainly export commodities. Cotton and cotton products,
such as raw cotton, cotton yarn, and cotton cloth, accounted for 89 per cent of the Egyptian exports in

Table 52. Production of Major Crops in Egypt,
1952-60

(1,000 metric tons)

Year	Cotton	Wheat	Corn	Rice	Onions
1952	447	1,089	1,506	517	267
1953	318	1,547	1,853	652	303
1954	348	1,729	1,753	1,118	370
1955	334	1,451	1,714	1,309	415
1956	325	1,547	1,652	1,573	403
1957	405	1,467	1,495	1,709	481
1958	446	1,412	1,758	1,082	462
1959	457	1,443	1,500	1,616	558
1960	478	1,499	1,691	1,486	544

Source: Central Committee for Statistics, Collection
of Basic Statistics (Cairo: S.O.P. Press,
1962), pp. 82-88.

1952 and for 78 per cent in 1960. Wheat and corn are
for local consumption and fall short of satisfying the
needs of the increasing population.

Here we have a situation where an agrarian
economy still imports most of its staples, i.e.,
wheat, corn, and flour. The imports of corn more than
doubled during a ten-year period, as can be seen from
Table 53 which shows the imports of wheat, corn,and
flour during the period 1952-60. From 43,000 tons in
1952, the imports of corn rose to 101,000 tons in
1961. The imports of flour almost tripled during the
same period, rising from 144,000 tons in 1952 to
473,000 tons in 1960. Although it appears from the
table that there has been some reduction in wheat
imports, the proportion is still large compared with

Table 53.   Imports of Wheat, Corn, and Flour,
1952-60

(1,000 metric tons)

Year	Wheat	Corn	Flour
1952	710	43	144
1953	467	9	86
1954	10	---	---
1955	---	---	---
1956	242	86	51
1957	710	75	93
1958	774	59	279
1959	730	107	424
1960	631	51	473

(---) Data not available.

Source: Central Committee for Statistics, Collection
of Basic Statistics (Cairo: S.O.P. Press,
1962), p. 88.

the domestic production and consumption.   Domestic
production of wheat in 1952 amounted to 1,089,000 tons.
With an import of wheat of 710,000 tons, domestic production of wheat satisfied only 60.5 per cent of total
domestic needs.   By 1960, domestic production of wheat
increased by about 40 per cent amounting to 1,499,000
tons.   In the meantime domestic needs also increased.
In 1960, imports of wheat totaled 631,000 tons.   Thus,
in spite of the increase in the production of wheat,
the economy still depends on imports for about 30 per
cent of its needs.   It should be noted that this took
place during the development period, when foreign exchange was needed for supplying the new industries
with machinery and equipment.   This situation sets

Table 54. Area of Principal Crops during the
Period 1940-60

(1,000 acres)

Year	Cotton	Wheat	Corn	Rice	Onions	Total
1940	1,749	1,563	n.a.	528	34	3,875
1950	2,050	1,424	1,506	727	37	5,848
1951	2,054	1,554	1,718	507	38	5,871
1952	2,042	1,455	1,769	388	33	5,687
1953	1,374	1,858	2,092	439	38	5,179
1954	1,639	1,863	1,976	633	48	6,159
1955	1,885	1,581	1,904	623	53	6,045
1956	1,716	1,630	1,906	716	50	6,017
1957	1,888	1,572	1,836	759	54	6,316
1958	1,977	1,479	2,029	538	54	6,077
1959	1,827	1,531	1,930	757	61	6,095
1960	1,944	1,511	1,890	733	61	6,140

Sources: Egyptian Federation of Industries, Yearbook
1950-51 (Cairo: S.O.P. Press, 1951), p. 213
and Yearbook 1955-56, p. 313; Central Committee for Statistics, Collection of Basic
Statistics (Cairo: S.O.P. Press, 1962), pp.
80-81.

some limit on the availability of foreign exchange, and
might impede development.

HIGH RATE OF SPECIALIZATION

One of the main problems of the Egyptian
economy, then, is not only the specialization in agriculture, but the dependence on a single crop, cotton.
Table 54 shows the area of principal crops during the

period 1940-60. Total crop area of these five crops averaged about six million acres during the ten years 1950-60. This amounts to about two-thirds of the total crop area for the Egyptian economy. Also within the total area of principal crops, cotton occupies about one-third.

The dependence of the economy on one main agricultural crop, cotton, subjects it to considerable instability, which is of two main types: production instability and price instability. Production instability results from the fact that cultivation of cotton in Egypt depends largely on the forces of nature. In the first place it depends on the irrigation from the Nile and the level of water during the flood. In the second place the cotton worm, the boll weevil, is always a threat to the farmer. If the crop is attacked by the worm, a good part of the crop will be spoiled and little can be done about it. To illustrate from the case of Egyptian agriculture, let us calculate an index number for the production of cotton for some years during the period 1951-61 with the production of 1951-52 as a base for comparison. This index number is shown in the following figures:[2]

Year	Index number	Year	Index number
1951-52	100	1956-57	89
1952-53	123	1957-58	112
1953-54	88	1958-59	123
1954-55	96	1959-60	126
1955-56	92	1960-61	132

From these figures we can see that after an increase of about 23 per cent from 1951-52 to 1952-53, the production of cotton fell below the level of 1951-52 during the following four consecutive years, after which it started rising again. These fluctuations are due to forces outside the control of the producer since the area cultivated with cotton is limited to about one-third of each owner's land.

Price instability also makes the dependence on

cotton risky. It is true that a good part of Egyptian cotton is of the long-staple variety, of which total supply is somewhat limited. Egypt is considered a major producer of long-staple cotton in the world. The other major producers are Sudan, Peru, and the United States. The share of Egypt in world production of long-staple cotton was 69.0 per cent in 1951-52, 67.7 per cent in 1952-53, and 56.5 per cent in 1959-60. In other words, Egypt produces more than half of the world production of long-staple cotton. Also long-staple cotton amounts to about one-half of total cotton production in Egypt. However, although Egypt's share in world production of long-staple cotton is more than 50 per cent, its share in total world cotton production averages only 4.5 per cent. Thus, the prices of cotton are determined by total world supply and demand outside the Egyptian market. The Egyptian producer does not have a completely monopolistic situation in the cotton market. Prices fluctuate with the variations in world production, demand, and especially the stock left from the previous years.

Wide fluctuations in the price of cotton and the average yield affect the national income of Egypt, as well as the proceeds from foreign exchange, which depend to a great extent on cotton exports. This is evident from Table 55 and Figure 11 which illustrate the changes in the output per acre and gross value of Egyptian cotton during the period 1950-58. Gross value of income from the cultivation of cotton fell from $437 million in 1950 to $198 million in 1953. By 1954 it increased to $238 million, but decreased to $229 million in 1955. After that it increased to $302 million by 1958.[3] These fluctuations are due mainly to price fluctuations, and in part to the change in productivity resulting from attacks by the cotton worm. Therefore, it is risky to depend on cotton to provide a good part of the national income and to obtain foreign exchange through exports. This risk is more important if we recognize the increasing competition in recent decades from synthetic products. As a result of this situation we find that during the development period and the ten-year plan, efforts were directed

Table 55.   Output per Acre and the Value of Egyptian
             Cotton, Selected Years, 1950-58

Year	Output per acre (1935-39 = 100)	Gross value (Million dollars)
1950	82.5	437.2
1951	78.3	387.5
1952	96.7	268.6
1953	102.7	197.6
1954	94.0	237.6
1955	78.7	229.3
1956	84.1	290.9
1957	95.2	313.0
1958	100.0	302.0

Source: Computed from National Bank of Egypt, Economic
          Bulletin,   Vol. XV, No. 1   (Cairo, 1962), pp.
          19-21.

toward gradual diversification in agriculture, in addition to the industrialization of cotton.

THE AGRARIAN REFORM

        A major   problem which existed in the agricul-
tural sector of the Egyptian economy prior to 1952 was
the extreme   maldistribution   of land   ownership, as we
have seen   in Chapter 2.   There was a decline   in the
productivity of large   estates, many of which were run
by inefficient   managers   in the   employ   of   absentee
owners.   An investigation   of the Fallah   (Peasants')
Department of the Ministry of Social   Affairs in Egypt
has revealed   that, "On the big estates   where records
are kept and where some of the land is operated by the
owner and   some of it is rented out,   the rent charges
were in some cases higher than the net output obtained
from the land operated by the owner."[4] An index of the

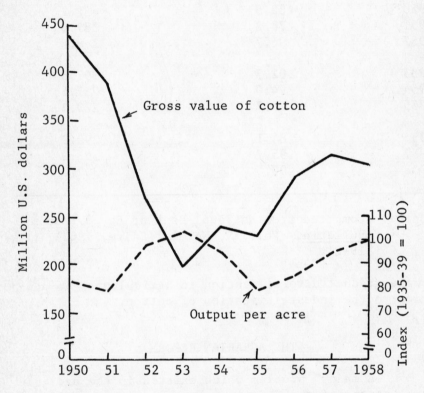

FIGURE 11.   AN INDEX OF OUTPUT PER ACRE
AND THE GROSS VALUE OF EGYPTIAN COTTON,
1950-58

average yield of agricultural crops taking 1913 as the
year for comparison (= 100) shows that it dropped to
90.6 in 1920 and 92.0 by 1944. On the other hand agricultural land was absorbing large portions of savings.
Since the supply of agricultural land is inelastic,
the concentration of land ownership in the hands of a
few caused a rise in the price and rent of land. Comparing average wage rates and land values in Egypt and
the U. S. for the year 1945, Dawood found that, "an
average acre of farm land in the U. S. was worth the
equivalent of less than ten days of the average farm
worker's wage. In Egypt an equivalent farm land area
claimed a price equal to about 20 years of the average
Egyptian worker's wages."[5]

In a study of the distribution of net income
from agriculture in 1946-47 among owners and tenants
in Egypt, the Division of Agricultural Statistics
found that out of a net income of $317.4, the owner
gets $264.5 while the tenant receives $52.9. In other
words, the owner receives the major part, 83 per cent,
of net income from agriculture.[6] The same study showed
that for 1945-46, the average net income per owner was
4.5 times that of the tenant.[7]

Before the 1952 Revolution, not only the disparities in land ownership became wider, but also we
find few landowners who actually tilled the land. The
situation can be seen better if we look at the distribution of all landowners and total area owned by size
of ownership and compare it with the distribution of
the number of owner-operators and the area they cultivated. The figures of Table 56 provide this information.

The maldistribution of land ownership in Egypt
in 1950 is evident from the first two columns of the
table. As the National Bank of Egypt reported, a further breakdown showed that the area owned by landlords
with estates of over 1,000 acres and who represented
only 0.01 per cent of all landowners amounted to 8.3
per cent of all agricultural land in 1952.However, the
striking phenomenon, as we can see from the table, is

Table 56. Distribution of All Agricultural Land and
Owner-Operated Land by Size of Ownership in 1950

Size of Ownership (acres)	All Agricultural Land		Owner-operated Land	
	Number of Owners (1,000)	Area (1,000 acres)	Number of owner-operators (1,000)	Area (1,000 acres)
Less than 1	1,875	719	179	95
1 - 5	599	1,263	362	835
5-10	83	592	67	463
10-21	42	582	28	392
21-52	21	667	14	441
52 & above	12	2,219	8	1,635
Total	2,632	6,042	658	3,861

Sources: Tables 5 and 6, pp. 33-34, above, and Department of Mobilization and Statistics,   Handbook of Basic Statistics (Cairo, 1963), p. 74.

that only one fourth of landowners operated   their
farms.   The fragmentation of landownership led to the
creation of many farms of less than one acre in size
whose operation is extremely uneconomical,   especially
if it is the only source of income for a rural large
family.   Only ten per cent of the small-size farms
(less than one acre) operated their farms.   The ratio
becomes less pronounced as we move up the scale of the
farm sizes, with the indication that the economical
unit was about 5-10 acres.

The above described situation leads to the deterioration of productivity for two reasons. First,
cultivation on small areas is not economical, and second, large estates in most cases are rented in small
plots or left to farm workers to manage.   In the case
of rented land,the owners make little capital improvements on the land, and try to extract as much rent as
possible from the land with as little input as

as possible, a situation that leads to the deterioration of land. In the case of land managed by hired farm workers we find a great deal of waste due to lack of supervision. If we add to this the lack of proper agricultural credit, we can account for the low yield of land, the failure of many major crops, and the decrease in income from agriculture.

In Egyptian agriculture, it seems that the efficient unit is the small-size farm. A survey undertaken in 1938 showed that the most productive and the most efficient size of farm was found to be five acres.[8] This is confirmed by the results of another study on cost, return, and efficiency of the different size of farms in 1947.[9] The findings of this study are summarized as follows:

Size of farm[10] (acres)	Per cent of total of farms	Average gross output per acre (dollars)
Less than 5 (Small)	81	81.4
5-50 (Medium)	18	91.8
50 and Over (Large)	1	84.9

These figures show that the most efficient and productive size farm is the medium one with an average of 12.4 acres. It was also found that,within the medium-size farms,the 5 - 10 acres size group had the highest average gross income of S 95.2

It is often ascertained that a direct relationship exists between land reform and agricultural productivity and output because of the two effects that land reform provides. In the first place, it provides greater incentive to the operator. Secondly, it leads to a more efficient farm management and better organization.

Actually, land reform is not new to underdeveloped but developing countries. It has been applied with some degree of success to several countries in Eastern Europe, Italy, Ceylon, Iran, Mexico, and some Latin American countries. Thus, one of the first tasks of the Egyptian Revolution, in the second month of its life, was the application of land reform measures to correct some of the social injustice resulting from the maldistribution of land, and at the same time to increase the productivity of land.

The Agrarian Reform Law was enacted on September 9, 1952, for the declared purpose of increasing the welfare of the population through the redistribution of agricultural land.[11] The law set a maximum limit of ownership at 208 acres. Meanwhile, the proprietor has the right to retain 104 acres more for his children provided the total does not exceed 312 acres. Associations and joint stock companies are exempted from the 104 acres limitation in order to encourage reclamation of additional land by these private enterprises. The law stipulated the compulsory expropriation of land holdings exceeding the maximum limits. Compensation or the purchase price for the expropriated land was set at a price equivalent to ten times the rental value of the land in addition to the value of the mobile and fixed assets such as buildings, machines and trees. Compensation was to be paid by the government in the form of state bonds bearing interest at 3 per cent, redeemable in thirty years. These bonds were to be registered bonds, and cannot be disposed of except to Egyptians. They also may be validly used in payment for fallow land purchased from the government, in payment of land tax, in succession duty, and the supplementary land tax as imposed by the law.

The land reform law also provided for the establishment of agricultural cooperatives by landowners owning less than 5 acres. These cooperatives, whose membership is compulsory, will provide farmers with credit, seeds, fertilizers, and farm machinery in addition to marketing their products. A minimum daily wage was also fixed by this law for agricultural workers, and for the first time they were given the right to form trade unions. A maximum annual rent per acre was set, and the rental value was not to exceed seven times the original land tax.

The redistribution of land proceeded simultaneously with the procedure of requisitioning. The expropriated areas were to be sold by the government to the new owners who were to pay the price of land in 30 years by equal installments. In addition to the compensation paid to the previous owners, the selling price included 15 per cent which represents the cost of requisition and administrative expenses plus 3 per cent annual interest. One of the most important measures provided by the Agrarian Reform Law was to safeguard against future subdivision of land by inheritance to less than five acres. This was necessary since the Moslem religion which is the religion of the majority in Egypt divides the inheritance among all the heirs, a matter that results after one or two generations in an extreme subdivision of land. Articles 23 and 24 of Chapter 3 of the law state that the smallest ownership should be limited in the future to five acres. In case the division of the property among the heirs will result in less than this limit, land should be given to the person who is actually engaged in agriculture, provided that the rest of the heirs are paid for their shares.

This law made about 6.4 per cent of the total cultivated area, or about 395,478 acres, suitable for distribution to the landless. Of this total amount, about 189,954 acres were actually taken over during the first year. A total of 15,570 acres have already been distributed in an average of slightly above three acres per family. This was in addition to about 51,900 acres sold directly to small holders by the owners up to the end of June 1953.[12] One of the major accomplishments of land reform in Egypt is the success in the distribution of 155,700 acres of "wakf" land, public domain land and reclaimed land during 1957-60.

Agricultural capital broadly defined by the United Nations, "comprises in addition to the land itself and the acquired knowledge of the potentials of the soil, supplies and equipment for current farm operations, houses and farm buildings and various infra-structure facilities--roads and (where possible) electric power, and frequently also community services especially to help ease the social strains in new settlements in isolated areas."[13]   The beneficiaries of land reform or the former tenants, the landless workers, and the persons new to agriculture needed substantial amounts of production capital in order to accomplish the goals of land reform. In order to solve the problem of capital after land reform in Egypt, beneficiaries were expected to join a system of supervised cooperatives which provide loans and furnish needs, livestock, fertilizers, and other services. Another major accomplishment is the consolidation of farm operation into major units of crop rotation, a system under which all farmers follow a uniform crop rotation in a new field layout.   The land is divided into several large areas consisting of a large number of small holdings to be cultivated with one crop. This was done outside the areas affected by land reform and aimed at overcoming fragmentation of land holdings and the difficulties of farming small units.

Up to 1961 the government permitted individuals and joint stock companies to own more than the maximum ownership limit set by the land reform law, provided that the excess ownership was of barren land under reclamation.   There was some abuse of the law with larger estates being farmed again in the name of relatives of an original owner and with advantage being taken of the exception set by the law regarding the ownership of barren land under reclamation. Therefore, the land reform law was amended in 1961 to limit maximum ownership to 104 acres of agricultural and barren land. Also it stipulated that no person or any of his family should hold more than 52 acres above the limit allowed by the 1961 amendment, whether that holding was through rent, inheritance, or any other means.

The land reform law of 1952 and its amendment led to the redistribution of a large amount of land among the landless. During the period 1952-61, an area of 358,410 acres which was requisitioned by the Public Organization for Agricultural Reform was distributed

to 135,174 families.   In addition,   another   139,031
acres   were reclaimed   by the   different agencies   and
distributed   among   53,043 families.   This brings the
total land   distributed among   188,217 families during
the period   1952-61   to   497,441 acres.   An area   of
150,510 acres   was sold directly by the original   owners to 35,000 families.   In 1962, 172,308   acres   were
to be distributed among 60,000 families.[14]

Table 57 shows the land   distribution   by size
of ownership for the postrevolution years (1956-60) as
compared with 1950 and shows the change as a result of
the land reform law. The distribution of land to the
landless increased the number of owners by 1956 to
2,948,100 as compared with 2,631,900 in 1950.   Most
of the increase was in the less than one acre farms.
By 1960, the number of landowners of less than one
acre declined, reaching 2,039,800 by 1960 as compared
with 2,123,000 in 1956.   Their weight in total landowners declined from 71.2 per cent in 1950 to 69.2 in
1960.   There has also been a rise in the number of
medium-size farms (1-5 acres), with their share in the
total increasing from 22.7 to 25.8 per cent during the
period 1950-60. The number of owners of large estates
of 52 acres and above (within the limit set by the
law) showed a decline from 12,100 in 1950 to 10,900 by
1960.   In addition, the law encouraged land reclamation. Land reclamation by the government and private
organizations amounted to   125,287 acres during the
fifties as compared with 55,638 acres reclaimed during
the forties. A report by the National Bank of Egypt
states that the annual average of land reclaimed by
the government and private organizations amounted to
125,287 acres during the fifties, as compared with
55,638 acres which were reclaimed during the forties.
A report by the National Bank of Egypt states that the
annual average of land reclaimed by the government,
companies and societies reached in the period 1955-59
some 17,761 acres as compared with an average of 6,673
acres annually during the period 1950-54.[16]

The results of the efforts expounded on the
redistribution of land during the development period
are reflected in the figures of output per acre of

Table 57. Land Distribution by Size of Ownership, 1950-60

(1,000 owners)

Size of ownership (acres)	1950	1956	1957	1958	1959	1960
Less than 1	1,874.7	2,123.0	2,058.3	2,074.7	2,045.8	2,039.8
1-5	599.2	660.1	659.5	662.0	706.8	741.9
5-10	83.2	81.0	81.1	81.0	81.0	82.9
10-21	41.5	48.5	49.8	49.4	48.3	46.9
21-52	21.2	23.3	24.3	23.6	24.5	23.9
More than 52	12.1	12.2	12.3	11.3	11.3	10.9
Total	2,631.9	2,948.1	2,885.3	2,902.0	2,917.7	2,946.1

Sources: Compiled from Central Committee for Statistics, Collection of Basic Statistics (Cairo: S.O.P. Press, 1962), p. 75; Department of Mobilization and Statistics, Handbook of Basic Statistics (Cairo, 1963), p. 71; and Table 5, p. 33 above.

field crops. Table 58 provides index numbers for the average output per acre from main crops for the period 1952-58 (1935-39 = 100). Most of the improvement took place in the production of cotton, wheat, rice, and sugar cane. There is still room for improvement in the yield of beans to supplement the deficiency in other foodstuffs, and onions, an export commodity that contributes to the proceeds of foreign exchange. The increase in the yield per acre, coupled with the increase in the cultivated area, led to the general increase in agricultural production. An index number for agricultural production (1935-39 = 100) shows that agricultural production rose from a level of 105 in 1950 to 136 by 1959. The level of animal production increased from 128 to 145 and that of foodstuffs from 109 to 143 for the same period.[17]

The success of land redistribution in Egypt can be seen from a report on land reform prepared by the United Nations' Food and Agricultural Organization and the International Labor Office which states that:

> Although the U. A. R. (Egypt) land reform has not been able to relieve the severe pressure of population on land or to ensure full employment for the agricultural labor force, the quality and profitability of employment have improved. Moreover, the new owners, as a result of better farming methods and of lower charges for land, have larger incomes than before the reform, and tenant incomes have risen as a result of the decrease in rental payments.[18]

THE COOPERATIVE MOVEMENT IN AGRICULTURE

Although the introduction of agricultural cooperatives started in Egypt in 1908, there have been some efforts in that field that date back to the last decade in the nineteenth century. In an agrarian economy with a large number of owners of small pieces of land, there was a need for some method of financing

Table 58.   Index Numbers for Average Output per Acre from Main Crops, 1950-58

(1935-39 = 100)

Crop	1950	1951	1952	1953	1954	1955	1956	1957	1958
Cotton	82.5	78.3	96.7	102.7	94.0	78.7	84.1	95.2	100.0
Wheat	83.9	91.4	87.8	97.6	108.8	107.6	111.4	109.5	112.0
Corn	86.3	82.3	84.7	88.2	88.2	89.7	86.3	81.1	86.2
Rice	115.3	82.8	89.6	100.0	119.0	141.7	147.9	151.5	135.6
Beans	74.0	96.5	93.4	93.0	101.0	97.5	81.2	95.1	96.3
Onions	78.6	98.1	93.5	91.6	94.8	87.7	87.0	87.7	83.1
Sugar cane	90.9	95.7	103.3	103.9	107.5	109.3	108.9	110.8	109.2
Total	88.7	77.1	95.2	100.1	102.9	101.4	100.6	104.7	104.1

Source: National Bank of Egypt, Economic Bulletin, Vol. XV, No. 1 (Cairo, 1962), p. 19.

these farmers. Thus in 1896 the government allocated a sum of $23,000 for the purpose of lending owners of not more than five acres small sums at an interest rate of 6 per cent. It seems that this effort was successful as Lord Cromer reported in 1899, "This trial proved two things; that the farmers were willing to accept any measures that facilitate borrowing at a low rate of interest, and that although repayment of loans was somewhat hard, yet it was possible."[19]

In spite of the success of this attempt, it was not repeated. Agriculture credit was left in the hands of the banks until the establishment of the National Bank in 1898.[20] This bank even took the function of lending to small farmers and expanded its loans. During the period 1899-1901, the National Bank issued loans to 34,000 persons. In addition, the government allocated the bank a sum of $57,500 to be loaned to small farmers.[21]

In 1902 the Agricultural Bank was established with a capital of 5.8 million dollars for the main purpose of helping the small farmers and lending to them at a rate of interest of 9-10 per cent.[22] The government guaranteed a minimum rate of interest of 3 per cent on the bank's loans to the farmers. However, this bank did not accomplish the goal for which it was established. Little help was given to the small farmers. The criterion for lending was based on the amount of collateral the farmers could offer to back these loans and this did not help the small farmers who did not possess any assets to offer as collateral. Agriculture credit declined as a result. The situation became worse with the 1907 economic crisis which resulted in the cessation of the flow of foreign capital investments in Egypt.[23]

Credit facilities available in Egypt did not help either agricultural labor or the tenants in climbing the agricultural ladder. Actually, the situation of agricultural credit deteriorated by the end of the first decade in the twentieth century. Most of the land of five acres or less was mortgaged. In 1912 real estate loans of some of the banks amounted to more than 120 million dollars. This led the government to issue in 1913 the famous law of the "Five acres." This law prohibits the seizure of farms which are less than five acres. Naturally banks stopped their loans to farmers with five acres and less.[24]

It could be said that cooperation in its modern form was actually introduced in Egypt in 1908 by a private philanthropist, Omar Lotfy, who was interested in the welfare of the peasants.[25] Up to this time, there was no cooperative legislation in Egypt. In 1909, Lotfy succeeded in persuading the "Khedevial Agricultural Society" to form a committee to study the possibility of introducing agricultural cooperation in Egypt. In the same year the committee submitted to the government a detailed memorandum and a draft of a cooperative law. However, nothing came out of this attempt in spite of Lotfy's continuous efforts to get it acted on.

When Lotfy gave up on the government's taking the initiative in introducing cooperatives in Egypt by passing the needed legislation, he decided to act anyway to introduce cooperatives there. In the absence of special laws and regulations, he had to establish cooperative societies governed by the law of joint stock companies, and that was an obstacle in itself. It was difficult to try to accomplish the objectives of cooperation within the law governing joint stock companies. However, Lotfy managed to obtain some exceptions such as the ability to decrease and increase capital. Other obstacles which were hard to overcome were the minimum value of share and the voting power according to the number of shares owned. In cooperatives each member has one vote irrespective of his holding of share. However, in 1909 he established the "Finance Cooperative Corporation" with a capital of $7,848 and with a maximum capital of $46,000. He also urged the establishment of consumers' cooperatives in cities and towns. During the period 1909-11 he managed to establish 14 agricultural cooperative societies for the purpose of lending to farmers and purchasing

inputs. These societies also aided the farmers in
marketing their products.

Following the First World War, the Egyptian
government directed some efforts toward helping the
farmers. In 1921, it allocated the sum of $230,000 for
the purpose of advancing loans without collateral to
the farmers owning not more than five acres to meet
production expenses at a rate of interest of 9 per
cent. The lending operation was carried through the
National Bank on behalf of the government. In 1922, a
sum of 1.15 million dollars was allocated to lend cotton growers who owned not more than 50 acres without
collateral. The rate of interest on these loans was 6
per cent and the Agricultural Bank acted in issuing
these loans on behalf of the government. The success
of all these efforts encouraged the government to
think seriously of adopting the agricultural cooperative system and cooperative credit in Egypt.

In 1923, the first cooperative law, applying
only to agricultural cooperatives, was passed. This
was amended in 1927 to cover cooperatives for other
purposes and to allow for the formation of cooperative unions. Up to 1923, cooperative development was
mainly the responsibility of the Ministry of Agriculture which registered societies and carried out subse-
quent inspection and auditing. At the same time (in
1923), the government reached an agreement with the
National Bank according to which the bank would advance the cotton growers loans secured by crops. These
were short-term loans for not more than three months
and at the set rate of .5 per cent monthly. Besides,
the Egyptian Ministry of Agriculture started selling
cotton seeds and fertilizers on time. In order to
encourage the cooperative movement, the government
also opened an account for the agricultural cooperatives to draw upon at a rate of interest of 4 per
cent. The rate of interest charged was divided equally between the government and the bank. This account
increased yearly until in 1930 it reached $805,000. As
a result, we find the number of agricultural cooperatives increased to 135 by 1925. By 1931 there were

539 cooperatives of all kinds with a membership of
53,000.[26] These were mainly agriculture since the
other kinds of cooperatives did not fully develop by
this time.

In 1931 the Agriculture Credit Bank was founded in which the government held 51 per cent of the
shares. The main objective of this bank was to advance
loans to small holders either directly or through cooperative societies. The bank started its operation
with the Agricultural Season of 1931-32. The bank's
credit operations were of four types.[27] First, short-
term credit was granted for a period of not more than
14 months to finance the farmer and the cooperatives
during the season of cultivation. Second, loans were
made for not more than ten years for the purpose of
buying livestock and machinery and for land improvement. Third, long-term loans were made up to twenty
years for land reclamation. Fourth, financing was
made available to any organization working for the
benefit of agriculture. These loans were secured by
collateral and were issued for fourteen months or
more.

In 1949, the bank's name changed to the Agricultural Credit and Cooperative Bank. Its capital was
increased to $5.75 million. Its operations were ex-
panded to cover any type of credit instead of agricultural credit only. Thus, by 1939 we find 792 cooperatives in Egypt, most of them agricultural, multipur-
pose societies with a membership of 78,000. Advances
and sales amounted to $2,587,000 and paid up capital
and reserves were $752,100. In this year (1939) the
official control of the cooperatives was transferred
to the Ministry of Social Affairs. It should be noted
that large landowners began to join the cooperatives
to benefit from the low rate of interest at which the
bank advanced loans to cooperatives. This enabled
them to control the cooperative.

The role of cooperatives expanded during the
Second World War. The government relied heavily on
them in the distribution of supplies and fertilizers.

In 1944, an amendment of the cooperative law transferred the function of audit and supervision to provincial cooperative unions which were formed over the
next four years and numbered 35 by 1950. This shows
how the cooperative movement expanded. Between 1933
and 1944 membership in cooperatives increased ten-
fold.[28] The expansion of the cooperative movement in
agriculture is evident from the following figures:

	1940	1944	1952
Number of societies	757	1,559	1,727
Number of members	70,517	517,053	498,653
Value of services ($1,000)	3,038	8,568	16,187

The Agrarian Reform Law which was issued immediately following the 1952 Revolution stipulated
that in all cases an agricultural cooperative made up
of peasants in the village should be formed among
farmers who had acquired requisitioned land in that
village and who did not own more than five acres. This
was instituted in the law to guarantee a continuous
improvement in the method of cultivation, providing
technical and material help in order to increase production. The formation of these societies immediately
after the distribution of the Agrarian Reform lands
enabled the small farmer to enjoy the advantages of
large ownership from the point of view of profiting by
the modern technical cultivation processes, use of
agricultural machinery, ameliorated irrigation of land
and better marketing systems. As an example of the
marketing efforts of these societies, the quantity of
cotton sold through cooperatives increased from 1,375
to 22,742 tons during the period 1952-1960. Even with
the damage that befell the crop in 1960-61, the cooperative societies sold 15,000 tons. Marketing also
extends to crops other than cotton.[29]

The following are some of the specific activities laid down by the law for the cooperative societies:[30]

(1)   extension of agricultural loans in regard to the needs of the land;

(2)   supply of inputs such as seeds, fertilizers, livestock, and agricultural machinery;

(3)   developing the use of select seeds, storage of crops, combating pests,and digging of waterways and canals;

(4)   marketing crops on behalf of the farmer;

(5)   provision of social services to the members and their families, such as the creation of rural centers, health units, consumer's cooperatives, and making available pure water and electric light in the village.

The 1952 laws, and the reorganization of the cooperative system during the early 1950's directed the attention of the government and the Agricultural Credit and Cooperative Bank toward further   development of the cooperative system. In 1954, they started reorganizing the cooperative societies. Experts from the Land Reform Organization participated in the management of these societies in cooperation with the bank representatives. This experiment was started with four societies as a first step--the number increased to 41 by 1956. The success of this trial resulted in the increase of memberships of these societies from 15,467 in 1954-55 to 19,048 members in 1955-56.[31]

In 1957, the Agricultural Credit and Cooperative Bank tried another system in three areas. According to this system, the Bank's operation was limited to the agricultural cooperative societies which in turn deal with the farmers and offer them credit facilities. To ensure the success of this system the bank exerted complete supervision over the cooperative societies. The success of this system encouraged the government to continue in that direction and adopt it in all areas. By 1961, agricultural credit became cooperative. In other words, tenants and land holders

cannot obtain any credit facilities except through the
cooperative society in their area. The success of
this system can be seen from the expansion in the cooperative movement as is evident from the following
figures.[32]

	1956	1961	Per cent increase
Number of societies	2,190	4,038	84
Number of members (1,000)	449	1,250	181
Areas served (1,000 areas)	2,171	3,503	61
Value of loans ($1,000)	46,952	74,920	50

While the number of societies almost doubled,
the number of members joined about tripled. Another
system initiated by the Agricultural Credit and Cooperative Bank is the designation of 16 agricultural
societies in selected areas as "Village Banks." In
addition to offering credit facilities they are authorized to accept deposits and savings. Actually the
"Village Bank" is a branch of the Agricultural Credit
and Cooperative Bank, which at the same time assumes
the function of the agricultural cooperative society,
such as providing farmers with seeds, fertilizers,
machinery, and credit. In 1961, a five-year plan was
designed according to which the 16 village banks were
to undertake projects totaling more than one-half million dollars to be spent on the improvement of irrigation and drainage systems, mechanization in agriculture, and improving livestock. By 1962, the number of
village banks increased to 27.

Cooperation in Egypt has become the tool of
state by which it can provide services to the people,
particularly in rural areas. It now has become an
accepted part of government policy through which it
sees that the whole estate is properly cultivated
according to plan. At the end of 1960, all cooperatives were placed under the authority of the Ministry
of Agrarian Reform which administers them through regional agrarian reform offices. Also, they were to be

reorganized as "supervised cooperatives." These co-operatives are set up on each estate, membership in which is compulsory. Membership in these cooperatives usually runs into the hundreds and may be over 1,000. They are run by a manager, an elected board of management and a supervisory committee.[33]

These supervised (agrarian reform) cooperatives were successful. A United Nations Study on co-operatives reports that these societies, "at least in their early years, have had considerable advantages over other agricultural societies."[34] Issawi concurs with that as he writes, "There seems little doubt that the new co-operatives have performed valuable services to their members and have reduced some of the disruptions which the removal of landlords control might have created."[35] It is expected that these cooperatives, in addition to their basic functions of credit, supply,and marketing, play a leading part in land settlement, improvement of agricultural techniques, diversification of crops,and increase in livestock production.

INCOME FROM AGRICULTURE

Employment, earnings,and income from agriculture are largely affected by factors other than those operating in agriculture alone. This makes it difficult to isolate the incidence of land reform, however. Table 59 shows total plant production, animal production,and total gross income from agriculture during the period 1945-60 in millions of dollars. There has not been an appreciable increase in income from agriculture during the postwar period. Gross income from agriculture increased from $625 million in 1945 to only $773 million in 1948 after a sharp decline during 1946 and 1947. During the period 1945-48, animal production accounted for less than one-fourth of total agricultural production.

Gross income from agriculture increased from 1948 to 1951 in which year it reached $1,088 million.

Table 59.   Gross Income from Agriculture
by Major Source, 1945-60

(Million U. S. dollars)

Year	Plant production	Animal production	Total
1945	491	134	625
1946	492	110	602
1947	515	135	650
1948	635	138	773
1949	709	219	928
1950	863	225	1,088
1951	863	225	1,088
1952	719	199	918
1953	703	182	885
1954	766	190	956
1955	761	207	968
1956	882	202	1,084
1957	891	229	1,120
1958	894	237	1,131
1959	950	250	1,200
1960	1,022	256	1,278

Sources: Compiled from Egyptian Federation of Industries, Yearbook 1950-51 (Cairo: S.O.P. Press,
1951), p. 214, and Yearbook 1953-54, pp.
276-77; National Bank of Egypt, Economic
Bulletin, XV, No. 1 (Cairo, 1962), p. 21;
Department of Public Mobilization and Statistics, Handbook of Basic Statistics (Cairo:
S.O.P. Press, 1963), pp. 92-93.

This sharp increase was due mainly to the rise in the price of cotton. Actually the production of cotton decreased by about seven per cent during the period 1949-51. It was followed by a sharp decline in the total value of plant production. This took place while the production of cotton increased by 22.9 per cent in 1951-52. Again this was due to the sharp decline in the price of cotton.

Gross income from agriculture started rising steadily beginning in 1954. While the share of animal production continued to provide about one-fourth of gross agricultural income, income from cotton increased by 44.5 per cent during the period 1953-60. Meanwhile plant production increased by 45.5 per cent and animal production by 40.58 per cent during the same period.

To sum up, the agricultural sector experienced considerable changes during the development period. The land reform laws, the land reclamation projects and the improvements in the means of irrigation and drainage all contributed to the expansion and the increase in the cultivable area. For example, canals increased from 13,954 to 15,606 kilometers during the period 1952-61 and drainage facilities from 7,580 to 8,522 kilometers during the same period.[36] The increase in productivity was accomplished through the selection of new types of seeds and pedigreed animals, the protection of plants and animals against pests and diseases, the dissemination of new cultivation methods, as well as the plant rotation system.

These efforts to develop the agricultural sector during the 1952-60 period were to continue during the ten-year plan (1960-70) for social and economic development. It was recognized that development in agriculture should proceed along with industrialization in order to ensure the success of the development programs. This is true for two principal reasons. First, agriculture provides most of the inputs for the Egyptian industries. Second, it provides foodstuffs and other consumer goods, the demand for which will

increase further as the economy proceeds along the
path of industrialization.

Notes to Chapter 9

[1] Central Committee for Statistics, Collection
of Basic Statistics (Cairo: S.O.P. Press, 1962), p.
130.

[2] Collection of Basic Statistics, op. cit., p.
89.

[3] National Bank of Egypt, Economic Bulletin,
Vol. XV, No. 1 (Cairo,   1962), p. 21.

[4] This shows also that tenants in Egypt fre-
quently are little better off than the agricultural
labor. Mohamed A. Ezzat, "The Land Tenure System of
Egypt," in Kenneth H. Parsons et al. (eds.), Land
Tenure, Proceeding of the International Conference on
Land Tenure and Related Problems in World Agriculture
(Madison, Wisc.: University of Wisconsin Press, 1956),
p. 101.

[5] Hassan A. Dawood, "Agrarian Reform in Egypt:
A Case Study," Current History, Vol. XXX (Cairo,
1956), 333.

[6] Ministry of Agriculture, Division of Agricultural Statistics, The National Income from Agriculture
(Cairo: Government Press, 1948).

[7] Ibid.

[8] Ezzat, op. cit., p. 102.

[9] Ibid., pp. 101-102.

[10] The average size of the farm in the first
group (small) was 1.4 acres, in the second group
(medium) 12.4 acres, and in the third group (large)
173.4 acres. Ibid.

[11]With the unity with Syria, a similar Agrarian Reform Law was issued for the Northern Region on November 26, 1958.

[12]National Bank of Egypt, Economic Bulletin, Vol. VI, No. 3 (Cairo, 1953), p. 215.

[13]United Nations, Department of Economic and Social Affairs, Progress in Land Reform, Third Report (New York, 1962), p. 6.

[14]Mohamed M. Hamdy, Some Reflections on Our Contemporary Economic System (Alexandria: Dar El-Maaref Press, 1963), pp. 145-46.

[15]See Table 5, p. 33 supra.

[16]National Bank of Egypt, Economic Bulletin, Vol. XV, No. 1 (Cairo, 1962), p. 15.

[17]Ibid., p. 18.

[18]Progress in Land Reform, op. cit., p. 4, (parentheses added).

[19]As quoted in Abdel-Rahman El-Rafie, Agricultural Cooperative Unions (Cairo: n.p., 1914), p. 167.

[20]The first bank to be founded in Egypt was the Egyptian Bank in 1856. This was followed by several other banks established with foreign capital.

[21]El-Rafie, op. cit., p. 168.

[22]Kamal H. Abul-Khair, Co-operation, Its Evolution and Philosophy (Cairo: National House for Printing and Publishing, n.d.), p. 86.

[23]Ibid.

[24]Sayed Marei, Agricultural Reform and the Population Problem in Egypt (Cairo: National House for Printing and Publishing, n.d.), pp. 177-78.

[25]Omar Lotfy was interested in Egyptian affairs and politics. He studied in Egypt and England. Following the 1907 crisis he went to Italy to study its agricultural cooperatives and its cooperative system of financing. When he returned to Egypt, he urged the Agricultural Society to study the possibility of introducing agricultural cooperatives in Egypt and continued to work for that goal.

[26]Charles Issawi, Egypt in Revolution (London: Oxford University Press, 1963), p. 164.

[27]Marei, op. cit., pp. 148-85.

[28]Issawi, op. cit., p. 164.

[29]Ministry of Agrarian Reform and Land Reclamation, Agrarian Reform and Land Reclamation in Ten Years (Cairo: National House for Printing and Publishing, n.d.), p. 37.

[30]Ibid., pp. 35-36.

[31]Marei, op. cit., p. 190. As an indication of the success of this system, Marei gives an example of one of these cooperatives (Shanatouf), which managed to increase the productivity per acre by 23 per cent during the period 1955-56.

[32]Central Bank of Egypt, Economic Bulletin, Vol. III, No. 2 (Cairo, 1963), pp. 190-91.

[33]United Nations, Economic and Social Council, "The Cooperation Movement in Africa," Fourth Session of the Economic Committee on Africa, Addis Ababa, February-March, 1962 (Mimeographed.), p. 6.

[34]Ibid., p. 7.

[35]Issawi, op. cit., p. 166.

[36]Collection of Basic Statistics, op. cit., pp. 95-96.

PART **III**

DEVELOPMENT STRATEGY
AND THE SUPPLY APPROACH

CHAPTER **10** INVESTMENT STRATEGY
AND DEVELOPMENT
PLANNING

Since the 1952 Revolution, two eras could be
distinguished in the development of the Egyptian economy. First, the era of Reconstruction which we have
called the Development Period (1952-60). Measures
taken during this period paved the way for the second
stage of development which is termed the Planning Era.
The latter started with a ten-year plan (1960-70) to
be implemented in two five-year phases.

Investment began to take place under a political, social, and economic framework different from
that which prevailed before 1952. The new administration intended to transform the economy into a socialist one and, in fact, initiated a great deal of legislation to accomplish that end. Before we examine investment strategy, however, a review of the new laws
and regulations which provided the socialist framework
of the Egyptian economy is in order.

THE INSTITUTIONAL FRAMEWORK OF
THE DEVELOPMENT PERIOD

Economic development is a complex phenomenon
involving shifts among different stages of technology,
standards of living, and levels of education. Most
important to note is that it is a product of a multitude of factors which act and interact upon each other
to produce a certain level of economic development.

279

However, the initiation of the development process depends largely on the simultaneity in producing changes in the economic, social, and political arenas. It is of vital importance to the process of development that changes in the factors affecting it do take place simultaneously, thus producing significant enough forces to initiate development. A change in any of these factors by itself might not be strong enough to overcome the obstacles encountered in the first stage of development. In this case, the attempt to develop will revert to the old low level equilibrium. The simultaneous changes in the economic, social, and political arenas, however, will reinforce each other, and therefore produce a push large enough to make development self-sustaining.

There is no doubt that the 1952 Revolution succeeded in initiating development during the first few years following the Revolution. As we have seen in Chapter 3, the Egyptian economy had been exposed since the beginning of the nineteenth century to several shocks that could have resulted in initiating development. However, such scattered efforts were set back by counteracting forces. The change that the Revolution produced in the economic, social, and political arenas, in a society which was actually ready for the change, helped mobilize all the development forces and embarked the economy on its development path in the 1950's.

Immediately following the Revolution, in an effort to develop the economy rapidly, several projects were adopted and put into effect without any predesigned plan. Most of the projects were studies individually by the Permanent Council for National production which was established in 1952. The Permanent Council for National Welfare Services was also in operation to change the social structure of the farm people by building schools and providing clinics, welfare, and recreation services. All these scattered efforts and especially those directed mainly toward industrialization did not give the desired results.

The Permanent Council for National Production, which superseded the former Economic Advisory Council, was formed as an independent agency of the Cabinet with the following functions:[1]

(1) to examine and recommend development projects in the fields of irrigation, land reclamation, electrification, mining, and industrialization, and to examine the means of internal and external financing of these projects;

(2) to present to the Cabinet, within a year of its inception, an integrated program of national economic development to be carried out over three years; pending the completion of this plan, the Council may present well conceived projects for immediate execution if it sees fit;

(3) to proceed with an early examination of the possibilities of increasing the local supply of food, grains, petroleum, sugar, animal products, and fertilizers with a view to overcoming existing bottlenecks.

The establishment of this Council was the first step toward economic development. Besides referring approved projects to the Cabinet, it was empowered to carry out certain schemes and launch pilot projects. The Council was authorized to issue bonds with government guarantee. Furthermore, it would participate in the formation of joint stock companies with the state guarantee of an annual return on paid-up capital. The Council enjoyed a large measure of autonomy in the administration. It was consulted about important measures of agricultural development.

In the agricultural sector, the Agrarian Reform Law of 1952 limited land ownership to a maximum of 208 acres. In 1961, it was amended limiting the maximum ownership of agricultural land to 104 acres. Many other pieces of social legislation have been enacted since 1952. New labor laws provided for the placement of unemployed workers, vocational training, collective bargaining, and the employment of women and minors. The Social Insurance Act brought all workers under social security.

During the four years following the Revolution, nothing much was said regarding the economic system or the degree of government control over the various private economic activities. The government was mainly concerned with studying projects needed for the development of the economy. By initiating and participating in such projects, directly and through the Industrial Bank, the government encouraged the undertaking of these projects with minimum interference on its part.

In 1956 the new Constitution outlined the economy's socialist framework. In the first place, it pointed out that the existence of large amounts of capital owned privately is detrimental to the state since capital tends to protect itself by changing the law toward its benefit. With this constitution, the nation entered the planning phase of its economy. Article 7 declares that "National economy is to be organized according to plans, which conform to principles of social justice, and which aim at promoting national productivity and raising the standard of living." Private economic activity was conditioned by the stipulation of Article 8 that "Private economic activity is free from state interference provided that it does not prejudice public interests or endanger the people's security or infringe upon their freedom and dignity." The constitution also put in the hands of the State the welfare function according to Article 17, reading: "The state endeavors to secure a decent living-standard for every citizen, with the aim of providing food, housing, health, cultural and social services for all." Article 26 of the constitution proclaimed "Natural resources, whether subterranean or in territorial waters, are the property of the State which it administers taking into account the exigencies of National defense and national economy." Hav-

ing declared the public ownership of national resources, the constitution also stipulated state control
over the other factor of production--labor. According
to Article 53, state regulation in the area of labor
included limitation of working hours, determination of
wage scales, insurance against work injuries, and arrangements concerning holidays and leisure hours.

With the union of Egypt and Syria on February
21, 1958, a provisional constitution of the U.A.R. was
promulgated. The economic and social structure outlined in this constitution did not differ essentially
from the 1956 constitution. The new constitution stated that social solidarity is the basis of society,
that planning is the basis for economic organization,
and that private property is inviolable.[2]

The five years following the Revolution witnessed a rapid growth of the public sector. During
that period, the "Egyptianization Laws"[3] which were
promulgated after the Suez Crisis led to the acquisition by the state of substantial interests in several
banks and insurance, commercial, and industrial companies. This necessitated a reconsideration of the
methods of administering and supervising public enterprises. Thus in 1957, the government felt the need to
establish a public body to control the state's interests in these various projects. In other words, the
purpose of the creation of a new organization was to
entrust to a single body the task of laying down the
policy for public investment in the various fields of
economic activity in order to ensure uniformity of
purpose. This inclination materialized in the creation
of the Economic Development Organization (EDO) which
essentially is a holding enterprise owning interests
in a very wide range of economic activities. The capital of the EDO consists of government participation
in various join-stock companies as well as public
establishments which are designated by a Presidential
Decision. In addition, it has the right to issue bonds
in Egypt and abroad and obtain loans from local and
foreign governments and financial institutions. The

Organization is charged with the supervision and control of other public institutions designated by a Presidential Decision without the transfer of their capital. In addition, it can set up new companies as well as own shares and debentures of existing ones. The main tools of control are built in the following regulations of the Organization:[4]

(1) The organization is represented on the board of directors of the various companies in proportion to its participation in their capital. In any case, the Organization should be represented by at least one director whenever its participation is not less than 5 per cent of capital.

(2) If the Organization owns at least 25 per cent of the capital of a company, the president of the board, the managing director or the director general of that institution is to be appointed by a Presidential Decision from three persons nominated by the institution after consulting the Organization.

(3) Decisions taken by the board or the general assembly of companies or the boards of public institutions are to be reported by the representatives of the Organization, within three days, to the president of the Organization who can refer them for reconsideration within one week of its notification.

(4) The accounts of the Organization are to be audited by the State Audit Department at the end of each year.

The adoption of the 1958 constitution by both Syria and Egypt laid down the basic elements for the socialist economy of the U.A.R. In order to complete the transformation to a socialist economy and to increase the government's role, several other holding enterprises were created in the public sector of Egypt. First we find the establishment of Misr Organization and El-Nasr Organization. This was followed by several other public organizations such as the Petroleum Authority, the Public Organization for Internal

Transport and Construction,and the Public Organization
for Desert Reclamation.

In 1961 a Presidential decree prevented the
government, public organizations, and companies in
which the government or public organizations participate to the extent of 25 per cent of the capital,
from assigning general contracts and public work to
companies other than those in which the government
and public organizations participate to at least 50
per cent of the capital, except by a decree from
the President. All public sector's contractual works
exceeding $69,000 were restricted to the firms which
belonged to the public sector. As most of the private
firms in the business of contractual works were dependent in their activities on the public sector's contractual works, they found it necessary to request the
government to accept their amalgamation with the public sector establishments in order to be able to continue their business relations with the public sector.
It was also decreed that labor must be represented on
the board of directors of corporations and a maximum
remuneration stipulated for the members of the board.
Furthermore, employees and workers of joint-stock companies, partnerships with shares,and limited liability
companies are entitled to 25 per cent of the establishment's net distributed profits.

The foreign trade sector was reorganized to
become virtually a government monopoly. Law No. 71/
1961 and its amendments put into the hands of the government the southern region's (Egypt's) cotton export
trade. This government monopoly of cotton trade was
effected through the establishment of the Egyptian
Cotton Commission (ECC). Besides, all cotton exporting houses were required to allow a government participation in their capital, rising to at least 50 per
cent. Furthermore, cotton pressing establishments were
nationalized. Similarly a monopoly was established in
the import trade. The right to import was restricted
to companies which belong to the public sector. Fac-
tories, the majority of which are partially or wholly
owned by the public sector, were authorized to import

directly the commodities and equipment needed for their own use. Since cotton is the major export commodity of the country, and the public sector owns or participates in the capital of all major corporations in Egypt, it can be safely stated that the government has practically complete control over foreign trade.

Actually, the year 1961 could be considered a major turning point in the Egyptian economy. It witnessed the largest nationalization movement ever experienced in Egypt. The nationalization laws radically changed the economy, with the public sector emerging as the main economic power to exercise complete control over the major part of the economy. First, all banks and insurance companies were nationalized, together with maritime companies and 50 other companies mainly engaged in basic and heavy industries. Second, 83 companies were partially nationalized through government's acquirement of at least 50 per cent of each company's capital. This group of companies is mainly engaged in light industries and contractual work. A third group of 145 companies and enterprises was also partially nationalized through government's acquisition of all holdings of any shareholder in excess of $23,000 (market value) worth of shares in all this group of companies.[5] The value of the shares becoming the property of the state was settled by means of nominal bonds drawn on the state for a period of 15 years at 4 per cent annual interest. This group consists mainly of companies in the textile industry and some other light industries which were owned by a limited number of individuals or families.

In order to ensure more efficiency through specialization and closer supervision of each sector as a whole, it was decided to reorganize the public sector by creating specialized agencies, each one to supervise a definite sector of the economy, to replace the previous types of organizations. In December, 1961, 38 specialized public organizations were established to undertake this function.[6] Each one of these organizations was charged with the task of supervising several companies which belong to one type of economic

activity. This helped to assign targets in the plan
to each one of these organizations.

The decade beginning with 1960 could be called
the planning period of the Egyptian economy. In order
to put the socialist framework outlined by the government into operation, a ten-year plan for comprehensive
economic and social development was mapped out, which,
beginning in 1959-60, was to continue through 1969-70.
This ten-year plan consists of two phases, one for
each five-year period, the first of which was put into
effect in 1959-60.

INVESTMENT ALLOCATION

Data on investment, whether by industry or
total, were scanty during the years before 1952. The
analysis in this section will be concerned only with
investment and output for the years covering the development period, 1952-60. During these eight years
several measures were enacted to encourage both domestic and foreign capital. However, other factors were
operating which affected the flow of investment and
foreign capital into the economy. The 1956 crisis, and
the nationalization movement which started by nation-
alizing the Suez Canal Company, not only stopped foreign capital from flowing into the Egyptian economy,
but also resulted in the flight of capital out of the
country. During this period, the government stepped
into the sphere of economic activities and undertook
several investments, either indirectly by participation with a large share in private enterprise, or directly through government organizations which were
established especially for this purpose and also to
manage the nationalized industries.

Table 60 shows the distribution of total investment in millions of dollars by economic and social
sectors during the period 1952-60. The data are given
for fiscal years (July-June) and are comparable to the
data on income which will be used in this section
which are also for fiscal years. From the table it c

Table 60. Investment in the Economic and Social Structure During the Period 1952-53 to 1960-61 (Millions of dollars)

Sector	52-53	53-54	54-55	55-56	56-57	57-58	58-59	59-60	60-61
Agriculture	15.9	12.6	13.8	20.0	28.8	33.3	37.5	38.4	47.6
Irrigation	15.6	21.4	21.4	21.4	16.3	15.4	19.5	19.8	28.1
High dam	—	—	—	1.2	0.9	1.1	2.8	9.7	19.5
Industry	67.9	62.5	77.3	113.2	71.5	81.8	109.9	113.4	154.1
Electricity	13.3	26.0	16.8	21.8	21.4	17.7	15.4	14.3	12.6
Transportation and communication	43.9	44.2	54.3	56.3	35.7	54.0	62.1	69.0	154.6
Suez Canal	—	—	—	—	9.2	11.5	13.8	13.3	13.6
Housing	86.7	105.8	115.0	119.6	115.0	110.4	92.0	71.5	41.9
Public utilities	6.7	6.2	10.6	11.7	14.7	17.7	23.9	17.2	17.7
Education, health, and social services	13.6	15.9	16.3	18.4	20.0	22.3	24.4	22.8	19.1
Other services	9.2	9.9	10.8	12.2	13.8	15.2	15.9	4.8	8.3
Total	272.8	304.5	336.3	395.8	347.3	380.4	417.2	394.2	517.1

Source: Department of Statistics and Census, Ten Years of Revolution: Statistical Atlas (Cairo: S.O.P. Press, 1962), Table 11.

be seen that total investment has been increasing
steadily since the beginning of the development period,
with the exception of the short period following the
nationalization movement and the 1956 crisis. The rate
of increase during the years 1952-60 varied considerably, but showed an upward trend. From 1952-53 to 1953-
54 it was 11.3 per cent and rose to 17.7 per cent just
before the nationalization and invasion caused a decrease during 1956-58. During the last two years of
the period, the rate of increase of total investment
recorded a high one of 31.2 per cent.

This considerable change in the movement of
total investment was not evenly distributed among the
various economic and social sectors. When the change
in the political framework of the country took place
in 1952, there was a great dissatisfaction among the
majority of the population, which falls in the low income groups. With such low levels of income, several
services such as health and education were not accessible or sufficient. Thus the new administration directed tremendous efforts toward public services and
the welfare sector in an attempt to raise the standard
of living of the majority of the population. Out of a
total investment of $272.8 million in 1952-53, $86.7
million went for housing, $6.7 million for public
utilities, and $22.8 million for education, health,
social, and other services. Investment in these noncommodity sectors of the economy amounted to more than
40 per cent of the total investment for that year.
This policy continued during the years following the
revolution until 1956-57 when investment in such services became $163.5 million out of a total investment
of $347.3 million, raising the ratio to about one-half
of total investment. However, beginning with the year
1957-58, the share of these sectors started declining
until by 1960-61 it was only $87 million, thus amount-
ing only to 17 per cent of total investment.

With respect to investment allocation for the
rest of the economy, or the basic sectors, industry
and electricity took first place. Investment in industry and electricity started with $81.2 million in

1952-53, less than one-fourth of total investments for
that year, and increased steadily until by 1960-61 it
almost doubled to $166.7 million, or about one-third
of total investment for that year. Agriculture, which
previously was considered the major occupation and
source of income, took second place with respect to
investment allocation. Investment in the agricultural
sector averaged less than 10 per cent of total investment for the whole period 1952-60.

The Egyptian economy was lacking many of the
social overhead outlays such as roads, means of transportation and communication, and power. Attention
during the development period was directed toward the
building of the infrastructure. The share of transportation, communication, and storage in total investment which was only $43.9 million in 1952-53, increased
to $154.6 million by 1960-61, thus rising from 16 to
30 per cent of total investment. In addition, other
facets of investment, which were also considered as
building the infrastructure, were opened in the middle
of the period, namely, the High Dam project and the
improvement of the Suez Canal. Investment on the
first, which apart from providing the electric power
for industry will add to the cultivable area of the
country, started in 1955-56[7] and has been increasing
steadily. Investment on the improvement of the Suez
Canal, a vital waterway both nationally and interna-
tionally, in addition to being a major source of foreign currency, started with the nationalization of the
company in 1956-57 at $9.2 million and increased to
about $13.6 million in 1960-61.

In general, a change took place with respect
to investment allocation in the Egyptian economy during the development period 1952-60, which focused on
building the infrastructure in both the economic and
social sectors during the first half of the period.
In the latter part, emphasis was placed mainly on the
commodity sectors with industry in the first place.

A final point should be noted here with respect to the movement of investment over time. Though

the volume of investment increased considerably during 1952-60, it does not show the same trend if taken as a percentage of national income. The following figures show total investment as a percentage of national income for the period 1952-60:[8]

Year	Investment/ income ratio (per cent)
1952-53	14.6
1953-54	15.6
1954-55	15.7
1955-56	17.6
1956-57	14.1
1957-58	14.5
1958-59	14.9
1959-60	13.2
1960-61	16.1

It is evident that investment, as a ratio of national income, showed to a great extent a constant rate over the 1952-60 period. For the whole period, the rate of investment as a percentage of national income averaged around 15 per cent.

INVESTMENT AND OUTPUT

Let us now examine the percentage distribution of investment among the various sectors as compared with the percentage distribution of output from each sector. Estimates of total output or gross national product are not available for the Egyptian economy. Therefore, we are going to use instead national income originating in each sector. The results will be biased (upward or downward) depending on the rate of depreciation in each sector.

Table 61 shows national income estimates by economic activity. Table 62 is computed from Tables 60 and 61 to show the percentage share of each of four

Table 61. National Income Estimates by Economic Activity for the Period 1952-53 to 1960-61 (Millions of dollars)

Activity	52-53	53-54	54-55	55-56	56-57
Agriculture	579.6	602.6	692.3	717.6	860.2
Industry and electricity	292.1	322.0	356.5	391.0	441.6
Construction	57.5	62.1	59.8	62.1	73.6
Transportation and communication	124.2	126.5	133.4	142.6	133.4
Housing	135.7	128.8	142.6	149.5	154.1
Commerce and finance	165.6	172.5	190.9	211.6	232.3
Other services	499.1	533.6	540.5	545.1	558.9
Total	1,853.8	1,948.1	2,116.0	2,219.5	2,454.1

Activity	57–58	58–59	59–60	60–61
Agriculture	876.3	837.2	931.5	926.9
Industry and electricity	501.4	552.0	618.7	683.1
Construction	87.4	98.9	108.1	101.2
Transportation and communication	149.5	165.6	211.6	234.6
Housing	156.4	161.0	167.9	170.2
Commerce and finance	250.7	266.8	301.3	338.1
Other services	568.1	579.6	625.6	683.1
Total	2,589.8	2,661.1	2,964.7	3,137.2

Source: Department of Statistics and Census, Ten Years of Revolution: Statistical Atlas (Cairo: S.O.P. Press, 1962), Table 9.

Table 62.   Percentage Distribution of National Income and Investment
by Sector, During the Period 1952–53 to 1960–61

Year	Agriculture	Industry and electricity	Transportation and communication	Rest of the economy	Total
			Income		
1952–53	31.3	18.8	6.7	43.2	100.0
1953–54	30.9	19.7	6.5	42.9	100.0
1954–55	32.7	19.7	6.3	41.3	100.0
1955–56	32.4	20.4	6.4	40.8	100.0
1956–57	35.1	21.0	5.4	38.5	100.0
1957–58	33.8	22.7	5.8	37.7	100.0
1958–59	31.5	24.5	6.2	37.8	100.0
1959–60	31.4	24.5	7.2	36.9	100.0
1960–61	29.5	25.0	7.5	38.0	100.0

Investment

1952–53	11.5	29.8	16.1	42.6	100.0
1953–54	11.2	29.1	14.5	45.2	100.0
1954–55	10.5	28.0	16.1	45.4	100.0
1955–56	10.8	34.1	14.2	40.9	100.0
1956–57	13.2	26.8	12.9	47.1	100.0
1957–58	13.1	26.2	17.2	43.5	100.0
1958–59	14.3	30.1	18.2	37.4	100.0
1959–60	17.2	32.4	20.9	29.5	100.0
1960–61	18.4	32.3	32.5	16.8	100.0

Source: Computed from Tables 60 and 61.

sectors both in total investment and national income
for the period 1952-60. The first sector, agriculture,
includes land reclamation, irrigation, and drainage.
Suez Canal operations and storage are included under
transportation and communication.   The last sector,
rest of the economy, includes housing, commerce and
finance, welfare, and other services.

Two findings are evident from this comparative
table. First, in regard to the size of the relative
shares of each sector in income and investment, there
is an inverse relationship between the size of the
sector's share in investment and its contribution to
national income. Investment allocated to the agricultural sector was the smallest percentage over the
whole period, starting with 11.5 per cent of total investment in 1952-53 and increasing to 18.4 per cent by
1960-61. However, the contribution of this sector to
national income is the largest--disregarding the rest
of the economy sector since it includes many different
economic activities--with its percentage share in national income averaging over 30 per cent for the whole
period. On the other hand, a large share of total investment was directed toward transportation and communication; but the contribution of this sector averaged around only 6 per cent of national income.   Industry and electricity produced over 20 per cent of
national income, and their share in total investment
averaged around 30 per cent.

The second finding is concerned with the trend
of investment and the resulting trend of income. The
steady increase in the share of both agriculture and
transportation and communication in total investment
over time did not result in a similar increase in
their relative contribution to national income. While
the share of the agricultural sector in total investment increased during the period 1952-60 from 11.5 to
18.4 per cent, its share in income did not show a similar increase. In fact, it averaged around 32 per cent
with a downward trend during the last three years of
the period. While the share of the transportation and
communication sector in total investment doubled from

16.1 per cent in 1952-53 to 32.5 per cent in 1960-61, its relative share in national income averaged around 6 per cent for the whole period. Only in the case of industry and electricity was there a degree of association between this sector's share in investment and its contribution to income.

Increments in Income and Investment. The stock of capital in the economy plays an important role in determining the output. Yet, investment in each period can be considered the instrumental factor behind the increase in output. Thus we are going to examine the increments in income which resulted from such yearly investment.

It would have been better to examine the ratio of increments in income to yearly investment. However, due to the wide fluctuations in income which might result from factors other than the change in the volume of investment, it becomes necessary to take an average for the period. Table 63 shows investment and the increase in income during the period 1952-60 by sectors and the ratio of the latter to the former in each sector. The figures in this table confirm the observation already stated about the agricultural sector, i.e., the considerable contribution of this sector to national income, in spite of its relatively small share in total investment. The ratio for this sector is 75 per cent as compared with 43 per cent for industry and 17 per cent for transportation and communication. In other words, the agricultural sector was the most productive sector in the Egyptian economy during the period 1952-60.

THE TEN-YEAR PLAN
(1960-70)

As a result of the scattered and sometimes unsuccessful efforts to develop the economy, and in order to achieve an integration of efforts among all agencies concerned, it was decided to resort to economic and social planning in an attempt to accelerate

Table 63. Average Increments in Income and Investment
by Sector for the Period 1952-60

Sector	Investment	Increments in income	Ratio of increments in income to investment (per cent)
	(Millions of dollars)		
Agriculture	462.6	347.3	75
Industry and electricity	1,011.1	434.7	43
Transportation and communication	635.5	110.4	17
Rest of the economy	1,257.0	391.0	31
Total	3,365.0	1,263.4	38

Source: Computed from data in Tables 60 and 61.

the rate of economic development. Actually, the popu-
larity of economic planning methods in the present
day is due mainly to the   dilemma of economic underdevelopment. Thus, several developing countries decided
to entrust economic planning with the difficult task
of upsetting the elements of stagnation and initiating
a series of new investments. That may result in a new
rising spiral of prosperity in Egypt and launch the
economy on its development path.

       The constitution of Egypt stipulates that the
national economy is to be organized according to plans
conforming to the   principles of social justice, and
aiming at a rapid improvement in the standard of living. As a result, it was decided to draw up a ten-year
plan to be executed in two five-year phases. Although
the first phase started in 1959-60, the actual work in
preparation for the plan started in 1957. In January
of that year, a decree established two agencies to undertake preparation of the plan. The first is the Supreme Council for National Planning under the leadership of the President of the Republic. This council
determines the economic and social targets of the plan
and approves the development plans in their various
stages. The second is the National Planning Commission
which is headed by the Minister of Planning Affairs.
The six departments of this commission are concerned
with economics, agriculture and irrigation, industry
and electricity, transportation and   communication,
and commerce and services.   The Commission is charged
with responsibility of preparation of the plan. After
the execution of the plan, the Commission must follow
up by submitting periodic reports to the Supreme Council. The main function of the Commission is the collection and preparation of all the technical and statistical data needed for the plan. This includes a
survey of the natural and human resources of the country. In addition, it undertakes a study of the allocation of investments to the various sectors as well as
the possible means of financing economic development.[9]

       Table 64 shows the targets for the plan at the
end of the two phases, 1964-65 and 1969-70, by major

Table 64. National Income by Sector in 1959-60 and Income Targets
by Sector at the End of the Two Stages of the Ten-Year Plan,
1964-65 and 1969-70   (Millions of dollars)

Sector	1959-60	1964-65	1969-70
Agriculture	920	1,178	1,442
Industry and electricity	628	1,242	1,845
Building and construction	120	117	172
Supporting economic structure	600	727	1,000
Commerce	292	373	610
Services	389	492	828
Total	2,949	4,129	5,897

Source: Compiled from National Planning Committee for Southern Region, The Frame of
the General Five-Year Plan for Economic and Social Development (July 1960–
June 1965) (Cairo: General Organization for Government Printing Offices,
1960), p. 11.

sectors. During the first five years an increase in income of about 58 per cent is expected, and by the end of the second phase the increase will amount to approximately 100 per cent of the 1959-60 level, the starting year of the plan. In other words, national income is expected to double during a period of ten years. From this table, the change from 1959-60 in the structure of output is noticeable. Instead of the agricultural sector providing about one-third of national income, industry and electricity by the end of the plan's two phases will occupy first place and agriculture, second place.

Planned Investment. Investment needed for the execution of this plan was estimated at $7,576 million. Table 65 shows the planned distribution of this total investment in the two phases by major sector and the sources of financing. Concentration of investment will be on industry and electricity, followed by investment in supporting the economic structure, i.e., the building of the infrastructure. Investment in agriculture ranks third, but still absorbs about one-fourth of total investment. It is expected that total investment will be financed by $2,748 million from external sources, while the rest which amounts to $4,827 million will be supplied from domestic sources. The share of external sources in financing investment is a little over one-third. Of special importance is the emphasis placed on industry and electricity. The share of these two sectors in total investment is over one-third during the ten-year plan. These two sectors are the ones which are badly in need of external capital. And indeed, it is planned that they will absorb more than one-third of the capital needed during the ten-year plan.

The targets assigned to the various economic sectors show the emphasis placed on heavy industries in particular. An index number of targets for production shown in Table 66 reveals that the production of heavy industries will triple by 1964-65 and more than quadruple by 1969-70. Considering the large amount of investment directed to this sector, we can see that

Table 65. Distribution of Investment by Sector and Source of Financing During the Two Stages of the Ten-Year Plan, 1960-65 and 1965-70   (Millions of dollars)

Sector	1960-65			1965-70		
	Foreign	Local	Total	Foreign	Local	Total
Agriculture	181.5	720.1	901.6	193.2	754.4	947.6
Industry and electricity	862.5	468.5	1,331.0	690.0	586.5	1,276.5
Supporting economic structure	366.4	772.6	1,139.0	287.5	1,069.5	1,357.0
Services	75.4	179.9	255.3	92.0	276.0	368.0
Total	1,485.8	2,141.1	3,626.9	1,262.7	2,686.4	3,949.1

Source: Compiled from National Planning Committee for Southern Region, The Frame of the General Five-Year Plan for Economic and Social Development (July 1960–June 1965) (Cairo: General Organization for Government Printing Offices, 1960), pp. 15-24.

Table 66. An Index of Production Targets
by Industry at the End of the Two Stages
of the Ten-Year Plan, 1959-60 to 1969-70

Industry	1959-60	1964-65	1969-70
Heavy industry	100	310	445
Light industry	100	137	185
Services	100	128	213
Commerce	100	128	196
Supporting economic structure	100	122	160
Agriculture	100	128	159

Source: National Bank of Egypt, Economic Bulletin,
Vol. XIV, No. 1 (Cairo, 1961), p. 9.

concentration during this period of planning is on
producer's goods and heavy industries in particular.
The production of the light industries, services, and
commerce will about double by the end of the plan. The
sector supporting the economic structure which includes transportation, housing, public utilities, securities, and defense is planned to increase only by
60 per cent as in the case of agriculture. This change
in the production composition comes after the concentration on building the infrastructure which took
place during the development period (1952-60). However, the planned increase in the production of agriculture seems to be somewhat low considering the expected growth in population. Because of the expected
increase in demand on agricultural products, food in
particular, and since we have seen that the return per
dollar invested in agriculture is comparatively high,
more efforts should have been directed toward the agricultural sector during the ten-year plan.

PLANNING FOR AGRICULTURAL DEVELOPMENT

Total planned investment in the agricultural sector during the first phase (1960-65) of the ten-year plan amounts to $901.6 million and will increase to $947.6 million for the second phase. This can be seen from the following figures which show in millions of dollars the distribution of investment in agriculture during the two phases of the plan.[10]

	1960-65	1965-70
Increase in productivity	119.4	188.6
Land expansion	398.8	598.0
Irrigation, drainage, and the High Dam	383.4	161.0
Total	901.6	947.6

Investment in agriculture during both phases of the plan which amounts to about one-fourth of total national investment is directed mainly toward horizontal expansion or the reclamation of more agricultural land. According to the plan, the High Dam will absorb over one-third of total planned investment in the first phase. It should be noted that foreign exchange requirements for agricultural development are relatively low. Foreign exchange needed for agricultural development amounts to only $181.5 million for the first phase, and $193.2 million for the second phase of the plan. This amounts to 20 per cent of its total investment as compared to 47.9 per cent which is the share of foreign capital in total investment for the rest of the economy during the first phase.[11]

The ten-year plan with respect to agriculture has two principal programs, the short- and the long-term program. The short-term program for agricultural expansion envisages the reclamation of about 540,798 acres by 1964-65 divided as follows:[12] 483,708 acres to be irrigated by summer irrigation, 25,950 acres to be irrigated by sprinklers getting their water from subterranean (artesian) wells, and 31,140 acres to be irrigated by waters made available by the High Dam.

The long-term plan is aimed at the reclamation of an additional large area of fallow land through the utilization of water provided by the High Dam. It is estimated that it will add about one million acres of arable land to the existing cultivated area and allow the conversion of an additional 726,000 acres from the basin to the perennial irrigation system.[13] The work on this major project was inaugurated in January 1960, with the aim of controlling the water run-off of the River Nile to the sea. The water saved will be used in the expansion of cultivated area and to provide for the production of low-cost power. An additional benefit will be the protection against severe floods, which is not only a humanitarian gain but will mean a reduction in economic loss. It will also improve navigation and drainage conditions and facilitate the development of fish culture and recreational facilities. The hydroelectric power plant is designed for an eventual installation of twelve main generating units. It is estimated that at the ultimate stage the total energy generated will be 10,000 million KW/H. This will help boost industrial development as well as improve the conditions of the villages. In January, 1964, a Ministry of the High Dam was established.

According to the ten-year plan, the value of agricultural output will increase from $1,320 million in 1959-60 to $1,693 million by the end of the first phase (1964-65) and to $2,093 million by the end of the second phase (1969-70). This will increase value added by agriculture from $920 million in 1959-60 to $1,178 million by 1964-65 and to $1,442 million by 1969-70.[14] Manpower needed by the end of the plan will rise from 3,245,000 persons to 3,800,000 persons thus increasing employment by over half a million workers. Total agricultural wages will increase from $310 million at the beginning of the plan to $393 million at the end in 1970.[15] It is expected that development in agriculture will proceed as planned especially because it does not require much foreign capital. Actually the first stage of the High Dam has already been completed.

EMPLOYMENT STRUCTURE DURING THE PLAN

In 1959-60 employment amounted to around 6 million persons. With a population of 26 million, the ratio of employment to total population becomes 23 per cent. By 1969-70, the end of the plan, employment is expected to amount to 8,936,000 workers. Since population is forecast to be 31.6 million in 1970, the ratio of employment to total population will become 28 per cent, an increase of about one-fifth.

With the concentration on industry and some other sectors of the economy during the ten years, one would expect the distribution of employed persons among the various sectors to undergo some change. Table 67 shows, by sector, the percentage distribution of employed persons during the ten-year plan. The agricultural sector, which absorbed 53.3 per cent of employed persons in 1959-60, will, by the end of the plan (1969-70), still absorb about one-half of the employed persons. In other words, agriculture will still be the major occupation but, on the other hand, will provide only one-fourth of national income. The share of industry in employed persons will increase from 10 to 11.7 per cent during the ten years of the plan. The only sector which will experience a considerable increase is services, whose share will increase from 13.3 to 16.1 per cent.

With regard to the share of labor in national income, we find that in 1959-60 income of labor amounted to $1,311 million. With a national income of $2,949 million, the share of labor amounts to 44 per cent. It is expected that by the end of the first phase of the ten-year plan (1964-65) the share of labor will drop to 42 per cent. By the end of the ten-year plan (1969-70), it will go up to 44 per cent, almost its level at the beginning of the plan. That is, the

Table 67. Percentage Distribution of Employed
Persons in 1959-60 and the Target
Distribution at the End of the Two
Stages of the Ten-Year Plan,
1964-65 and 1969-70

Sectors	1959-60	1964-65	1969-70
Agriculture	54.3	54.3	49.9
Industry	10.6	12.1	11.7
Construction	2.8	2.3	2.5
Supporting economic structure	8.4	7.9	7.9
Commerce	10.6	10.4	11.9
Services	13.3	13.0	16.1
Total	100.0	100.0	100.0

Source: National Planning Committee, Southern Region,
The Frame of the General Five-Year Plan for
Economic and Social Development (July 1960–
June 1965) (Cairo: General Organization for
Government Printing Offices, 1960), p. 13.

share of labor income in total national income will
not increase as a result of this development plan.
However, with the increase of employed persons from
5,975,000 to 8,936,000, the average earning per employed person will increase from $219 to $290 during
the ten years of the plan.[16]

Notes to Chapter 10

[1]National Bank of Egypt, Economic Bulletin,
Vol. VI, No. 1 (Cairo: 1953), p. 44.

[2]U.A.R., Constitution (1958) Art. 3, 4, 5, and 6, Sec. 2.

[3]The Egyptianization Laws for the banks provide that the banking business may be carried only by Egyptian Joint-Stock Companies. The paid-up capital should not be less than $1.15 million owned by Egyptians. The board of directors as well as managers should be Egyptians. The same regulations apply to all insurance undertakings and all Egyptian joint-stock companies. Travel agencies, air companies, and foreign representatives of enterprises undertaking public works or industrial activities in Egypt are exempted from the provisions of this law.

[4]National Bank of Egypt, Economic Bulletin, Vol. X, No. 1 (Cairo: 1957), pp. 37-38.

[5]National Bank of Egypt, Economic Bulletin, Vol. XIV, No. 3 (Cairo: 1961), pp. 276-77.

[6]National Bank of Egypt, Economic Bulletin, Vol. XIV, No. 4 (Cairo: 1961), pp. 387-88.

[7]The actual work on the High Dam project started in 1960 after extensive preparation. This project, which is expected to increase the yearly national income by $644 million, will be completed by 1968. Projects for generating electric power are expected to be completed by 1972.

[8]Computed from data in Tables 60 and 61.

[9]National Bank of Egypt, Economic Bulletin, Vol. X, No. 1 (Cairo: 1957), p. 40.

[10]National Planning Committee, Southern Region, The Frame of the General Five-Year Plan for Economic and Social Development (July 1960-June 1965), (Cairo: General Organization for Government Printing Offices, 1960), pp. 26-28.

[11]Ibid., p. 24.

[12]Information Department,   The Yearbook 1963 (Cairo: National Publication House, 1964), p. 145.

[13]Information Department,   Land Reclamation (Cairo: Al Shaab Printing House, 1963), p. 4.

[14]The Framework of the Five-Year Plan, op. cit., p. 11.

[15]Ibid., pp. 13-14.

[16]National Planning Committee, Southern Region, The Frame of the General Five-Year Plan for Economic and Social Development (July 1960-June 1965), (Cairo: General Organization for Government Printing Offices, 1960), pp. 13-14.

CHAPTER **11** THE ROLE OF
EXTERNAL CAPITAL

Before 1952, the inflow of long-term capital, grants, and other loans into the Egyptian economy was insignificant. For example, during the five years (1946-51) preceding the development period, United States "nonmilitary" grants, long-term capital, and other assistance to Egypt amounted only to $10 million. However, during the development period (1952-60) attempts were made to attract foreign capital to the Egyptian economy through loans, grants, or technical assistance from both eastern and western countries and international agencies, such as the International Bank for Reconstruction and Development.

EXTERNAL FINANCING OF DEVELOPMENT

In trying to assemble data on the loans and grants to Egypt during the period 1952-60, we were faced with two major difficulties. In the first place, a great deal of discrepancy exists among the various sources with respect to the amounts granted to Egypt. The second difficulty is that, since the unity between Egypt and Syria in 1958, some statistics do not distinguish between the two regions. Some of these statistics--even those collected for periods before 1958 --have not previously appeared separately.

Information on the amount of loans and grants was derived from various sources: some from the borrowing country, Egypt; others from the lending

countries. The first source of figures for all coun-
tries excluding the United States and Soviet Russia is
the Economic Bulletin of the National Bank of Egypt.
Other sources are the United States Department of
State publications, the Department of Commerce, and the
Agency for International Development. Some information
was available from the economic section of the Egyptian
Embassy in the United States.

United States economic assistance took the
form of grants, credits, and other assistance. Grants,
as defined by the United States Office of Business
Economics, are transfers for which no payment is expected, or which, at most, involve an obligation on
the part of the receiver to extend aid to the United
States or other countries to achieve a common objective. Credits are loan disbursements or transfers
under other agreements which give rise to specific
obligation to repay, over a period of years, usually
with interest. Other assistance represents the transfer of United States farm products in exchange for
foreign currencies, less the government's disbursements of the currencies as grants, credits, or for purchases.[1] The latter includes economic assistance under
Public Law 480 (Food for Peace). According to this law
there are three titles. Title I provides for the sale
of surplus agriculture commodities for local currencies of the country involved and specifies the ways in
which these currencies may be used. Title II authorizes the funds for the transfer of commodities to help
friendly people to meet famine or other urgent or ex-
traordinary relief requirements. Title III authorizes
the donation of surplus commodities to voluntary relief agencies such as CARE for free distribution to
needy people. Egypt, which was the third largest sig-
natory of Title I agreements, was to receive wheat and
flour amounting in value to $532 million by 1953.[2] The
value of grains imported by Egypt under Public Law 480
amounted to $48.3 million in 1959 and to $72.7 million
in 1960.[3] It should be noted also that up to 1960 Title II was not used by Egypt and an amount of $60 mil-
lion was used under Title III.[4] Economic assistance
under Public Law 480 is included in the United States

loans and grants to Egypt. Most Soviet and European
satellites assistance to Egypt was in the form of interest-bearing credits rather than grants.[5]

The data collected on foreign loans and grants
are summarized in Table 68 which shows the amounts of
foreign loans and grants advanced to Egypt, 1952–60,
in millions of dollars. Soviet Russia and its European
Satellites seem to be the major contributors with
their percentage share in total loans and grants
amounting to 56 per cent. Actually, Soviet Russia is
the major contributor of loans and grants; its share
amounts to more than one-half of the total. More than
67 per cent of Russia's assistance was planned for the
first and second stages of the High Dam project.[6] At
this point it should be noted that the Economic Bulletin of the National Bank of Egypt estimated the
foreign facilities and loans granted to Egypt up to
March 1961 at $427.8 million.[7] However, a study on
the Communist Economic Policy in the less developed
areas, by the United States Department of State, revealed that by the end of 1959 $653 million in Soviet
Bloc credit had been advanced to Egypt. To this, in
January 1960 was added another $187 million.[8] In order
to resolve this discrepancy, total loans advanced by
the Soviet Satellites are subtracted from the total
estimated by the Department of State, the remainder,
$767.6 million is taken to show Russia's contribution
in total loans to Egypt. The rest of the Soviet Bloc
contributed less than 5 per cent of the total.

Western Bloc countries come next, providing
about 40 per cent of the total loans and grants. The
first creditor of this region is the United States with
its share amounting to about 19 per cent of total loans
and grants which is about one-third the share of Russia.
Most United States loans and grants were extended
mainly by the Export-Import Bank of America and the
various United States Government programs. West Germany is the second major contributor in this region with
its share of 8.16 per cent. The International Bank for
Reconstruction and Development extended $56.5 million

Table 68.   Foreign Loans
and Grants (1952-60)[a]

Country or agency	Amount (millions of dollars)	Per cent of total
Western Bloc		
United States	281.0	18.79
West Germany	122.1	8.16
Italy	78.9	5.27
Japan	39.1	2.61
France	23.0	1.54
United Kingdom	12.4	0.83
Holland	11.5	0.77
Switzerland	9.2	0.61
Sweden	7.6	0.51
Others	14.5	0.97
Total	599.3	40.06
Eastern Bloc		
Soviet Russia	767.2	51.29
East Germany	21.9	1.46
Czechoslovakia	21.2	1.42

(continued)

Table 68 (continued)

Country or agency	Amount (millions of dollars)	Per cent of total
Hungary	13.6	0.91
Yugoslavia	16.1	1.08
Total	840.0	56.16
International Bank (IBRD)	56.5	3.78
Grand total	1,495.8	100.00

[a]For a discussion of the methods of estimation and the sources, see text, pp. 311-12.

Sources: National Bank of Egypt, Economic Bulletin, Vol. XIV, No. 2, 1961; United States Department of Commerce, Balance of Payments Statistical Supplement (Washington, D. C., 1963); United States Department of Commerce, Foreign Grants and Credits by the United States Government, No. 69 (Washington, December 1961); Bureau of Public Affairs, Communist Economic Policy in the Less Developed Areas, Department of State Publication No. 7020 (Washington, July 1960), pp. 25-26; United States Department of State, Mimeographed document on P.L. 480, U.A.R. Desk, Agency for International Development, (Washington, D. C., 1962.)

(3.78 per cent of total loans obtained) for financing
the improvement projects of the Suez Canal.

Adjusting total investment from fiscal years
to calendar years, total investment is found to amount
to $4,244.6 million during 1952-60. External loans and
grants amounted to $1,495.8 million, a ratio of about
46 per cent to total investment.   But, before we can
say that this is the share of external financing in
development during that period, domestic saving must
be considered.

SAVINGS AND INVESTMENTS
1952-60

Data on savings in underdeveloped countries
are usually inadequate and unreliable, Egypt is no exception.   This is due to the fact that in most cases
private savings are treated as a residual--a matter
that widens the margin of error.

In an attempt to estimate savings in Egypt for
the development period (1952-60), we had to rely on
limited data for the period 1950-56 which we also used
on basis for extrapolation.   In the 1957 supplement to
World Economic Survey,[9] the United Nations Department
of Economic and Social Affairs reported the Egyptian
National Planning Commission's estimates of total savings for the period 1950-56. According to this report
total domestic savings--private and public--have been
calculated as total investment adjusted by the foreign
balance. Public savings have been calculated as public
investment adjusted by the government deficit or surplus, while private savings have been treated as a res-
idual, i.e., the difference between domestic and public
savings. The following are the figures on public, private, and total domestic savings in millions of U.S.
dollars.[10]

Year	Private	Public	Total
1950	278.3	32.2	310.5
1951	156.4	-39.1	117.3
1952	211.6	-41.4	170.2
1953	142.6	82.8	225.4
1954	151.8	115.0	266.8
1955	248.4	27.6	276.0
1956	282.9	-71.3	211.6

In order to estimate total domestic savings for the period 1957-60, we used the above figures on total savings and the national income figures from Chapter 6 (Table 32 above). From these two sets of figures the ratio of savings to income was calculated and it amounted to 10.9 per cent. This was rounded off and the average savings ratio is taken to be 10 per cent. An estimate of savings for this period 1957-60 was then obtained by applying the savings ratio to national income figures (Table 32) for the same period. This helped us to extend the National Planning Commission's estimates of saving through the year 1960 as can be seen from the following figures.

	Total Domestic Savings
Year	(million U. S. dollars)
1952	170.2
1953	225.4
1954	266.8
1955	276.0
1956	211.6
1957	252.3
1958	262.7
1959	281.3
1960	305.2

Total domestic savings for the period 1952-60 amounted to $2,251.5 million. Total investment (adjusted to calendar years) for the period 1952-60 amounted to $3,244.6 million, giving an average of $360.5 million for each of the nine years of the period. However, there were some fluctuations in the rate of

investment over the period showing a tendency to increase over time. On the other hand, domestic savings,
which was low during the first part of the period,
started increasing, with the exception of 1956, probably due to the unrest caused by the Suez Crisis in
1956. From $170 million in 1952, savings almost doub-
led by 1960 reaching $305 million. An amount of
$1,495.8 million in loans and grants was advanced to
Egypt during this period, giving an average of $166.2
million per year.

[margin note: inaccurate statement]

Total loans and grants for the period, which
represent the external financing of investment, added
to total domestic savings which amounts to $2,252.5,
gives a figure of $3,748.3 million. This exceeds by
$503.7 million the amount invested in the economy for
the whole period. In other words, about 13 per cent of
the total capital available for investment was not invested. There are two possible explanations for this.
First, part of domestic savings does not find its way
to the capital market to be invested; instead, it is
hoarded either in the form of currency or precious
metal. In underdeveloped countries, however, it is
important to maintain a distinction between savings
and savings available for investment. The two are separated by a gap caused by hoarding. Hoarding of precious metals and stones is one of the main forms of
holding assets in underdeveloped economies. The acquisition of jewelry and of gold and silver coins represents a high degree of safety, besides giving a certain class distinction. The hoarding attitude is encouraged by the absence of sound financial institutions; people keep their savings at home in the safest
form. Thus a considerable part of savings in underdeveloped countries is lost insofar as investment is
concerned.[11] This is not unusual, especially in the
rural areas of Egypt. The political unsettlement and
the nationalization movement also contributed to that.
In other words, the rate of savings invested is somewhat exaggerated. Harbison and Ibrahim reported that
out of a total savings per year that was in excess of
10 per cent of national income, only one-half of this
savings would normally flow into channels which would

[margin note: What about $2,251.5]

contribute significantly to the country's economic development.[12]   Second, most of the industrial projects
which required external financing were completed in
stages, such as the High Dam project. Thus there is a
possibility that, although $1,495.8 million in loans
and grants was advanced to Egypt up to 1960, only a
portion of it was used during that time. For example,
the Economic Bulletin of the National Bank of Egypt,
which estimated the total amount of foreign facilities
and loans at $1,020.7 million, states that until March
1961 only $401.6 million were used. Thus, over 60
per cent of the total loans and grants advanced were
not used during the period.   On the other hand,   the
difference could be an   exaggeration in the estimation
of domestic savings.

Whatever the case may be, both hoarding and
not using foreign capital available for investment are
harmful to the process of development, since those
hoarding do not participate in actual investment or in
increasing consumption expenditure which is a stimulant
on the demand side.   That part of income which is not
saved should be spent on consumption, thereby producing
an increased demand, which, in turn, is needed to push
the wheel of economic activity. A second liability is
that unused available foreign funds become an additional burden on economy if they are interest-bearing.
A delay in using these loans does not stop the interest charges assumed after the loans are contracted.
In other words, interest will accumulate on nonpro-
ductive funds.[13]

To summarize, the above estimates show that
with respect to the saving-investment relationship during the period 1952-60, $503.7 million available for
investment was either hoarded (from domestic savings)
or not used (from external capital).   To be on the
safe side, we can assume that half of it was hoarded
and the other half was not used.   The amount of foreign capital used in investment becomes now $1,244 mil-
lion, while the contribution of domestic savings is
$2,000 million.   This brings the share of foreign

financing in total investment during the development period to roughly a little over one-third.

It is true that the percentage share of foreign capital in financing investment amounts to 40 per cent according to the last adjustments, giving a ratio of foreign to domestic capital of 2:3. However, we noted that there exists some discrepancy in the data on foreign and domestic capital. On the other hand, at that early stage of development, part of the foreign capital available for financing investments was not used because of the lack of preparation. Therefore, in order to avoid exaggeration in the share of foreign funds in the capital mix, we are going to assume that the ratio of foreign to domestic capital was 1:2.

This combination of domestic and foreign capital resulted in the growth of national income from $1,853.8 million in 1952 to $3,052.1 million in 1960. With an increase in population from 21.6 million in 1952 to 26.1 million in 1960, per capita income increased only from $86 to $117. The growth in per capita income during the nine years of the development period was 36 per cent, an average of 4 per cent per year. It should be noted here that in Chapter 6, the average annual compounded rate of growth of national income at constant prices was 4.89 per cent and that of per capita income at constant prices was 2.37 per cent.

THE ROLE OF EXTERNAL CAPITAL
(1952-60)

The results with respect to the capital mix can be summarized as follows:

(1) Investment expenditure during the nine years of the 1952-60 period amounted to $3,244.6 million.

(2) The ratio of foreign loans and grants to domestic sources of financing in the capital mix was 1:2.

(3) Investment resulted in an annual rate of
national income growth during that period of 7 per cent,
or about 4 per cent for per capita income.

Suppose now that development during the 1952-
60 period depended on domestic savings for its financing
with no foreign funds available . What would have been
the course of national income growth during the period
and what level would it have attained are the questions
raised.   In order to consider these questions, three
assumptions are necessary.

First, the ratio of savings to income is 10 per
cent. Although this might be considered a rather high
ratio since it is based on what took place during the
development period when foreign capital participated
in development, this assumption is necessary at the
outset and will be relaxed later.

Second, foreign capital in terms of loans and
grants is not allowed a role during this period; however, we will assume that the economy could provide
the capital mix (foreign and domestic) by exporting
goods and services.

Third, the ratio of the increments in income
to investment during the development period (1952-60)
resulting from the participation of both foreign loans
and domestic savings in investment will be the same
even though only the latter took place.   This ratio
for the economy as calculated in Chapter 10 was 38 per
cent.[14]

The increase in income each year will be equal
to the investment during the year (which is equal to
savings) multiplied by the income/capital ratio prevailing during the 1952-60 period which was 38 per
cent. In other words, let

Y_i = income at time period i,
ΔY_i = the increase in income during time period i,
I_i = investment at time period i, and

$\frac{Y}{C}$ = income/capital ratio (a constant).

Thus, the increments in income each year are given by:

$$\Delta Y = (I_i) \; (\frac{Y}{C})$$

Income in each year is given by:

$$Y_i = Y_{i-1} + (I_i) \; (\frac{Y}{C})$$

If we calculate the income accordingly, the results found in Table 69 show the hypothetical yearly income based on our assumption and in the absence of foreign loans.

From this table it can be seen that by the years 1960-61 income is only $2.5 billion as compared with $3.1 billion which actually resulted when foreign loans participated in investment. With a population of 26.5 million, the corresponding per capita national income is $94 and $118, a reduction of about 20 per cent. Under the above assumption, the yearly rate of national income growth during the period 1952-60 drops from 7.7 to 3.9 per cent. In other words, the absence of foreign investment, one-third of total investment, resulted in reducing the rate of growth of income by 50 per cent.

The other alternative which could have occurred, assuming that development took place with no foreign investment, is that the $3.1 billion level of national income obtained actually in the year 1960-61 will be realized over a longer period. A look at the table reveals that this level of national income could be attained approximately by the year 1966-67. In order to build the necessary capital from domestic saving to attain a $3.1 billion level of income the period was prolonged from nine to fifteen years, an increase of two-thirds from the original period. This extension results in reducing the average yearly rate of growth of national income to 4.6 per cent. Moreover,

Table 69.   A Comparison of Actual Income
and an Estimate of Hypothetical Income in the Absence of Foreign Loans[a]
(in billions
of dollars)

Year	Hypothetical income	Actual income
1952–53	1.9	1.9
1953–54	1.9	1.9
1954–55	2.0	2.1
1955–56	2.1	2.2
1956–57	2.2	2.5
1957–58	2.2	2.6
1958–59	2.3	2.7
1959–60	2.4	3.0
1960–61	2.5	3.1
1966–67	3.1	

[a]Calculated on the basis that the increase in income
each year is equal to investment during the year multiplied by the income investment ratio prevailing during 1952-60 which was 38. The equation used is:
$Y_i = Y_{i-1} + I_i \left(\frac{Y}{C}\right)$. See the text, pp. 320-21.

with a population of 41.2 million by 1966-67, per capita income will be reduced to $100 compared with $118
which it attained in 1960-61.

The result from either alternative is to reduce the average yearly rate of national income growth,
and the effect of population growth leads to a further
decrease in per capita income, so that rate of national
income growth is expected to be even smaller. A further reduction in the rate of growth is expected if we

do not maintain two of the assumptions specified at
the outset.

The first assumption regarding the ratio of
saving to income, which was assumed to be 10 per cent,
should be discussed now.   This ratio of saving to income was based on the results of the development period in which income was considerably higher and consequently so were savings. Since there are no data
available on saving for another period, it was necessary to resort to this ratio.   Thus, if the ratio was
smaller than 10 per cent, and it could have been, we expect less income in each period.   This may finally
lead to a lower rate of growth.   The other assumption
regarding the ratio of the increments in income to investment was also based on the results of the development period, since data for previous periods were un-
available. This ratio was somewhat higher when development was taking place and is expected to be smaller
if development depends only on domestic sources for financing. Since the increase in income depends in each
period on these two coefficients, the ratio of saving
to income and the ratio of the increments in income to
investment, we can conclude that if these two coefficients were smaller than what was assumed, the reduction in income and its rates of growth would have been
larger or the longer would have been the period to at-
tain the same level of income.   The third assumption
which allowed the economy to provide the foreign currency needed for development through the balance of
payment might not have been possible. With imports exceeding exports during the years 1951, 1952, and 1956,
and the urgent need to provide wheat for consumption,
the Egyptian economy could not have obtained the necessary equipment needed for development or to maintain
the capital mix. The latter puts a limitation on the
development capacity of the economy.

EXTERNAL CAPITAL REQUIREMENTS FOR DEVELOPMENT

Most of the work on the role of external capital in development usually starts with an estimation

of the amounts of foreign capital needed to accomplish a certain development target.   In many cases, this is based on arbitrary assumptions regarding the desired rate of growth of national income, and taking into consideration the savings capability of the economy. Thus, an examination of external capital requirements for development planning in the Egyptian economy is in order.

A United Nations report has estimated the capital required by underdeveloped areas in industry and agriculture to raise their national income per capita by 2 per cent annually.[15]Their estimate is based on the following arbitrary assumptions:

(1) New employment outside of agriculture is provided by an annual transfer out of agriculture of 1 per cent of the total working population into nonagricultural employment;

(2) The amount of capital required for each person absorbed in nonagricultural employment is $2,500; and

(3) As to development of agriculture, it is assumed that these countries should spend 4 per cent of their national income on agricultural extension services, research, and investment in agricultural capital.

Using these arbitrary assumptions, we estimated the external capital needed annually in industry and agriculture to raise national income per capita in Egypt by 2 per cent at $196 million.[16] Thus for a period of ten years, a total of about $2 billion dollars in foreign capital is needed for that target of development.

Another attempt, by P. N. Rosenstein-Rodan in his paper on international aid for underdeveloped countries resulted in a similar estimate.[17] His estimates are based on what he called the absorptive capacity or the ability to use capital productively in the various projects comprising a development program.[18] With a

capital output ratio (k) of 3:1 and provided that gross
national product (Y_O) and its rate of growth (r)--as-
sumed according to its estimated absorptive capacity--
in addition to the average (S_O/Y_O) and marginal rates
of saving (b) are given, Rosenstein-Rodan estimated
foreign capital inflow requirements (F) for 112 underdeveloped countries and territories in six different
areas of the world during three five-year periods: 1961-
66, 1966-71, and 1971-76. Using the above notations,
he constructed the following formula to calculate foreign capital inflow requirements to achieve a set
growth rate during each five-year period:[19]

$$F = (kr - b) \ \Sigma Y + 5Y_o \ (b - S_o/Y_o).$$

With respect to Egypt, foreign capital inflow required
for development during these three periods is $866.4
million, $1,092.9 million, and $673.2 million, respectively. In other words, for the ten years (1961-71)
which almost coincide with the Egyptian planning period (1960-70), foreign capital required in terms of aid
and private investments amounts to $1,959.3 million or
about two billion dollars, a figure which is equal to
our estimate using the United Nations approach. In the
following pages, we are going to see that external capital required, as estimated in the ten-year plan amounts
to $2,748.5 million. Since Rosenstein-Rodan estimated
the margin of error for his figures to be ($\pm$) 25 per
cent, we can conclude that there is little disagree-
ment as to the large magnitudes of external capital
needed to enable the underdeveloped countries to get
over the hump during the early stages of development.

Since the amounts needed of foreign capital
for the development plan during the ten years do not
differ considerably using different approaches, we are
going to raise here another question. Taking into
consideration the results of the development period
(1952-60), the question to be raised is: Could the
Egyptian economy achieve these set targets with the
capital mix designed in the plan? First, the capital
required for development, whether domestic or foreign,
should be considered.

The share of domestic financing during the planning period estimated at $4,827.5 million is the expected saving for this period. The question is, then, could that amount be saved with the new expected increased levels of income; and if so, would it all be invested, or would a good portion of it be hoarded as apparently happened during 1952-60.

No estimates for national income were given in the plan's framework for the years between 1959-60 and 1969-70, except for the year 1964-65. Assuming a constant income increase during each five years, the first five years show a total income of $21 billion and for the second period a total income of $26 billion. The amount of domestic financing expected for the first period was $2.1 billion, and $2.7 billion is expected for the second phase. Since the domestic financing of investment should be equal to savings at the end of the period, this gives an average rate of savings of about 10 per cent. This again confirms our earlier estimate of domestic savings.

GROWTH DURING THE PLANNING PERIOD

Now, we are in a position to examine the ten-year plan in the light of the results obtained earlier in this chapter and under the same assumptions regarding the capital mix. The objective is to find out what will happen to the path of national income growth if foreign loans are not available during that ten-year period.

Investment planned during the period 1960-70 amounts to $7,576 million, about one-third of which is expected to be financed by foreign loans and grants, and the other two-thirds from domestic savings. Investment during the ten years is expected to raise national income from $2,949 million (1959-60) to $5,897 million (1969-70). The following figures show the distribution of total investment by major economic sector during this period.[20]

Sector	Amount of Investment
Agriculture	1.8
Industry and electricity	2.6
Transportation and communication	1.2
Rest of the economy	1.9
Total	7.5

In Chapter 10, Table 64 shows the ratio of the increments in income to investment during the period 1952-60 by major economic sectors. Assuming that these ratios apply to the period 1960-70, and that the productivity per unit of investment in the different sectors will remain the same, what will be the increase in national income which results from planned investment during the ten years of the plan? The increase in income for each of the four sectors is obtained by multiplying planned investment for each sector by the ratio of the income increments to investment for the period 1952-60. With regard to total increase in income, it is obtained as the sum of the increments in income in the four sectors. This is preferred to obtaining the total by using an over-all income investment ratio of 38 per cent since disaggregation allows some differences in the level of productivity of the various sectors. The following figures give a summary of the results:

Sector	Income/ investment ratio (per cent)	Increase in income in billions of dollars
Agriculture	75	1.4
Industry and electricity	43	1.1
Transportation and communication	17	0.2
Rest of the economy	31	0.6

From this, it can be seen that though investment in industry and electricity amounts to more than
one-third of total investment for the period, the
largest increase in income comes from the agricultural
sector. Adding the increase in income to the income
of the initial year 1959-60 which was $2.9 billion, the
income in the year 1969-70 becomes $6.2 billion which
exceeds the expected figures of the plan by $0.3 bil-
lion. This difference, which amounts to only about 5
per cent of the estimate, could be caused by the difference in the method of estimation.

The point now is, what would be the path of national income if the economy depended only on domestic
savings in development with no participation from foreign sources? The three assumptions introduced earlier in this chapter must be retained here. The ratio
of savings to income is assumed to be 10 per cent. This
percentage will not make the figure of domestic financing amount to the estimated $4,827.5 million, since
this was calculated taking into consideration the increase in income which would be larger in the case of
participation of foreign capital. Also, the other two
assumptions are retained: The ratio of increments in
income to investment for the whole economy is 38 per
cent; foreign funds needed to import equipment and
technical knowledge could be provided through the balance of payment, keeping the capital mix within the
same ratio of 1:2.

Table 70 shows the expected national income in
the absence of foreign investment as compared with
planned income under the above three assumptions, and
using the same equation employed earlier on page 321.
The first possibility, as a result of not using foreign capital during the planning period, is that national income by 1969-70 will be only $4.3 billion.
This is about $1.6 billion less than the target of the
plan which is $5.9 billion. This also reduces the rate
of growth of income from 100 per cent to 45 per cent, or
about one-half. As a result per capita income increases
from $115 (1959-60) to $129 (1969-70), an increase only of 13 per cent during the ten years.

Table 70. A Comparison of Planned Income
with an Estimate of Hypothetical Income
in the Absence of Foreign Loans[a,b]
(Billions of dollars)

Year	Hypothetical income	Planned income
1959–60	2.9	2.9
1960–61	3.1	3.2
1961–62	3.2	3.5
1962–63	3.3	3.8
1963–64	3.4	4.1
1964–65	3.6	4.4
1965–66	3.7	4.7
1966–67	3.8	5.0
1967–68	4.0	5.3
1968–69	4.1	5.6
1969–70	4.3	5.9
1978–79	6.0	

[a]Although they are based on the same assumptions, the
hypothetical estimates in this table are different
from those in Table 69 for the period in which they
overlap.   The reason is that this table starts with
actual national income realized in 1959–60, which is
different from the hypothetical one computed for the
same year in Table 69.

[b]Calculated on the basis that the increase in income
each year is equal to investment during the year multiplied by the income/investment ratio prevailing during 1952–60 which was 38 and using the equation:
$Y_i = Y_{i-1} + I_i \left(\frac{Y}{C}\right)$.

The other possibility which could occur in the absence of foreign capital is that the target set to be reached in ten years, i.e., by 1969-70, will be a-chieved instead by approximately 1978-79. Prolonging the period from ten to nineteen years results in a 90 per cent increase in the time period needed to achieve the target of the plan. Instead of a 10 per cent aver-age yearly rate of increase in national income during the period 1960-70, this rate will decrease to about one-half (5.4 per cent) for the prolonged period. More-over, with a population of about 40 million in 1978-79, per capita income will not exceed $136.

In summarizing, it can be said that foreign capital helped to speed up the rate of income growth: Otherwise, it may have been absorbed by the increase in population. We have seen that the amount of foreign loans and grants needed during the planning period (1960-70) was only one-third of total planned invest-ments. In fact, if such investments take place, and if productivity remains the same, the income resulting in 1969-70 might exceed the planned level. But it seems that more than the estimated $2,288.5 million in foreign loans and grants is needed during the second stage of development of the Egyptian economy. Loans and grants advanced to Egypt up to 1960 amounted to $1,495.8 million. The repayment of these loans and the interest started in 1963. This throws an additional burden on the economy during its second stage of develop-ment.

The repayment of the loans advanced to Egypt up to 1960 will last for thirteen years (1963-76).[21] The burden of repaying these loans is somewhat higher during the first three years (1963-65) and amounts to $130 million yearly. Then, for the next three years, it will decrease to about $90 million. After 1968, the amount of repayment will continue to decrease. Then it will go up again by 1970. This alternation will continue until the loans are paid off in 1976.

It should be noted that these loans, amounting to $1,495.8 million, originated during the first stage

in the development of the economy.   On the assumption
that about $920 million will be repaid during the ten
years of the plan which ends in 1970 and adding the
amount of foreign capital needed for the plan, this
will bring the total amount of foreign capital needed
during the 1960-70 period to $3,668.5 million.   For
this reason there is a need for large amounts of foreign capital during the initial stages of development.

Notes to Chapter 11

[1]United States Department of Commerce, <u>Foreign
Grants and Credits by the United States Government</u>,
No. 69 (Washington, D. C., December, 1961), p. S-8.

[2]United States Department of Agriculture, De-
velopment and Trade Division, <u>Public Law 480 and other
Economic Assistance to United Arab Republic (Egypt)</u>,
ERS-Foreign 83 (Washington, D. C.:   Economic Research
Service, 1964), p. 3.

[3]United States Congress, <u>The 14th Semiannual
Report on Activities of the Food-For-Peace Program
Carried on Under Public Law 480, 83rd Congress, as
Amended; Message from the President to the United
States</u>, 87th Congress, 1st Session, House Document No.
223 (Washington, D. C.:   U. S. Government Printing
Office, 1961).

[4]This information is obtained from a mimeo-
graphed document from the United Arab Republic Desk,
Agency for International Development,   United States
Department of State, Washington, D. C.

[5]United States Bureau of Public Affairs,
<u>Communist Economic Policy in the Less Developed Areas</u>,
Department of State Publication No. 7020 (Washington,
D. C., July, 1960), p. 15.

[6]National Bank of Egypt, <u>Economic Bulletin</u>
Vol. XIV, No. 2, (Cairo, 1961), p. 198.

[7]<u>Ibid</u>., p. 197.

[8]United States Bureau of Public Affairs, Communist Economic Policy in the Less Developed Areas, op. cit., p. 25.

[9]United Nations, Department of Economic and Social Affairs, Economic Developments in the Middle East 1956-57, A supplement to World Economic Survey 1957 (New York, 1958).

[10]Ibid., p. 13.

[11]The Clapp report (final report of the United Nations Economic Survey Mission for the Middle East, 1949) mentions in respect to the gold hoards in Syria, for instance, that though no official estimates of their scope is available, their total was believed in some well-informed quarters to be no less than $150 million in 1949. Alfred Bonné, Studies in Economic Development (London: Routledge and Kegan Paul, Ltd., 1957), pp. 197-198.

[12]Frederick Harbison and Ibrahim A. Ibrahim, Human Resources for Egyptian Enterprise (New York: McGraw-Hill, 1958), p. 33.

[13]Bureaucracy, a characteristic of government business and government officials, adds to the burden and cost of loans. A government official in an underdeveloped country complained that after a foreign loan was contracted with a bank, extra interest (for three days) was charged on the loan by the lending bank. Inquiring about the reason for this action, it was found that after the loan was granted, the official did not complete the necessary papers, a matter that caused the three days' delay during which the bank could not make use of the money. This could involve large amounts of interest. On a loan of $150 million at an annual interest rate of 4 per cent, a delay of three days results in an extra charge of over $15,000.

[14]Table 63, p. 298, supra.

[15]United Nations, Department of Economic Affairs. Measures for the Economic Development of Underdeveloped Countries (New York: May, 1951).

[16]For details of calculations, see Magdi El-Kammash and Ernst W. Swanson, "Income Effects of Loan Transfers from a Developed to an Underdeveloped Country," a paper presented at the meeting of the Southern Economic Association, November 12-14, 1964, Atlanta, Georgia, pp. 19-24 appeared as Reprint 67-6, Department of Economics, North Carolina State University, Raleigh, N. C. (March, 1967).

[17]P. N. Rosenstein-Rodan, "International Aid for Underdeveloped Countries," Review of Economics and Statistics, XLIII (May, 1961), pp. 107-137.

[18]Rosenstein-Rodan is an advocate of the balanced growth theory which is one of the pillars of the supply approach to economic development examined in this work with respect to the Egyptian Economy. He maintains that the program approach, and not the project approach, in development planning renders the various projects interrelated and reinforcing. Hence the need for external capital to initiate such a program. Ibid., p. 108.

[19]Ibid., p. 107-108.

[20]National Planning Committee for Southern Region, The Frame of the General Five-Year Plan for Economic and Social Development (July 1960-June 1965) (Cairo: General Organization for Government Printing Office, 1960, p. 15.

[21]The source of this information on repayment is a confidential report by the World Bank to which I did not have access. However, this information was obtained from a reliable source with access to this report, who read to me this information from the report on the condition that reference would not be made to him as a source of this information.

CHAPTER **12** THE WAY AHEAD

The purpose of this study was to examine the
process of development of the Egyptian economy with
special reference to the supply approach to economic
development. Emphasis was placed mainly on the factors
that contributed to such development in order to eval-
uate the advantages of supplying the economy with such
factors, particularly capital and entrepreneurship.
The year 1952, which witnessed the Revolution, sepa-
rates two distinct periods in the history of development in the country. The first is a period of stagnation which existed before the 1952 Revolution and extends back to the nineteen thirties. The second is the
period of reconstruction, development, and economic
planning which took place after 1952. The following
section gives a summation of the main characteristics
and developments during these two periods.

THE EGYPTIAN ECONOMY IN RETROSPECT

Before the middle of the century, the Egyptian
economy was agrarian, with two-thirds of its capital
invested in agriculture and, largely, agricultural land
per se. Population had been--and is still--growing at a
considerably high rate, which now approaches 3 per
cent annually. Such a high rate resulted from the reduction in mortality, an aftereffect of the improvement
in sanitation and health conditions--while birth rates
experienced hardly any appreciable reduction. With
little migration, the population pressure on land and

other natural resources increased. In an economy that depends largely on agriculture, the increases in population and arable land have not been proportionate. This has tended to crowd the thin green ribbon of Nile-watered land and its Delta--areas which have produced Egypt's food since the dawn of history.

Farming in Egypt was characterized by two extremes of land ownership: numerous small holdings on one side and a few larger estates on the other end of the spectrum. These extremes are the result of an evolution that took place over centuries in Egypt's land tenure system. Actually, the Egyptian farmer did not gain the right of private property until the second half of the nineteenth century. Another characteristic of the Egyptian agricultural sector is the complete dependence on one major crop, cotton. It was introduced at the beginning of the nineteenth century and became the major source of national income and the chief export commodity. Although there has been some gain in productivity in cotton production, the wide fluctuations in cotton prices in world markets and the frequent attacks of the crop by the boll weevil caused economic instability for the Egyptian economy.

It should be emphasized that before 1952, the Egyptian economy was not growing at what could be termed a "reasonable" rate. A great population growth was coupled with an almost stationary real national income. In fact, when compounded, the average annual rate of growth of per capita income, stated at constant prices (1953 = 100), was very small and equalled 0.01 per cent during the period 1937-52. The only years before 1952 in which the economy flourished were the war years. Thereafter the economy assumed the previous state of relative stagnation with a declining rate of growth of per capita income during 1947-52.

The 1952 Revolution demarks considerable changes in long-run economic structure of Egypt and its political framework. It was not until that year that a systematic drive for development was launched. Government machinery was set up for the purpose of efficient execution of the development plan. However, before 1952, we distinguished the five most important phases.[1] They are summarized here so that the ensuing developments will be better understood. They are:

First: the industrialization period which began in 1805 and declined by the middle of the century;

Second: the period characterized by the improvement in one type of social overhead, transportation, and the financial troubles growing out of the opening of the Suez Canal and ended with the British occupation in 1882;

Third: the Egyptian economy remaining predominantly agrarian, a period that existed until the beginning of the First World War;

Fourth: a period of industrialization dependent on domestic capital initiated by Bank Misr which paved the way for the prosperity of the Second World War and managed to bring about legislation favorable to manufacturing industry; and

Fifth: a period of stagnation that followed the Second World War and continued until 1952.

Thus, by the end of the first half of the twentieth century, the Egyptian economy evidenced certain distinct characteristics of underdevelopment. In the first place, agriculture was the dominant industry with a skewed distribution of land ownership. In an agrarian economy, agriculture could not produce enough of the main food item, wheat, for its population; thus importation of this commodity in large quantities occurred yearly. With little development in industry, the result was a marked imbalance among industrial sectors as compared with other countries. Employment in "tertiary" industries was relatively large.

Second, entrepreneurial ability of the type needed for industrial development was lacking. This

absence of entrepreneurs may be attributed to the sentimental attachment to land   and to   the prestige land
bestows on landowners in agrarian societies. Moreover,
investors attach a high degree of liquidity to land, a
matter that makes it a more preferable form of wealth.
We note thus the formation of a sizable rentier group,
while nonland investments are viewed as bearing a high
degree of risk and uncertainty.   Third, investment in
social and economic   overhead facilities   was not carried far enough   to provide a stimulant   to industrial
development.   This is evident from the deficiencies in
investment in transportation and communication, power,
irrigation and drainage, soil conservation, and education, especially technical education and training.

        As already noted,   the year 1952 separates two
distinct   periods   in the   history   of development   of
Egypt.   With the political change   that took place in
1952,   the new administration tried to create a milieu
favorable for development.   Several measures such   as
the land reform,   labor and   investment laws   were enacted.   Some agencies were created to study the feasibility of new industries.   The state also decided   to
take a   positive role in   reinforcing the provision of
social   and economic overhead.   In addition,   several
projects were launched in order to fill the "entrepreneurial gap" that existed.   All these efforts did not
result   in the   private entrepreneurs expanding   their
activities.   It should be noted that, at this stage of
development, the Egyptian experience   did not   parallel
that of Turkey in which state intervention at the early
stages of development brought with it conditions favorable to the conduct of private entrepreneurs.[2]

        The   failure   of the   private entrepreneur   to
live up to its expectations coupled with the political
disturbances   as well   as the   Suez crisis resulted in
undertaking further steps to change the   economic system.   From a quasi-governmental administration of the
newly introduced industries, we find a tendency toward
the   Egyptianization and nationalization   of major industries. This was culminated by the socialistic measures contained in the 1958 Constitution.   This era of

reconstruction we have called the "development period" (1952-60). All these measures paved the way for the second stage of development of the Egyptian economy. This stage is termed the Planning Era which started in 1960 with a ten-year plan (1960-70) to be implemented in two five-year phases.

With the new regime, several measures were introduced in an effort to transform the economy into state socialism with planning as the major instrument for development. Nonetheless, the economy was kept open for foreign loans and grants for the purpose of development. Although the amount forthcoming was somewhat limited by the nationalization laws, considerable quantities of foreign loans and grants were invested in the economy during the initial development period. This inflow is expected to continue throughout the entire planning period.

The participation of foreign capital in investment for development of the Egyptian economy helped in two important ways:[3] First, it paved the way for initiation of the development plans. Second, it helped to speed up the rate of industrial growth so that the development was effected in a much shorter period of time than would otherwise been the case; in turn, the effect of the increase in population was counteracted. It may thus be said that, while the growth rate was pushed up, the nation achieved this goal only through a large inflow of foreign capital and grants. It would appear that there was no opportunity for the nation "to lift itself by its own bootstraps." The issue of whether "capital is made at home" is thus highly debatable.[4]

As a final observation, it may be said that capital importation may therefore enable Egypt to increase income to a level where it may start repayment of the loans in a later period without repayment having adverse effects upon the growth of the economy. Spengler considers that an external limit on how much foreign capital can be used effectively arises from the fact that, "the annual increment of gross foreign investment in a country must exceed the sum which that country is required to pay abroad each year in the form of interest and amortization charges or cumulated foreign investment."[5] It is probable that essentially all underdeveloped regions tend to face this prospect, unless by government edict population growth is forced to a virtual standstill.

PROBLEMS IN DEVELOPMENT

The principle objective of the Egyptian plan is to double national income over a period of ten years (1960-70) with a 40 per cent increase by the end of the first phase of the plan (1965). This results in an average annual rate of growth of 7 per cent during the first five-year plan. Another objective to be accomplished, along with the increase in national income, is to secure a more equitable distribution of income.

Although the first five-year plan ended in 1965 and the execution of the second five-year plan has already begun, there are not as yet detailed reports on the accomplishments of the plan at the end of each year. Such data can be helpful in evaluating planning strategy during the first phase. Only from the statements of the Minister of the Treasury and Planning can we get an idea about the results of the development plan for the second year.

The first phase of the ten-year development plan met with some obstacles in its second year of execution, according to the report available for the second year.[6] The cotton crop was attacked by the cotton worm. The lack of water for irrigation brought with it an unexpected deficiency in the rice crop. Income from agriculture declined by $149.5 million. This resulted from a decline of $112.7 million in cotton, $23 million in rice, $2.3 million in sugar cane, and $11.5 million in livestock. The effect of this shortage spread to other sectors which depended on the production of these agricultural crops according to the

plan.   The effect on other sectors amounted   to $24.2
million distributed as   follows: $9 million   in the
cotton and food industries, $12.9 million in commerce,
and $2.3 million   in the   transportation   and finance
sector.

In the plan income was to increase by 7 per
cent annually,   during the first phase   of the plan,
which would have been an increase   of 14.5 per cent by
the end of the second year of the plan.   Actual income
in the second year of the plan amounted only to $3,245
million,   an increase of only $296.7 million from the
income   at the   beginning of   the plan.   Thus the increase in income by the end of the second year amounted
only to 10 per cent instead of the planned 14.5 per
cent.   As a result, the frame of the plan was revised
to take care of the shortages.   Reports on the first
half of the third year show that the economy is beginning to catch up with the plan.

At the time of writing this chapter, data on
actual investment, total output, and national income
during the first five-year plan was made available by
the central Organization for Public Mobilization and
Statistics.   These detailed tables are to be found in
Appendix B which shows yearly actual investment and
realized   income by sector in current and constant
prices of 1959-60 during the first five-year plan.   It
should be noted that since the publication of the
Frame of the General Five-Year Plan for Economic and
Social Development (July 1960-June 1965) by the National Planning Committee,   there have been some revisions
of the national income estimate for the base year
1959-60. For the sake of accuracy, we are going to use
the revised figures in the following comparisons and
evaluation of the results of the plan.   This accounts
for the discrepancy the reader will notice between the
figures of the base year in this section and those in
Table 64 (page 300).

Actual Investment.   Total investment planned
for the five years amounts to $3,629.9 million. Out of

this total, an amount of $901.6 million is to be directed toward agricultural development including irrigation and drainage projects and the construction of the first phase of the High Dam. The share of industry and electricity in total investment during the five years amounts to $1,331 million. The preliminary figures on actual investment show that there has been a slight deviation from the planned figures. The following comparison shows actual and planned investment in millions of dollars in addition to the per cent realized, i. e., the percentage ratio of actual to planned investment, for major sectors of the economy.

	Planned Investment	Actual Investment	Per Cent Realized
Agriculture	902	817	91
Industry and Electricity	1,331	1,189	89
Rest of the Economy	1.394	1.474	106
Total Investment	3,627	3,480	96

According to these figures unfulfilled investment amounts only to $147 million. In other words, 96 per cent of planned investment was realized. This in itself seems to be good results, yet there has been some structural change in the distribution of actual investment. In agriculture only 91 per cent of planned investment was realized. The corresponding figure for industry and electricity is 89 per cent. Since the figures for the whole economy amount to 96 per cent, this means that for the rest of the economy sector, which is comprised mainly of services such as housing, public utilities, transportation and communication, etc., actual investment exceeded planned investment. This can be seen from the above figures which give the realization at 106 per cent. Such a change could result partially from the increase in population and the consequent increase in demand on services. Another factor possibly contributing to such a change is the degree of availability of external capital. Investment in services is labor using, while investment in industry, electricity, and to a lesser degree agriculture is capital using. The limited amount of capital available from external sources could have necessitated such a structural change in investment.

Income Realized. Table B-2, Appendix B shows actual yearly income by sector in millions of dollars during the first five-year plan. Apparently, realized income by 1965, which amounts to $4,433 million, exceeds planned income which is $4,129 million. This apparent excess is due to the increase in the general price level. Real national income in the prices of the base year 1959-60 and for each year of the first five-year plan is shown in Table B-3, Appendix B. Actual real income in 1964-65, which amounts to $4,053 million, is below planned income of $4,129 for that year by less than 2 per cent. Instead of a planned increase of 40 per cent during the five years 1960-65, actual growth amounts to 37 per cent. It should be noted that we are using here the revised national income estimate for the base year 1959-60 as noted earlier.

Table 71 gives a sectoral comparison of real national income and national income in current prices at the end of the five-year plan with the base year 1959-60. Although the over-all deviation of actual national income from planned income is very small, there are considerable deviations if we look at the individual sectors. Annual average national income growth rate during the five years is 6.5 per cent instead of the planned 7 per cent. The total commodity sector shows a rate of 6.3 per cent and the total services sector a rate of 6.7. However, if we look at the agricultural sector, we find that the rate is 2.7 per cent and for industry it goes up to 8.9 per cent.

Obstacles to Development. On the whole, the results of the Egyptian first five-year plan are quite satisfactory, considering that this is the first experience in development planning for the country. But

Table 71. A Sectoral Comparison of National Income at the End of the Five-Year Plan (1964-65) with National Income at the Base Year (1959-60)

(Millions of dollars)

	National income at the base year, 1959-60[a]	National income 1964-65[a] (current prices)	Real national income 1964-65 (1959-60 prices)
Agriculture[b]	932	1,215	1,081
Industry	589	974	901
Electricity	23	53	51
Construction	108	213	214
Total commodity sector	1,652	2,455	2,247
Transportation and communication[c]	214	399	349
Trade, commerce, and finance	297	387	373
Housing	168	182	186
Public utilities	15	18	16
Other services	610	892	882
Total service sector	1,304	1,878	1,806
Total (all sectors)	2,956	4,333	4,053

[a] Preliminary.
[b] Including irrigation, drainage, and the High Dam project.
[c] Including Suez Canal improvements.

Source: See Appendix B, Tables B-2 and B-3.

the structural change both in investment and income
could have some implications on future planning and
the course of economic growth. It seems that the economists and planners in Egypt are aware of some of
these problems. Dr. El-Kaissonny, Deputy Prime Minister
for Finance and Economic Affairs, pointed out some of
these problems in his 1965-66 budget message.

Following the 1952 Revolution there has been
an increase in consumption rates as a consequence of
the increase in national income and the tendency toward
more equitable distribution of income. Total consumption in current prices increased from $2504 million in
1959-60 to $3370 million by 1964-65, an increase of 34.6
per cent. This took place while national income at
current prices increased by only 33.6 per cent during
the same period. The following figures, which show the
percentage increase in some of the main consumption
goods between 1953 and 1964, are self-evident:

Commodity	Per Cent Increase
Wheat and flour	82.6
Corn	90.2
Cotton seed oil	62.8
Margarine	124.2
Tea	51.9
Sugar	44.3
Cotton cloth	54.2
Silk	69.2
Woolen cloth	224.0
Blankets	59.3

During the first four years of the plan, imports of wheat and flour nearly quadrupled from $42.3
million to $166.3 million. If we consider the increase
in population, we find that consumption per capita is
increasing over time, a matter which is going to present an obstacle to development for two reasons. First,
the increase in consumption limits the capacity to
save. Although part of planned investment should be
financed from external sources, the main objective is to
depend gradually on domestic savings which is expected

to increase during the course of development. A low
rate of saving, coupled with the increase in population
which Egypt is experiencing certainly will not result
in any appreciable economic growth per head. Second,
production in most of the projects undertaken during
the first stages of development planning does not ma-
terialize until a later date. In the meantime, the purchasing power resulting from such investment expenditure increases demand. With the limited amounts of
consumer goods available during that stage, the increase in purchasing power in turn tends to raise the
price level and may result in the increase in importation, a matter that reduces the amounts of foreign exchange available for development purposes.

This brings us to a final point regarding the
strategy of investment. World surplus of agricultural
products and especially that of the United States,
which is used to provide the underdeveloped nations
with their needs, is being depleted. If this trend
continues, and a worldwide shortage of food products
emerges, then we may witness, in the not very far future, a reversal in the terms of trade between industrial and agricultural commodities. In other words,
the widely accepted conclusion by some economists, especially Hans Singer, that "It is a matter of historical fact that ever since the seventies the trend of
prices has been heavily against sellers of food and
raw materials and in favor of the seller of manufactured articles"[8] may not hold any more. This means
that developing countries should plan to supply their
own food products needs locally. And, if the terms
of trade between agricultural and industrial products
are expected to change, they may be better off to exploit the export market. Earlier we noticed that little investment was directed to agriculture as compared
with industry during the first five-year plan and that
the country has been constantly importing wheat, corn,
and other agricultural food products. It seems that
Egypt should direct more attention to the agricultural
sector to feed its growing population until some
checks are developed to reduce the population pressure.

TOWARD A SUPPLY APPROACH TO ECONOMIC DEVELOPMENT

In analyzing the development process of the
Egyptian economy we have seen that emphasis during the
first period of development was placed on building the
social and economic overhead structure.   In addition,
efforts have been made to effect balance among the
major economic sectors.   This program, coupled with
the economies resulting from creating several industries simultaneously, has thus actually helped to initiate development and to speed up its rate.   From the
analysis of the Egyptian economy, its process of development, and from the international comparisons we have
from time to time introduced, we are now in a position
to stress some of the factors that are crucial to the
process of development of underdeveloped countries.
The three main economies which aided the Egyptian process are: The economies of a balanced development, the
economies of social overhead, and external economies.
All these economies should or can be placed on the supply side.

The concept of "balanced development"[9]--rather
than "balanced growth" --refers to the economies derived from the growth and expansion of markets. These
economies presumably result from the interdependence of
different sectors of an economy, particularly agriculture and industry. External economies in the Marshallian
sense, are considered as arising within the context of
partial equilibrium analysis under the assumption of a
fixed demand curve.   In the actual process of development to which underdeveloped countries may be subject,
however, the assumption of a fixed demand curve becomes
unrealistic because these countries usually enjoy an
increase in real income. This increase, the result of
expansion and/or creation of industries, will more than
likely generate demand for the products of other industries.   Consequently, the end result is an expansion
in the size of the market for other industries. Without complementary investments to meet the increase in
demand, the effect may be largely inflationary.   Here
we find, especially in its early stages, a major obstacle to development.   Moreover, we must not overlook

the secondary effects of the expansion of the markets. The increase in the consumer's demand for goods and services will make the production of the needed pro- ducers' goods profitable. When all these effects spread throughout different parts of an economy, the net re- sult is the beginning of the "take off" to use Rostow's classification of the stages of development.

Balanced development creates economies by raising the marginal productivity of capital in various industries rendering large-scale production feasible as a result. The absence of such a pattern sets limits to any attempt to develop and may indeed dampen its effects.

It is true that each country or region is en- dowed with certain types of resources which could de- termine those industries that are feasible within its economic structure. Few countries have the same struc- ture with respect to the output of the various sectors of the economy. Nevertheless, whatever the resources, there should be a degree of proportionality among sec- tors especially the commodity and service sectors.

Another major bottleneck that exists on the supply side in underdeveloped countries is incomplete- ness in the infrastructure or the social overhead out- lays. As Spengler points out, such activities "would not be carried out to the point where marginal social costs and marginal social benefits became approximately equal."[10] Thus, "if they were not carried far enough, investment in industrial and related capital, to which the indicated form of capital overhead are complemen- tary, is slowed down."[11] Underdeveloped economies all too often lack adequate means of transportation and communication, electric power, and numerous other so- cial and economic overhead assets that are as a rule prerequisite to economic development and progress. Little is invested in education either general or tech- nical. Between developed and underdeveloped countries, there usually exists a wide gap in such services.

Markets which the buyer or seller faces are
often characterized by certain monopolistic forms.
Market imperfections in the agricultural sector stand
in the way of attaining an efficient allocation of resources. As nearly as we can determine through our
analysis, this state of affairs is due largely to an insufficiency in capital financing. In the manufacturing
industry a similar situation quite commonly exists.
There are horizontal and vertical linkages among individual firms in the same industry, as well as among
industries. Economies resulting from such interdependence cannot be realized in underdeveloped countries.
Lack of efficient means of transportation and communication, imperfection of knowledge, and shortage of capital all contribute toward this restrictment upon entrepreneurial effectiveness and, hence, economic growth.

The supply approach which finds its origin in
the writings of the classical and neoclassical schools
of economic thought attributes the state of underdevelopment to an insufficiency and/or lack of certain
factors of production that are considered to be strategic to the process of development. In particular,
lack of capital and technical knowledge in underdeveloped countries are the two main obstacles in the way
of accelerating development. A sizable, balanced development program could help underdeveloped economies
initiate development. However, it has been shown that
such a program, even assuming a modest growth target,
requires amounts of capital beyond the means of underdeveloped countries; thus, the need for external means
of financing is amplified. Although underdeveloped
countries have to depend to a great extent on internal
efforts in development, external capital, if made a-
vailable to them during the initial stages of development, could help accelerate the rate of growth of the
economy during their initial periods of expansion.

THE ROLE OF THE STATE

The discussion of economic development usually
brings with it the controversial questions about the

The discussion of economic development usually brings with it the controversial question about. —

role of the state, and the effectiveness of public decisions in increasing economic growth.   This controversy is naturally of ancient origin. Even the extreme
liberals have accepted the idea that government has to
undertake certain minima of economic activities.   According to Adam Smith, these primarily fall in the domain of public works, as well as in the traditional
duties as to the provision of defense, justice, and
education.   According to Spengler, historically,   in
countries where a laissez-faire philosophy prevailed,
the state participated in economic activities such as
provision of education, electric power generation,
flood control, and the building of transport systems.[12]
However, Spengler recognizes the great change in the
economic role of the state that has taken place in recent centuries.[13] As he states it, "the scale of government has advanced with technology, while the intensity of government has grown with the evaluation of
instruments of social and economic control."[14]   Since
it is commonly admitted that the state's role must be
large, the question then becomes, "how large this role
may become before the public economy metastasizes and
swallows up the private economy."[15]

       The state is one of the interdependent ele-
ments composing the indivisible social structure called
society.   It is an association that came into being,
as have other associations, because it could serve
rather specific ends.[16] Yet the role of the state and
the specific economic ends it is expected to serve vary
with the nature of the regnant social system.[17]   An
integral part of the process of development is the
change in social institutions, and values and attitudes
of people. The role of the state is expected, therefore, to be different and certainly wider than   that
which had prevailed in the case of underdevelopment.
The absence of entrepreneurial ability, the deficiency
of capital formation, the incapability of the price
system to achieve an optimum allocation of resources,
in addition to the significant rigidities and discon-
tinuities, are all factors that call for state action
at the early stages of development.

According to our findings from the Egyptian experience, it is more than implicit that the state will not confine its activities to the traditional sectors of defense, health, and education. It tends to perform two other main functions deemed essential to initiating development. The first of these is the expansion of the domain of public works to include all the prerequisites for modern complex industrial systems. Examples of this are the production and distribution of electric power, transportation and communication, irrigation and drainage systems, vocational and industrial training centers, and research in agriculture and industry. The second function is the promotion--and if necessary the undertaking--of other activities which might be indirectly connected with several industries, yet are basic to most of them. The public enterprise sector seems to be becoming increasingly involved in the promotion of development, for example, of such basic industries as mining, petroleum and natural gas, and coal mining.

The first function surely could be undertaken without any damage to the free enterprise system, as history has demonstrated. State intervention in this sector is justified and based on the classical reasons mentioned earlier.

The changes in the industrial structure of the present developed countries brought with them certain other transformations. More industries of the second type (the basic industries), which in the early periods of the Industrial Revolution were considered the domain of private investments--and they led the major economic changes--are no longer viewed with suspicion. Since the early decades of the Revolution such industrial developments have evolved as tend to regard such basic industries as essential for development. It hardly need be said that the chief reason for this change in view rests upon their value for building the modern industrial complex. Indeed, we may say without too much quibbling that they are becoming more and more a part of the growing structure of social and economic overhead outlays.

State intervention in economic life to build up the infrastructure is a view now accepted by several economists, including Nurkse, Mason, and Hirschman. Although Hirschman advocated unbalanced growth through starting investment in directly productive activities (leaving investment in social overhead to be induced), he resorted to state action to promote investments in the former. This he implied when he stated "We have not debarred ourselves from undertaking <u>public investments</u> in DPA (directly productive activities) should we find that the more efficient development sequence is set in motion in this way."[18] Edward S. Mason supports his argument for the thesis with examples of developmental experiences in other countries. Referring to the early American period of development, Mason states that "both state and federal governments were called upon to undertake tasks that by reason of the size of the area and the sparseness of the population, were beyond the capabilities of private enterprise."[19] In another place he assesses the relationship between the degree of backwardness and government action by reporting that "Gerschenkron, in an essay that has become classic in the field..., relates an increasing role of the state to the degree of backwardness found in society in which the growth process is being initiated."[20]

It is true that the high rates of growth of western countries were associated with conditions such as the prevalence of democratic institutions and the existence of a strong middle class, all of which may be absent in the now developing countries. In these cases the state remained the agency of the national community and did not dominate it. But it should be remembered that the process of development and growth at that time took the Schumpeterian form of innovations and pioneering private entrepreneurship. In such situations, the state's function was mainly to create a milieu favorable to economic development. This is somewhat different from the process of development which the presently underdeveloped countries experience. To them, the adaptation to already established

technology may be essential; hence, the need to precondition the underdeveloped economy for such an adaptation process which involves the buildup of the social and economic overheads already accumulated and
taken for granted in the developed countries. On the
assumption that the state knows what these relation-
ships are, its action could provide such structures
and ensure a balance among sectors. In addition, the
state has had to play the role of the pioneering entrepreneur in order to create a motivation mechanism
that may stimulate the rise of the private entrepreneur. This could be achieved through "the simultaneous
expansion of sectors which are complementary and
through favoritism of sectors which enhance profitability in other sectors."21

The second type of activities referred to
above raises the question as to how the state is to
undertake such investments. It implies that intervention on the part of the state in the market mechanism
is essential if the balance needed in its social overhead outlays is to be secured. There are several levels of intervention in the economic sphere open to the
state. These range from the provision of social and
economic overheads, application of direct and indirect
levels and controls, government operation of enterprises to central planning.22

According to classical theory, a purely competitive market mechanism is supposed capable of controlling production and distribution in the public interest. In theory, this mechanism may restore and
effect balance between the different parts of the e-
conomy. If there is shortage in one part--such as in-
sufficient social overhead facilities--suppliers in
this part are making abnormal profits. This extra
profit will draw investors from other sectors where
they may be faced with low profits or even abnormal
losses. The market mechanism will take its course
without need for intervention on the part of government if the conditions underlying this theory prevail
in the economy. This does not seem to be the case with
underdeveloped countries, however. There are three

main obstacles that tend to inhibit the purely competitive market mechanism from inducing investment to
move to those parts suffering from capital deficiency.
In the first place, the initial shortages are general,
not partial, as is evident in the actual scarcity of
physical capital. The shortage in one part of the e-
conomy cannot be remedied by drawing resources from
another part since, because of indivisibility of factors, there is no real excess of factors in another
part. There are critical shortages in underdeveloped
countries that are difficult to remedy: consider the
need for investment finance, skills, and entrepreneurial
ability. These are general shortages and exist in almost
all parts of the underdeveloped economy, and they set:

(1) definite boundaries around the possibility of factor mobility among sectors; and

(2) a (low) ceiling on the maximum rate of
development. In the second place, the main characteristics essential to the operation of pure competition
within industry are almost nonexistent in the small
monopolistic markets of underdeveloped countries. Finally, the mobility of labor is limited by social barriers, traditions, and customs.

The state may of course initiate or speed up
the rate of development in the first stages of the
"take-off." Construction of basic industries and the
necessary social overhead facilities is more likely to
reduce the cost and increase the profitability of
other industries. It is not implied in this scheme of
state intervention that the economy must be subjected
to complete, rigid planning and state control. This
scheme may really be realized partly through state direction and partly through the market mechanism within
the framework of a general developmental plan. There
are numerous possible ways open to the state to put
such a policy in effect. First, the state may acquire
large amounts of foreign funds and it becomes a pro-
moter of those basic essentials. Most international
agencies such as the International Bank for Reconstruction and Development and the Import-Export Bank grant

loans to governments for construction of public works.
Second, it could establish corporations in which the
government participates by contributing part of the
capital and by selling state securities in the money
market. Probably, its "best bet" is to invite foreign
investors to buy the state securities on the assurance
of government participation. Third, industrial development corporations established for financing of promising projects and for expanding existing ones have
been proven successful in many countries. Finally,
the manipulation of taxes, state subsidies, licenses,
foreign exchange, interest rates, and so on are other
instruments which the government could manipulate to
build and encourage investment in the infrastructure
vitally needed for further development. Here, government action will be complementary rather than competitive with private enterprise.

The Egyptian model of development planning
provides an example of the changing role of the state.
Up to the middle of the twentieth century, the Egyptian
economy was dominated by the laissez-faire philosophy
in which the government undertook a minimum of economic activities. The underdevelopmental nature of
the economy did not allow the price system to allocate
optimally the resources destined for investment. The
result was little growth of the economy, especially
since a tremendous increase in population was concurrently happening.

With the 1952 Revolution there has been a considerable change in the economic and social system of
Egypt. To begin with, the new administration enlarged
the role of the state in order to undertake the necessary social and economic overheads with the purpose
of developing the economy. In addition it encouraged
the flow of foreign capital as well as the increase in
domestic capital formation. However, it could not
break the monopolistic forces that were dominating the
economy and which at the same time tried to put obstacles in the way of the new administration. On the
other hand, the private entrepreneur failed to live up

to the state's expectations.   Hence we find   a diversion toward Egyptianization   and Nationalization which
was culminated   by the   declaration   of the   socialist
system of the Egyptian economy and   the development in
the form of central planning.

Still, the economy now is not completely dominated by the state.   In the first place,   the agricultural sector is primarily privately owned and operated
through private cooperatives.   Second, the industrial
sector is not totally operated by the government. Only
those industries of strategic value to the development
of the economy are operated by the state.   Though   the
government   is the   largest owner,   however, there   is
still private ownership   in some of   these industries.
At the   same time,   small industries   are still widely
privately owned and operated. Finally, there is little
interference   with consumer   sovereignty, and the distribution of goods   and   services takes place   in   the
market.

The question whether   such an   economic system
is capable   of providing a milieu favorable for development cannot   be answered on   the basis of this short
experience   in development.   There has   been   quite a
change in   administration, political organization, and
government machinery. During the first five-year plan,
investment strategy was designed to lay the basic foundations of the economy through building the infrastructure.   Most of these investments, such as the High Dam
and land reclamation projects,   will start   paying off
during   the next five   or ten years.   If the economy,
then, can keep   its population rate   of growth   within
the existing limit--if   not   lower--it is   hoped   that
the desired rate of economic growth will not be difficult to accomplish by the end of the second   five-year
plan.

Notes to Chapter 12

[1]Magdi M. El-Kammash,   "On the   Take-off Stage

of the United Arab Republic Economy," Arab Journal, II (Fall 1965), 11-16.

[2]It should be noted that, at this stage of development, the Egyptian experience did not parallel that of Turkey in which state intervention at the early stages of development brought with it conditions favorable to the conduct of private entrepreneurs. See Robert W. Kerwin, "Etatism in Turkey, 1933-35," in Hugh G. J. Aitken (ed.), The State and Economic Growth (New York: Social Science Research Council, 1959), pp. 237-54, especially pp. 252-54.

[3]Magdi M. El-Kammash and Ernst W. Swanson, "Contributions of External Loans to Development," a paper presented at a seminar on Intersectoral Relations in Economic Development, sponsored by the Agricultural Development Council, Raleigh, North Carolina, November, 1964; published in Faculty Discussion Papers, FDP 67-3 (February, 1967).

[4]This is so because the rate of capital formation in underdeveloped countries is small. As Spengler points out, "...a savings rate of 4-5 per cent is too low to permit much if any economic growth per head when population is growing appreciably." Joseph J. Spengler, "Capital Requirements and Population Growth in Underdeveloped Countries: Their Interrelations," Economic Development and Cultural Change, IV (July, 1956), 313.

[5]Ibid., pp. 313-14.

[6]U. A. R. Documentation Research Center, Arab Political Encyclopedia, Documentation and Notes, Eleventh year, January-February, 1963 (Cairo: The National Publication House, 1963), pp. 50-52.

[7]U. A. R. Central Organization for Public Mobilization and Statistics, Selections from U. A. R. Statistics 1951-52 through 1964-65 (Cairo: Dar Memphis for Printing, 1965), p. 116. For planned investment see Table 65, p. 302, supra.

[8]H. W. Singer, International Development: Growth and Change (New York: McGraw-Hill, 1964), p. 165.

[9]We prefer to use here the term "balanced development" rather than "balanced growth" which is the term usually employed in the literature, since we are dealing with underdeveloped but developing countries. This term also is in accordance with our distinction between development and growth as outlined in Chapter 1.

[10]Joseph J. Spengler, "The State and Economic Growth: Summary and Interpretation," in Hugh G. J. Aitken (ed.), The State and Economic Growth, op. cit., p. 375.

[11]Ibid., p. 376.

[12]Spengler, "The State and Economic Growth," op. cit., p. 376. The first three activities are more amenable to public than private enterprise while the last is not likely to be undertaken under the auspices of private enterprise on a sufficiently large scale even if quite amenable to it. Ibid.

[13]Joseph J. Spengler, "The Role of the State in Shaping Things Economic," in Tasks of Economic History, a supplement to the Journal of Economic History, VII, 1947, p. 127.

[14]Ibid., p. 125.

[15]Ibid., p. 130.

[16]Ibid., p. 124.

[17]Ibid. Also see Joseph J. Spengler, "Social Structure, The State, and Economic Growth," in Simon Kuznets, Wilbert Moore, and Joseph J. Spengler (eds.), Economic Growth, Brazil, India, Japan (Durham, N. C.: Duke University Press, 1955), p. 370.

[18]Albert O. Hirschman, The Strategy of Economic

Development (New York: Yale University Press, 1961), p. 89.   (Italics and parentheses mine.)

[19]Edward S. Mason,   "The Role of Government   in Economic   Development,"   Paper and Proceedings   of the Seventy-Second Meeting of the American Economic   Association, _American   Economic   Review_,   L   (May, 1960), p. 641.

[20]_Ibid._, p. 637.

[21]Joseph J. Spengler,   "Economic   Factors   in Economic Development," _American Economic Review_, Papers and Proceedings of the 69th Annual Meeting, XLVII(May, 1957), p. 53.

[22]Alexander   Eckstein,   "Individualism   and the Role of the State in Economic Growth," _Economic Development and Cultural Change_, VI (January, 1958), pp. 81-87,   reprinted in DeVere E. Pentony (ed.),   _The Underdeveloped Lands_ (San   Francisco: Chandler   Publishing Company, 1960), p.145.

APPENDIXES

APPENDIX A

THE IMPLICATION OF ISLAMIC LAW
ON POPULATION CONTROL

A religious aversion is dominant among the majority of the Moslems that makes them resent any attempt to control their numbers. In fact, there is still a strong conviction that a large family is encouraged by the Islamic religion. This is supported by such verses of the Koran as "wealth and sons are the allurements of the life of this world" (X VIII-42),[1] "To whom I granted resources in abundance, and sons to be on his side!" (L XXIV-12, 13.) But a case can be made that these verses and many others as well as the Hadith of the prophet have been misunderstood or misinterpreted. For example, when God says that "wealth and sons...." He adds, "but the things that endure, good deeds, are best. In the sight of thy Lord, as rewards, and best as (the foundation for) hopes" (X VIII-46.) Before examining the stand of the Islamic religion on the question of population control, a brief reference to Islamic jurisprudence is in order.

ISLAMIC JURISPRUDENCE

The Sources of Islamic Law. The fundamental sources of Islamic jurisprudence (Shariah) are the text of the Book (the Holy Koran) and the Traditions (the Sunnah). It is generally accepted by the leaders of the Moslem schools and the jurists that these two texts are given priority over two other sources peculiar to certain schools, which are the consensus of opinion (ijma) and analogy (qiyas). Controversy among the jurists, however, resulted in some other sources that came out of situations which were not provided for in the primary four sources of law. The other sources are based on reason and their origin is found in the study of the reason behind the rules. Some jurists rejected, while others accepted these new sources, which are: Preference (istihsan); public interest

(al-masalih al-mursalah); and the continuation of a
rule (istishab).

The Holy Book, the Koran, is the first and
fundamental source of Islamic jurisprudence. Although
they might differ sometimes on interpretation of some
verses of the Koran, all the Moslem Schools of Law and
the jurists agree on this.   The Koranic chapters
(Surahs) deal with matters relating to religion and
God's Unity, detailed Islamic legislative material,[2]
theological matters, and regulations relating to prayer
and worship, prohibition laws of certain matters. It
also contains the laws relating to marriage, divorce,
inheritance, and family planning.

The Sunnah, or the Traditions of the prophet
is regarded as the second most important source of
Islamic jurisprudence after the Koran. It is considered
supplementary to, and explanatory of, the Koran, and
it interprets its general provisions.   It consists of
the sayings, deeds, or tacit approvals of the founder
of Islamic Shariah, the prophet.

The traditions were not recorded as in the case
of the Koran.   Actually, the prophet warned against
that, lest the people take it and disregard the Koran.
It was later classified, however, and compiled according to the reliability source of authority for their
narration.   Another major compilation is that of Imam
Malik which is classified according to various topics
of jurisprudence.

Consensus of opinion (ijma) is generally
accepted by the majority of the jurists as the third
source of Islamic law.   It is the agreement of the
Moslem Juriconsults on a judicial rule in which they
based their consensus upon the Koran and the Sunnah as
well as upon reason.   Consensus made great contributions to Islamic law since it resulted in such changes
as would suit the needs of changing times and usages.

With the expansion of the Islamic State, new
cases came up which sometimes were not provided for in

these first three sources. Thus the jurists have to turn to reason, logic, and opinion; hence the new source, analogy (qiyas). From the rules they deduced their causes in order to be able to apply the same rule to another problem whenever the cause for both was identical.

There has been a great deal of conflict between the schools to the extent to which analogy could be relied upon. Except when it conforms to certain conditions, it may not be considered valid as a source of law.

The Moslem Schools of Law. There are four Schools of Law which are known as the Sunni Schools of jurisprudence. First, the Hanafi School was founded by Abu Hanifah Numan ibn Thabit (699-767 A.D.), the Great Imam. The school was known as the "People of Opinion." It broadened the Shariah rules by means of analogy (qiyas) and preference (istihsan). It is the official school for Fatwas in Egypt, Syria, and Lebanon. As to religious matters, it is the predominant school in Turkey and among the Moslems of Balkans, Afghanistan, Pakistan, India, and China.

The Maliki School is the school of tradition and started in Medina with the thinking of Imam Malik ibn Anas al-Asbahi (713-795 A.D.). His main work is the book on Traditions which he arranged according to the topics of jurisprudence. In his interpretation of the Sunnah, he would rely upon the Koran, the Traditions, the practices of the peoples of Medina and on the sayings of the Companions. In the absence of explicit texts, he would have recourse to analogy and to al-Masalih al-mursalah (public interest).[3]

The Shafié School was founded by Imam Mohamed ibn Idris al-Shafié (767-819 A.D.). He was a pupil of Imam Malik in Hijaz and studied with all of the Companions of Imam Abu Hanifa in Iraq. He rejected the Hanafi's principle of preference (istihsan) and the Maliki's principle of public interest (al-masalih al-mursalah) and accepted deduction (istidlal) in

addition to the four sources of law.   Imam al-Shafié
was the first to compile the sources of law.   In his
now famous treatise, <u>al-Risalah</u>, he dealt with the
origins of jurisprudence.

The Hanbali School was founded by Imam Abu
Abdullah Ahmad ibn Hanbal (780-855 A.D.) in Baghdad.
He was one of the most distinguished of the students
of Imam al-Shafié.   He was very firm in his faith and
was renowned for his adherence to the strict text of
the Koran and the Traditions.   The main sources for
his school are: "The texts of the Koran and the
<u>Sunnah</u>, the <u>Fatwas</u> of the Companions; if there was
nothing to contradict them, the sayings of certain of
the Companions when these were consistent with the
Koran and the <u>Sunnah</u>, <u>daif</u>, and <u>mursal</u> traditions (the
former have a weak chain of transmission, while the
latter lacks the name of some of the transmitters),
and finally reasoning by analogy (<u>qiyas</u>) wherever it
is necessary."[5]   Today it is the official school of
the kingdom of Saudi Arabia.   Its followers number
about 5 million in the Arabian Peninsula, Palestine,
Syria, Iraq, and other countries.[6]

THE RELIGIOUS BELIEFS

The misinterpretation of the Koran and the
Islamic religion as a whole is not a recent phenomenon,
but something that started during the thirteenth century with the end of the Abbasid period.   In the dawn
of the Islamic era, the learned from among the Companions interpreted the Koran and Sunnah following either
consensus or analogy.   This gave rise to the various
schools of law and the jurists.   The science of jurisprudence flourished and attained its golden age with
the emergence of the Abbasid state in the eighth century. However, this came to a halt with the end of the
Abbasid period and the decline of Arab civilization
that followed.   During this period of stagnation, the
door was closed in the face of interpretation.   Imitation based on ignorance prevailed which in most cases
clung to trivial matters.   With the passage of time,

the source became so distant that these trivial matters
soon swelled into independent streams and became rooted
as part of the religion.   This made Islamic jurisprudence appear as backward. A great deal of superstition
and sayings crept into the Islamic religion, and in
time some laymen looked upon them as an integral part
of the religion.   The reform movement started in the
nineteenth century in an attempt to return to the
sources and the true spirit of the Shariah and to make
it cope with the modern progress and civilization.

Religious matters and beliefs are not something that can be changed easily by a law or even a
reform movement. Ignorance, imitation, and the introduction of trivial matters that were wholly unrelated
to Islamic jurisprudence became deeply rooted in the
minds and the hearts of those people who label themselves as Moslems. Moreover, they accepted these
rules as a matter of faith without discussion or question. Take Turkey, for example. Turkey was the capital
of the Islamic world. However, the reform of the
Nationalist Kemalist movement took on a new secular
trend with the purpose of destroying the Islamic
system in the country. One of the outcomes is that
the Turkish Civic Code is the Swiss Code with minor
changes. Despite all these efforts the Turks still
regard Islam as their religion. While the question of
faith is separated from the sphere of law which became
secularized, we find among the majority of the Turks
that the Islamic religion and teachings are predominant
and they still stay close to it in their everyday life,
especially in matters of family planning, which is our
concern in this book.

Family laws lie at the heart of the Islamic
jurisprudence, which is both a religious and a legal
system. Two divisions are evident in the Islamic
jurisprudence: The first is concerned with the hereafter[7] and the second with the affairs of this world.
To the latter belong family laws[8] as well as criminal
and commercial laws. This division is known today as
personal statutes.

Whether correctly interpreted or not, the teaching of the Islamic religion has a great deal of influence on the people's attitudes toward the problem of birth control and family planning. Only those acts which they believe are sanctioned by their religion are practiced, irrespective of the law. Thus a study of family planning and birth control among the Moslem people should focus on an examination of the opinions of the Moslem jurists and their interpretations of the Koran and Sunnah. This may help find some way to apply effectively family planning among the Moslem people.

THE MOSLEM JURISTS ON BIRTH CONTROL

In his elaborate study on the Islamic religion and family planning, Professor El-Sharabasy[9] raised the question: Under what circumstances does the Shariah sanction birth control. Before answering this question, we have to find the causes that give rise to birth control.

Most of the jurists agree on a number of factors that justify the practice of birth control. The following are considered the most important:[10]

First: If a woman has become pregnant immediately following a previous pregnancy, thus affecting adversely her health and that of her offspring;

Second: If either of the parents is afflicted with a hereditary disease that might be transmitted to the offspring;

Third: If frequent pregnancies might endanger the health of the mother or delay her recovery from an illness;

Fourth: If the family income is too low to allow a large family. In other words, when more children may lower the standard of living of the family. This point was emphasized by Imam El-Gazaly as grounds

for birth control because a large family causes poverty
and poverty would affect belief.[11]

What follows is an examination of these four
factors in the light of the Moslem texts (Koran and
Sunnah) and the opinion of jurists. The purpose is to
find out which of these are sanctioned according to
Shariah and under what circumstances. Emphasis is
placed particularly on the letters of Islamic jurisprudence in contrast to some of the common practices
which may have developed among some of the Moslems as
a result of ignorance or misinterpretation of the
Koran.

THE MOSLEM RELIGION AND FAMILY PLANNING

Before we discuss the stand of the Moslem religion on family planning, we should clarify the mean-
ing of that term. Family planning or what sometimes
is referred to as birth control does not mean a master
plan on the state level striving to restrict the population to a certain constant number over a period of
time. By family planning here we mean birth control
on the family level depending on its needs and its
circumstances. In other words, we dismiss the idea of
a law that restricts each family's size to a certain
number irrespective of their circumstances.

It should be noted at the outset that there is
no verse in the Koran that sanctions or prohibits
directly birth control. Efforts therefore must be
directed to the use of analogy, interpretation, and
consensus of opinion and the "Traditions" in order to
find the rule of the Islamic religion on this matter.

In doctrine, the Islamic religion forbids the
killing of the soul. Abortion, or the bringing down
of the child after the creation of the soul, is therefore forbidden. Most of the Moslem jurists agree,
however, that the soul is not created before the expiry
of the first 120 days because it has to pass by seven

stages according to the deduction of al-Imam Ali from the following verses of the Koran:

> Man We did create
> From a quintessence (of clay);
>
> Then We placed him
> As (a drop of) sperm
> In a place of rest,
> Firmly fixed;
>
> Then We made the sperm
> Into a clot of congealed blood;
> Then of that clot We made
> A (foetus) lump; then We
> Made out of that lump
>
> Bones and clothed the bones
> With flesh; then We developed
> Out of it another creature.
> So blessed by God,
> The Best to create!
> (XXIII-12-13-14)

The Maliki School, on the other hand, restricts the period to 40 days (instead of 120). However, we find a great deal of variation with respect to the permission or prohibition of birth control before the creation of the soul, with or without a valid cause. Dr. Madkour summarized the different views regarding abortion before the creation of the soul as follows.[12]

First: According to some of al-Hanafi's jurists and some of the Shafi's it is permitted without a reason, though some of them make it conditional with a cause.

Second: It is permitted only with a cause. This is the view of some of Shafié and Hanafi.

Third: According to some of the Maliki School it is not desirable though permissible. However, others prohibit it completely.

BIRTH CONTROL DURING THE EARLY DAYS OF ISLAM

There is a great deal of evidence in the Sunnah about the practice of birth control which was called al-a'azl (or withdrawal).   Actually some of the Companions practiced this method of birth control with the knowledge of the prophet who did not prohibit it. In Sahih al-Bukhari, several hadith (Traditions) are found which relate the cases where some of the Companions or the Moslems asked the prophet about al-a'azl. In some instances he sanctioned it; in others he did not say anything against it, which is taken as tacit approval.   Imam Abu-Al-Kayne mentions that "all the Hadith are explicit in sanctioning al-a'azl." However, some of the jurists sanctioned al-a'azl on the condition that it is practiced with the approval of the woman.

In sanctioning birth control (al-a'azl) if accompanied by a valid cause, the Moslem jurists are using reason and resorting to the text of the Koran. They justify this on the principle that "action that might cause harm should be avoided." Here is evidence from the Koran.

> And spend of your substance
> In the cause of God
> And make not your own hands
> Contribute to your destruction;
> But do good
> For God loveth those
> Who do good.
> (II-195)
>
> And strive in his cause
> As ye ought to strive
> (with sincerity and under discipline)
> He has chosen you, and has
> Imposed no difficulties on you
> In religion, it is the cult
> of your father Abraham.
> (XXII-78)

Some jurists also take an indirect hint from the following verse in the Koran:

> The mothers shall give suck
> To their offspring
> For two whole years,
> If the father desires
> To complete the term.
> (II-233)

As confirmation to this, the prophet in al-Hadith asked his Companions not to indulge in sexual intercourse during the time the mother is nursing the child, which is two years according to the Koran. This may be interpreted to mean that if another pregnancy would impair the health of the child or the mother, then it should be avoided, and such avoidance would not be against the religion.[13]

Besides health reasons for birth control, the economic factor was emphasized by one of the Companions Amre Ibn Al-A'ss. In his famous speech to the people of Egypt, he warned against four evils, the last one is the increase in the number of children and its effect on the family.[14] This also was emphasized by another Companion Abdulla Ibn Abbas in his saying that one of the main reasons for poverty is having too many children. These are just a few illustrations of the recognition of the Moslem community, the jurists, and the Companions of the problem of population increase and how they sanctioned birth control under certain circumstances as a remedy for it.

THE ISLAMIC RELIGION AND THE MODERN METHODS OF BIRTH CONTROL

A great deal of discussion is centered now around the question on whether the modern methods of birth control are sanctioned by the Islamic religion. As pointed out before, al-a'azl (or the withdrawal) was sanctioned by the prophet and most of the Companions and the Jurists. The withdrawal in essence is a

method to prevent conception, or the fertilization of
the egg cell by the sperm. Of course, that method was
used because at that time it was the only known and
sanctioned method. Therefore, by deduction (qiyas) we
can say that anything that does the same thing as
al-a'azl is also sanctioned. For example, Ibn Abdeen
quoted one of the famous Hanafi jurists who stated
that it is permissible for the woman to block the
mouth of the uterus in order to prevent the sperm from
reaching the egg cell.[15] More recently, we find that
the highest Islamic authority, the Rector of **Al**-Azhar
University, permits the use of legitimate contraceptive
devices that do not cause harmful side effects. Other
Moslem jurists and Imam share the same view.

NOTES

[1] All translations of the verses from the Holy
Koran are based on: A. Yusif Ali, The Holy Quran,
Text, Translation Commentary, (Washington, D. C.: The
American International Printing Company, 1946).

[2] Phillip K. Hitti, The History of the Arabs
(New York: St. Martin's Press, 1964), p. 124.

[3] This last source is unique to this School. S.
Mahmassani, Falsafat Al-Tashri Fi Al-Islam, Translated
by Farhat J. Fiadeh (Leiden: E. J. Brill, 1961) p.
26.

[4] The Koran, the Sunnah, Consensus of Opinion,
analogy. See Appendix B on sources of Law in
Islam.

[5] Mahmassani, op. cit., pp. 30-31.

[6] Ibid., p. 32.

[7] Religious matters such as belief, prayer,
almsgiving, fasting, and pilgrimage.

[8] It includes marriage, divorce, and related

matters such as birth control, alimony, child custody, guardianship, inheritance, and others.

[9]Ahmed El-Sharabasy, Religion and Family Planning (Cairo: Ministry of Social Affairs, Public Relations Office, 1966), in Arabic.

[10]Ibid., pp. 50-51.

[11]Imam Abu-Hamid Ibn Mohammed El-Gazaly, Ihya Elome El-Din (Cairo: Commercial Press, n.d.), Vol. 2, p. 48.

[12]Mohammed Salam Madkour, The Islamic View of Birth Control, A Comparative Study of the Moslem Schools (Cairo: Dar Al-Nahda Al-Arabia, 1965), p. 93.

[13]Imam Mahmoud Shaltout, Al Fatawi: A Study of the Problem of the Contemporary Moslem in His Private and Public Life, (Cairo: Dar Al-Kalam, 1964), pp. 296-297.

[14]Ibn Abdel-Hakam, Fetouh Masr, p. 139, and Ibn Tagri Bordi, Al-Negoum Al-Zahira, Vol. 1, p. 72. Also see Al-Manar, Vol. 7, No. 1, March, 1904, p. 52.

APPENDIX B

STATISTICS OF NATIONAL INCOME

AND INVESTMENT EXPENDITURES

DURING THE YEARS OF THE

FIRST-FIVE-YEAR PLAN 1960-65

AND THE BASE YEAR 1959-60

Table B.1.　Investment Expenditure by Sector during the Five-Year Plan, 1960-70 and the Base Year 1959-60

(Millions of dollars)

Sector	1959-60	1960-61	1961-62	1962-63	1963-64	1964-65[a]	Total for the five-year plan[a]
Agriculture[b]	67.9	87.4	119.6	170.2	234.6	204.7	816.5
Industry	113.4	155.9	115.7	185.2	242.4	229.8	929.0
Electricity	14.3	12.9	14.5	27.4	81.9	122.4	259.1
Construction	-	-	-	8.0	10.4	12.0	30.4
Total commodity sectors	195.6	256.2	249.8	390.8	569.3	568.9	2,035.0
Transportation and communication[c]	82.3	172.0	163.8	123.7	103.7	113.4	676.6
Trade, commerce, and finance	-	-	11.5	8.5	14.9	9.9	44.8

Housing	71.5	43.9	86.9	86.5	86.0	68.1	371.4
Public utilities	17.2	17.7	23.4	31.0	18.9	25.1	116.1
Other services	27.6	28.5	42.3	49.0	63.5	52.7	236.0
Total service sectors	198.6	262.1	327.9	298.7	287.0	269.2	1,444.9
Total (all sectors)	394.2	518.3	577.7	689.5	856.3	838.1	3,479.9

[a]Preliminary figures.

[b]Including irrigation, drainage, and the High Dam project.

[c]Including Suez Canal improvements.

Source: U. A. R. Central Organization for Mobilization and Statistics, United Arab Republic Yearbook for Public Statistics 1952-65 (Cairo: Dar Memphis, 1966), p. 210.

Table B.2. National Income by Sector in Current Prices during the Period 1959-60[a]

(Millions of dollars)

Sector	1959-60	1960-61	1961-62	1962-63	1963-64	1964-65
Agriculture[b]	931.5	926.2	857.9	978.0	1,092.5	1,215.1
Industry	589.5	656.9	712.7	807.1	902.3	973.8
Electricity	22.6	28.1	37.5	42.3	44.4	53.3
Construction	108.3	101.6	169.3	192.0	220.8	213.0
Total commodity sectors	1,651.9	1,712.8	1,777.4	2,019.4	2,260.0	2,455.2
Transportation and communication[c]	213.7	235.1	268.9	305.2	359.3	399.1
Trade, commerce, and finance	297.2	333.9	348.7	354.2	369.1	386.4
Housing	167.9	169.7	175.2	178.5	181.0	181.9

Public utilities	14.7	15.6	16.1	17.0	17.5	18.4
Other services	610.6	669.1	659.2	720.1	814.2	892.2
Total service sectors	1,304.1	1,423.2	1,468.1	1,575.0	1,741.1	1,878.0
Total (all sectors)	2,956.0	3,136.0	3,245.5	3,594.4	4,001.1	4,333.2

[a] Preliminary figures.

[b] Including irrigation, drainage, and the High Dam project.

[c] Including Suez Canal improvements.

Source: U. A. R. Central Organization for Mobilization and Statistics, United Arab Republic Yearbook for Public Statistics (Cairo: Dar Memphis, 1966), p. 212.

Table B.3. Yearly Real National Income by Sectors (at 1959-60 Prices)
during the Planning Period 1960-65

(Millions of dollars)

Sector	1960-61	1961-62	1962-63	1963-64	1964-65[a]
Agriculture[b]	926.2	857.9	980.7	1,041.6	1,081.0
Industry	656.9	712.7	757.2	850.1	901.6
Electricity	101.6	169.3	192.1	220.8	213.9
Construction	28.1	37.5	42.3	42.8	50.6
Total commodity sector	1,712.8	1,777.4	1,972.3	2,155.3	2,247.1
Transportation and communication[c]	235.1	268.9	292.3	331.2	349.6
Trade, commerce, and finance	333.7	348.7	354.2	341.1	372.6
Housing	169.7	175.2	178.5	181.0	185.6

Public utilities	15.6	16.1	17.0	17.5	16.1
Other services	669.1	659.2	709.1	763.8	882.1
Total service sectors	1,423.2	1,468.1	1,551.1	1,634.6	1,806.0
Total (all sectors)	3,136.0	3,245.5	3,523.4	3,789.9	4,053.1

[a]Preliminary figures.

[b]Including irrigation, drainage, and the High Dam project.

[c]Including Suez Canal improvements.

Source: U. A. R. Central Organization for Mobilization and Statistics, Selections from the United Arab Republic Public Statistics 1951-52 to 1964-65 (Cairo: Dar Memphis, 1965), p. 116.

BIBLIOGRAPHY

BOOKS

Abd-al-Rahman, B. Hassan Al-Hanafi. Adjaib Al-athar fi Taradjim-wal-Akhbar (The Great History of Egypt in the 12th and 13th Moslem Centuries). n.p., Government Press, 1297 Higry (1880 A.D.).

Abul-Khair, Kamal H. Co-operation: Its Evolution and Philosophy (in Arabic). Cairo: National House for Printing and Publishing, n.d.

Aitken, Hugh G. J. (ed.). The State and Economic Growth. New York: Social Science Research Council, 1959.

Al-Hitta, Ahmed. Economic History of Egypt (in Arabic). Cairo: n.p., 1957.

Anis, Mahmoud A. The National Income, Output and Expenditure of Egypt for the Years 1937-1945. Cairo: Nile Printing House, 1950.

Bonné, Alfred. Studies in Economic Development. London: Routledge & Kegan Paul Ltd., 1957.

Briabanti, Ralph, and Spengler, Joseph J. (eds.). Tradition, Values and Socio-Economic Development. Durham, N. C.: Duke University Press, 1961.

Clark, Colin. The Conditions of Economic Progress. London: Macmillan and Co., Ltd., 1940.

Cleland, Wendel W. The Population Problem in Egypt. Lancaster, Penn.: Pennsylvania Printing Co., 1936.

Crouchley, A. E. Economic Development of Modern Egypt. London: Longmans, Green and Co., 1938.

Egyptian Federation of Industries. Livre d'or de la

federation Egyptienne de L'Industrie.   Cairo:
Imprimerie Schindler, 1948.

El-Gazaly, Imam Abu-Hamid Ibn Mahmoud, Ihya Elome El-
Din. Vol. II. Cairo: Commercial Press, n.d.

Ellis, Howard S. (ed.). Economic Development for
Latin America. New York: St. Martin's Press,
1961.

El-Rafie, Abdel-Rahman. Agriculture Cooperative Unions
(in Arabic). Cairo: n.p., 1914.

Enke, Stephen. Economics for Development. Englewood
Cliffs, N. J.: Prentice-Hall, Inc., 1963.

Hamdy, Mohamed M. Some Reflections on Our Contemporary
Economic System. Alexandria: Dar El-Maaref
Press, 1963.

Harbison, Frederick, and Ibrahim, Ibrahim A.   Human
Resources for Egyptian Enterprise. New York:
McGraw-Hill Book Co., 1958.

Harbison, Frederick, and Myers, Charles A. Education,
Manpower and Economic Growth. New York:McGraw-
Hill Book Co., 1964.

_____, and _____. Manpower and Education.   New
York: McGraw-Hill Book Co., 1965.

Hauser, Philip M. (ed.). Population and World Politics.
Glencoe, Ill.: The Free Press, 1958.

Hirschman, Albert O. The Strategy of Economic Development. New York: Yale University Press, 1961.

Hitti, Philip K. The Near East in History. Princeton,
N. J.: D. Van Norstrand Co., Inc., 1961.

Institute National De La Statistique Et Des Études
Economiques. Meménto economique, l'Egypte.
Paris: Presses Universitaires de France, 1950.

Issawi, Charles. Egypt: An Economic and Social Anal-
      ysis. London: Oxford University Press, 1947.

_____. Egypt in Revolution. London: Oxford
      University Press, 1963.

Kemmerer, Donald L., and Jones, C. Clyde.   American
      Economic History. New York: McGraw-Hill Book
      Co., 1959.

Keynes, John Maynard. The General Theory of Employ-
      ment, Interest and Money. New York: Harcourt,
      Brace and Co., 1938.

Kuznets, Simon, Moore, Wilbert E., and Spengler, Joseph
      J. Economic Growth, Brazil, India, Japan.
      Durham, N. C.: Duke University Press, 1955.

Leheita, Mohamed Fahmy. Modern Economic History of
      Egypt. Cairo: n.p., 1938.

Leibenstein, Harvey. Economic Backwardness and Economic
      Growth. New York: John Wiley and Sons, Inc.,
      1957.

Lewis, William Arthur. Aspects of Industrialization.
      ("National Bank of Egypt Fiftieth Anniversary
      Commemoration Lectures.") Cairo: N.B.E.
      Printing Press, 1953.

Marei, Sayed. Agrarian Reform in Egypt. Le Caire:
      Imprimerie de L'institut Francais d'Archéologie
      Orientale, 1957.

_____. Agricultural Reform and the Population
      Problem in Egypt. Cairo: National House for
      Printing and Publishing, n.d.

Marshall, Alfred. Industry and Trade. London:
      Macmillan Co. Ltd., 1919.

_____. Principles of Economics. 8th edition. New
      York: The Macmillan Co., 1948.

Matthew, Roderic D., and Arkawi, Matta. Education in
    Arab Countries of the Near East. Menasha,
    Wisc.: George Banta Publishing Co., 1949.

Mill, John Stuart. Principles of Political Economy.
    5th London ed. New York: D. Appleton and Co.,
    1872.

Mudd, Stuart (ed.). The Population Crisis and the Use
    of World Resources. Bloomington: Indiana
    University Press, 1964.

Myrdal, Gunnar. An International Economy. New York:
    Harper & Brothers Publishers, 1956.

Nelson, Eastin (ed.). Economic Growth. Austin:
    University of Texas Press, 1960.

Nurske, Ragnar. Problems of Capital Formation in
    Underdeveloped Countries. Oxford: Basil
    Blackwell, 1953.

Parsons, Kenneth H., Penn, Raymond J., and Raup,
    Philip M. Land Tenure. (Proceeding of the
    International Conference on Land Tenure and
    Related Problems in World Agriculture.)
    Madison, Wisc.: University of Wisconsin Press,
    1956.

Pentony, DeVere E. (ed.). The Undeveloped Lands: A
    Dilemma of the International Economy. San
    Francisco, Calif.: Chandler Publishing Company,
    1960.

Rosier, C. L'Urbanisme ou la science de l'agglomer-
    ation. Paris: Dunod, 1953.

Rostow, W. W. The Stages of Economic Growth. Cambridge:
    Cambridge University Press, 1961.

Said, G. M. The Road to Socialism. Cairo: Arab
    Renaissance Press, 1962.

Samy, Amin. The Nile Almanac. Egypt: Government
      Press, 1915.

Schackle, G. L. S. Expectations in Economics.
      Cambridge: Cambridge University Press, 1949.

Shannon, Lyle W. (ed.). Underdeveloped Areas. New
      York: Harper and Brothers Publishers, 1957.

Singer, H. W. International Development Growth and
      Change. New York: McGraw-Hill Book Co., 1964.

Smith, Adam. An Inquiry into the Nature and Causes of
      the Wealth of Nations. Cannan's ed. New York:
      The Modern Library, 1937.

Spengler, Joseph J., and Briabanti, Ralph (eds.).
      Tradition, Values and Socio-Economic Develop-
      ment. Durham, N. C.: Duke University Press,
      1961.

Spengler, Joseph J., and Duncan, O. D. (eds.). Demo-
      graphic Analysis. Glencoe, Ill.: The Free
      Press, 1956.

                    ESSAYS IN COLLECTIONS

Aubrey, Henry A. "Investment Decisions in Under-
      developed Countries," in Capital Formation and
      Economic Growth. Princeton: National Bureau
      of Economic Research, November, 1955.

Beer, George L. "Egyptian Problems," in African
      Questions at the Paris Conference. New York:
      The Macmillan Co., 1923.

Byé, Maurice. "The Role of Capital in Economic Devel-
      opment," in Economic Development for Latin
      America, ed. Howard S. Ellis. New York: St.
      Martin's Press, 1961, pp. 110-24.

Davis, Kingsley. "Institutional Patterns Favoring High Fertility in Underdeveloped Areas," in Underdeveloped Areas, ed. Lyle W. Shannon. New York: Harper and Brothers Publishers, 1957, pp. 88-95.

Eckstein, Alexander. "Individualism and the Role of the State in Economic Growth," in Economic Development and Cultural Change, VI (January, 1958), and The Underdeveloped Lands - A Dilemma of the International Economy, ed. DeVere E. Pentony. San Francisco: Chandler Publishing Co., 1960, pp. 141-49.

Ezzat, Mohamed A. "The Land Tenure System of Egypt," in Land Tenure, eds. Kenneth H. Parsons et al. Proceeding of the International Conference on Land Tenure and Related Problems in World Agriculture, Madison, Wisc: University of Wisconsin Press, 1956, pp. 100-103.

Fleming, J. Marcus. "External Economies and the Doctrine of Balanced Growth," in The Economics of Underdevelopment, eds. A. N. Agarwala and S. P. Singh. Bombay: Oxford University Press, 1958, pp. 272-94.

Issawi, Charles. "Population and Wealth in Egypt," in Demographic Analysis, eds. J. J. Spengler and O. D. Duncan. Glencoe, Ill.: The Free Press, 1956, pp. 689-703.

Kerwin, Robert W. "Etatism in Turkey, 1933-50," in The State and Economic Growth, ed. Hugh G. J. Aitken. New York: Social Science Research Council, 1959, pp. 237-54.

Kiser, Clyde V. "The Demographic Position of Egypt," in Demographic Studies of Selected Areas of Rapid Growth. New York: Milbank Memorial Fund, 1944, pp. 97-122.

Notestein, Frank W. "The Population of the World in the Year 2000," in Demographic Analysis, eds. J. J. Spengler and O. D. Duncan. Glencoe, Ill.: The Free Press, 1956, pp. 34-43.

Rizk, Hanna. "Population Growth and Its Effects on Economic and Social Goals in the United Arab Republic," in The Population Crisis and the Use of World Resources, ed. Stuart Mudd. Bloomington: Indiana University Press, 1964, pp. 169-75.

Rosenstein-Rodan, P. N. "Notes on the Theory of the 'Big Push,'" in Economic Development for Latin America, ed. Howard S. Ellis. New York: St. Martin's Press, 1961, pp. 57-67.

_____. "Problems of Industrialization of Eastern and South-Eastern Europe," in The Economics of Underdevelopment, eds. A. N. Agarwala and S. P. Singh. Bombay: Oxford University Press, 1958, pp. 245-55.

Singer, Hans W. "The Concept of Balanced Growth and Economic Development: Theory and Practice," in Economic Growth, ed. Eastin Nelson. Austin: University of Texas Press, 1960, pp. 71-86.

Spengler, Joseph J. "Social Structure, The State and Economic Growth," in Economic Growth, Brazil, India, Japan, eds. Simon Kuznets, Wilbert E. Moore and Joseph J. Spengler. Durham, N. C.: Duke University Press, 1955, pp. 363-87.

_____. "Population as a Factor in Economic Development," in Population and World Politics, ed. Philip M. Hauser. Glencoe, Ill.: The Free Press, 1958, pp. 162-89.

_____. "The State and Economic Growth: Summary and Interpretation," in The State and Economic Growth, ed. Hugh G. J. Aitken. New York:

Social Science Research Council, 1959, pp. 353-382.

_____. "Theory, Ideology, Non-Economic Values, and Politico-Economic Development," in Tradition, Values and Socio-Economic Development, eds. Ralph Briabanti and Joseph J. Spengler. Durham, N. C.: Duke University Press, 1961, pp. 3-56.

_____. "The Economics of Population Growth," in The Population Crisis and the Use of World Resources, ed. Stuart Mudd. Bloomington: Indiana University Press, 1964, pp. 73-93.

ARTICLES AND PERIODICALS

Abu-Laghod, Janet L. "Migrants' Adjustment to City Life: The Egyptian Case," American Journal of Sociology, LXVII (July, 1961), 22-32.

_____. "Urbanization in Egypt: Present State and Future Prospects," Economic Development and Cultural Change, XXIII (April, 1965), 313-43.

Adler, Richard. "Les Lignes principales du problém de la population d'Egypte et leur coordination," Egypte Contemporaine, XXXIV (March, 1943), 161-204.

Anis, Mahmond A. A Study of the National Income of Egypt, a special issue of Égypte Contemporaine, (November-December, 1950).

Arab Review. "Socio-Economic Aspects of Agrarian Reform in the United Arab Republic," a special issue of The Scribe, The Arab Review, Agrarian Reform and Land Development, VIII (July, 1964), 15-32.

Bauer, P. T., and Yamey, B. S. "Economic Progress and

Occupational Distribution," Economic Journal,
LXI (December, 1951), 741-55.

_____ _____. "Economic Progress, Occupational Distribution, and Institutional Wage
Rigidities: A Comment," Review of Economics
and Statistics, XXXV (November, 1954), 461-62.

Buntle, M. H. "L'Hypertrophic urbaine," Bulletin de
l'Institut International de Statistique, Actes
De La 32e Session De Statistique, XXXVII (Tokyo,
1960), 521-28.

Central Bank of Egypt. Economic Bulletin, Vol. III,
No. 2, Cairo: 1963.

Chenery, Hollis B. "The Role of Industrialization in
Development Programs," American Economic
Review, papers and proceedings XLV (May, 1955),
40-57.

Chenery, Hollis B., and Watanabe, Tsunehiko. "International Comparisons of the Structure of
Production," Econometrics, XXVI (October,
1958), 487-521.

Cook, R. C. "Egypt's Population Explodes," Population
Bulletin, XII (July, 1956), 57-69.

Crouchley, A. E. "The Development of Commerce in the
Reign of Mohamed Ali," Égypte Contemporaine,
XXVIII (February-March, 1937), 305-318.

_____. "A Century of Economic Development, 1837-
1937, A Study in Population and Production in
Egypt," Égypte Contemporaine, XXX (February-
March, 1939), 133-55.

Davis, Kingsley, and Golden, Hilda H. "Urbanization
and Development of Preindustrial Areas,"
Economic Development and Cultural Change, III
(October, 1954), 6-24.

Dawood, Hassan.   "Agrarian   Reform   in   Egypt: A Case
        Study," Current History,   XXX (Cairo, 1956),
        331-38.

Egyptian Federation of Industries.   Yearbook 1950-51
        to 1955-56, Cairo: S.O.P. Press, 1951-56.

El-Badry, M. A.   "Some Demographic Measurements for
        Egypt Based on the Stability of Census Age
        Distribution," Milbank Memorial Fund Quarterly,
        XXXIII (July, 1955), 268-305.

_____.   "Some Aspects   of Fertility in Egypt,"
        Milbank   Memorial   Fund   Quarterly,   XXXIV
        (January, 1956), 22-43.

_____.   "Census Regional   Fertility Data in Egypt:
        Appraisal and Mapping," Egyptian Statistical
        Journal, IV (Cairo, 1960), 4-30.

El-Kammash, Magdi M.   "Stockwell's Infant Mortality
        Index for Measuring Economic Development: A
        Comment," Milbank Memorial Fund Quarterly, XL
        (January, 1962), 112-19.

_____.   "On the Measurement of Economic Development
        Using Scalogram Analysis," Papers and Proceed-
        ings, Regional Science Association, XI (1963),
        309-334.

_____.   "On the Take-off Stage of the United Arab
        Republic Economy," Arab Journal, II (Fall,
        1965), 11-16.

Eman, André. "L'Industrie Egyptienne Sons La Dynastie
        De Mohamed Ali," in Livre D'or De La Federation
        Egyptienne De L'Industrie. Cairo: Schindler,
        (1948), 81-86.

Fleming, J. Marcus.   "External Economies and the
        Doctrine of Balanced Growth,"Economic Journal,
        LXV (June, 1955), 241-56.

_____. "External Economies and the Doctrine of Balanced Growth: A Rejoinder to Professor Nurkse," Economic Journal, LXVI (September, 1956), 537-39.

Hoselitz, Bert F. "The City, Factory and Economic Growth," Papers and Proceedings, American Economic Review, XLV (May, 1955), 166-84.

Industrial Bank. Quarterly Bulletin of the Industrial Bank, Vol. I, No. 1, Cairo, 1957.

Issawi, Charles. "Population and Wealth in Egypt," Milbank Memorial Fund Quarterly, XXVII (January, 1949), 98-113.

Johnson, D. Gale. "The Functional Distribution of Income in the United States," Review of Economics and Statistics, XXXVI (May, 1954), 175-82.

Journal of Economic History, A Supplement. The Tasks of Economic History. Vol. VII, 1947.

Kiser, Clyde V. "The Demographic Position of Egypt," Milbank Memorial Fund Quarterly, XXII (October, 1944), 383-408.

Kuznets, Simon. "Economic Growth and Income Inequality," American Economic Review, XLV (March, 1955), 1-27.

_____. "Quantitative Aspects of the Growth of Nations, IV: Distribution of National Income by Factor Shares," Economic Development and Cultural Change, VIII (April, 1959), 81-83.

Maddox, James G. "Private and Social Costs of the Movement of the People Out of Agriculture," Papers and Proceedings, American Economic Review, L (May, 1960), 393-402.

Mason, Edward S. "The Role of Government in Economic

Development," papers and proceedings of the seventy-second meeting of the American Economic Association, American Economic Review, L (May, 1960), 636-48.

Mushkin, Selma J. "Health as an Investment," Journal of Political Economy, Supplement, LXX (October, 1962), 129-57.

National Bank of Egypt. Economic Bulletin, Vols. II-XV (Cairo: 1949-62).

Nurkse, Ragnar. "Some International Aspects of the Problem of Economic Development," American Economic Review, XLII (May, 1952), 571-83.

Rosenstein-Rodan, P. N. "Problems of Industrialization of Eastern and South-Eastern Europe," Economic Journal, LIII (June-September, 1943), 202-11.

_____. "International Aid for Underdeveloped Countries," Review of Economics and Statistics, XLIII (May, 1961), 107-38.

Rottenberg, S. "A Note on Economic Progress and Occupational Distribution," Review of Economics and Statistics, XXXVI (May, 1953), 168-70.

Schultz, Theodore W. (ed.). Journal of Political Economy, A supplement, Investment in Human Beings, LXX (October, 1962).

Seal, Patrick, and Beeson, Irene. "Babies along the Nile," The New Republic, Vol. 154, No. 9 (Washington, D. C., May, 1966), 10-11.

Sjaastad, Larry A. "The Costs and Returns of Human Migration," Journal of Political Economy, Supplement, LXX (October, 1962), 80-93.

Skinner, William G. "Cultural Values, Social Structure, and Population Growth," in United Nations, Department of Economics and Social Affairs,

Population Bulletin of the United Nations, No. 5 (New York, 1956), pp. 5-12.

Spengler, Joseph J. "Capital Requirements and Population Growth in Underdeveloped Countries: Their Interrelations," Economic Development and Cultural Change, IV (July, 1956), 305-34.

_____. "Economic Factors in Economic Development," American Economic Review, papers and proceedings of the 69th annual meetings, XLVII (May, 1957), 42-56.

_____. "The Role of the State in Shaping Things Economic,"in Tasks of Economic History, a supplement to the Journal of Economic History, Vol. II, 1947.

Strassmann, Paul. "Economic Growth and Income Distribution," Quarterly Journal of Economics, LXX (August, 1956), 425-40.

Swaroop, S. "Growth of Population and Health Programmes in Asia and the Far East," United Nations, Department of Economics and Social Affairs, Population Bulletin of the United Nations, No. 5 (New York, 1956), pp. 13-27.

Usher, Abbott Payson. "The Resource Requirements of an Industrial Economy," Journal of Economic History, VII (May, 1957), 35-46.

Young, Allyn A. "Increasing Returns and Economic Progress," Economic Journal, XXXVIII (December, 1928), 527-42.

Youngson, A. J. "Marshall on Economic Growth," Scottish Journal of Political Economy, III (February, 1956), 1-18.

DOCUMENTS

Abdel-Rahman, A. G.   The Egyptian Normal Life Table

No. 2. Cairo: Government Press, 1958.

Egypt, Department De La Statistique Generale. Annuaire Statistique de Poche, 1942. Le Caire: Imprimerie Nationale, 1943.

Egypt, Department of Agriculture. "The Economic Structure of Egypt." Cairo, 1951. (Mimeographed.)

Egypt, Department of Statistics. Statistical Pocket Yearbook, 1952. Cairo: Government Press, 1953.

Egypt, Department of Statistics and Census. Population Census of Egypt, 1937 General Tables. Cairo: Government Press, 1942.

_____. Population Census of Egypt, 1947, General Tables. Cairo: Government Press, 1952.

Egypt, Permanent Council for Public Welfare Services, National Planning Commission. The Population Problem in Egypt. (Cairo, 1955).

Egyptian Embassy. Egypt News Bulletin. Washington, D. C. (April, 1950).

Egyptian Ministry of Agriculture, Division of Agricultural Statistics. The National Income from Agriculture, Cairo: Government Press, 1948.

Hauser, Philip (ed.). Urbanization in Asia and the Far East. Proceedings of the Joint UN/UNESCO Seminar on Urbanization in the ECAFE Region (Calcutta: UNESCO Research Center on the Social Implications of Industrialization in Southern Asia, 1957).

International Labor Organization. Yearbook of Labor Statistics. Geneve: 1959.

Makar, R. The Egyptian Life Table No. 3 for 1947. Cairo: Government Press, 1957.

Massachusetts Institute of Technology, Center for
      International Studies. <u>The Objectives of
      United States Economic Assistance Program</u>.
      Washington, 1957.

United Arab Republic. <u>U. A. R. Constitution</u>, 1958.

United Arab Republic, Central Committee for Statistics.
      <u>Collection of Basic Statistics</u>. Cairo: S.O.P.
      Press, 1962.

_____. <u>Population Trends in the United Arab Repub-
      lic</u>. Cairo, 1962.

United Arab Republic Central Organization for Public
      Mobilization and Statistics. <u>Selections from
      The United Arab Republic Public Statistics
      1951-52 to 1964-65</u>. Cairo: Dar Memphis,
      1965.

_____. <u>United Arab Republic Yearbook for Public
      Statistics 1952-65</u>. Cairo: Dar Memphis, 1966.

United Arab Republic, Department of Public Mobilization
      and Statistics. <u>Handbook of Basic Statistics</u>.
      Cairo: S.O.P. Press, 1963.

United Arab Republic, Department of Statistics. <u>Vital
      Statistics</u>, Vols. I and II. Cairo: Government
      Press, 1963.

United Arab Republic, Department of Statistics and
      Census. <u>Annuaire Statistique</u>. Cairo: National
      Press, 1948.

_____. <u>Annuaire Statistique, 1959</u>. Cairo: Govern-
      ment Press, 1960.

_____. <u>Ten Years of Revolution, Statistical Atlas</u>.
      Cairo: S.O.P. Press, 1962.

United Arab Republic, Documentation Research Center.
      <u>Arab Political Encyclopedia</u>. Documents and

Notes, Eleventh Year, Jan.-Feb., 1963. Cairo: The National Publication House, 1963.

United Arab Republic, Information Department. Land Reclamation. Cairo: Al Shaab Printing House, 1963.

_____. The Yearbook, 1963. Cairo: National Publication House, 1964.

United Arab Republic, Ministry of Agrarian Reform and Land Reclamation. Agrarian Reform and Land Reclamation in Ten Years. Cairo: National House for Printing and Publishing, n.d.

United Arab Republic, Ministry of Education, Department of Statistics. Comparative Statistics on Education. Cairo: S.O.P. Press, 1961.

United Arab Republic, Ministry of Social Affairs. Magazine of Social Affairs. Cairo: Government Press, 1942.

United Arab Republic, Planning Committee for Southern Region. The Frame of the General Five-Year Plan for Economic and Social Development, July, 1960-June, 1965. Cairo: General Organization for Government Printing Offices, 1960.

United Nations. Agriculture in the World Economy. Rome, 1955.

_____. Report on World Social Situation. New York, 1957.

_____. Science and Technology for Development, Vol. VI, Education and Training. New York, 1963.

_____. Yearbook of National Accounts Statistics. New York, 1962.

United Nations, Department of Economic Affairs. Domestic Financing of Economic Development. New

York, 1950.

_____. Measures for the Economic Development of Underdeveloped Countries. New York, 1951.

_____. National Income and Its Distribution in Underdeveloped Countries, Statistical Papers, Series E, No. 3. New York, 1951.

_____. Review of Economic Conditions in the Middle East, 1951-52. Supplement to World Economic Report. New York, 1953.

United Nations, Department of Economic and Social Affairs. A Study of Industrial Growth. New York, 1963.

_____. Demographic Yearbook, 1957, 1959, 1963. New York, 1957, 1959, 1963.

_____. Economic Developments in the Middle East, 1954-55 to 1959-61. Supplements to World Economic Surveys, 1955-61. New York, 1956-62.

_____. Population Bulletin of the United Nations, No. 5. New York: 1956.

_____. Processes and Problems of Industrialization in Underdeveloped Countries. New York, 1955.

_____. Progress in Land Reform, Third Report. New York: 1962.

_____. Statistical Yearbook 1956, 1957, 1958, 1959, 1960, 1961, 1963. New York, 1956, 1957, 1958, 1959, 1960, 1961, 1963.

United Nations, Department of Social Affairs, Population Division. The Determinants and Consequences of Population Trends. New York: 1953.

United Nations, Economic and Social Council. "The Cooperative Movement in Africa," Fourth Session of the Economic Committee on Africa, Adis Ababa, February–March, 1962. (Mimeographed.)

United Nations, Statistical Office. _Monthly Bulletin of Statistics_, VIII (June, 1954).

_____. _Monthly Bulletin of Statistics_, XVII (September–December, 1963).

_____. _Per capita National Product of Fifty-Five Countries, 1952–54_, Statistical Paper, Series E, No. 4. New York, 1957.

_____. _National and per capita Income, Seventy Countries, 1949_, Statistical Paper, Series E, No. 2, New York, 1950.

UNESCO. _Basic Facts and Figures 1959_. Paris, 1960.

_____. _World Illiteracy at Mid-century_. Paris, 1957.

United States, Bureau of Public Affairs. _Communist Economic Policy in the Less Developed Areas_, Department of State Publication No. 7020 (Washington, D. C., 1960).

United States, Bureau of the Census. _Historical Statistics of the United States, 1789–1945_. Washington, D. C.: U. S. Government Printing Office, 1949.

United States, Department of Commerce. _Statistical Abstracts of the United States, 1948_. Washington, D. C.: U. S. Government Printing Office, 1948.

_____. _Statistical Abstracts of the United States, 1955_. Washington, D. C. U. S. Government Printing Office, 1955.

United States Congress. _The 14th Semiannual Report of the Food-for-Peace Program Carried on under_

Public Law 480, 83rd Congress, as Amended;
Message from the President to the United
States, 87th Congress, 1st Session, House
Document No. 223. Washington, D. C.: U. S.
Government Printing Office, 1961.

United States, Department of Agriculture, Development
and Trade Division. Public Law 480 and Other
Economic Assistance to United Arab Republic,
(Egypt). ERS--Foreign 83, Economic Research
Service. Washington, D. C., July, 1964.

United States, Department of Commerce. Balance of
Payments Statistical Supplement. Washington,
D. C., 1963.

_____. Foreign Grants and Credits by the United
States Government, No. 69. Washington, D. C.,
December, 1961.

                        OTHERS

El-Kammash, Magdi M., and Ernst W. Swanson. "Income
Effects of Loan Transfers from a Developed to
an Underdeveloped Country," a paper presented
at the 1964 Meeting of the Southern Economic
Association, Atlanta, Ga., November, 1964.
(Mimeographed.) Appeared as Reprint 67-6,
Department of Economics, North Carolina State
University, Raleigh, N. C. (March, 1967).

_____ ___ _____. "Contributions of External
Loans to Development," a paper presented at a
Seminar on Intersectoral Relations in Economic
Development, sponsored by the Agricultural
Development Council, Raleigh, N. C., November,
1964. (Mimeographed.) Published in Faculty
Discussion Papers, FDP 67-3 (February, 1967).

El-Shafie, M. Ahmed. "Population Pressure on Land and
the Problem of Capital Accumulation in Egypt,"

unpublished Ph.D. dissertation, University of Wisconsin, 1951.

Hussein, Hassan M. "Evaluation of Progress in Fertility Control in U. A. R.," a paper contributed to United Nations World Population Conference, Belgrade, Yugoslavia, 1965. (Mimeographed.)

Sjaastad, Larry A. "Income and Migration in the United States," unpublished Ph.D. dissertation, University of Chicago, 1961.

United States, Department of State, Agency for International Development, U. A. R. Desk. "United Arab Republic Foreign Assistance Obligations and Loan Authorization." Washington, D. C., 1962. (Mimeographed).

Zikry, A. M. "Fertility Differential of the U. A. R. Women," a paper contributed to the United Nations World Population Conference, Belgrade, Yugoslavia, 1965. (Mimeographed).

INDEX

INDEX

ABOUT THE AUTHOR

Magdi M. El-Kammash, Associate Professor of Economics at North Carolina State University at Raleigh, has had wide experience in teaching and research both in Egypt and the United States. His professional experience began when he was a member of the research staff of the Industrial Bank of Egypt. In addition, he served in the United Arab Republic as a consultant and member of several committees of the National Council of Production, the National Council of Public Services, the Planning Commission, and the Ministry of Commerce. His research experience in the U.S.A. began with his graduate work at Duke University. While working there toward a Ph.D. degree, he served as a Research Associate with the Department of Sociology and then as a Research Statistician with the Department of Economics.

A contributor to journals in both the United States and Egypt, he also has translated two books from English to Arabic. His articles have appeared in the Papers and Proceedings of the Regional Science Association, the Milbank Quarterly, the Arab Journal, and the Journal of Economics and Accountancy. He has traveled extensively in the U. S. and abroad, participating in conferences and professional meetings on development.

Professor El-Kammash studied economics and statistics at Cairo University. He is the recipient of several awards from Cairo University and the Institute of Banking Studies, in addition to scholarships from the Egyptian Government, Duke University, and the Ford Foundation. In 1964, he was awarded a Ford Foundation Fellowship for Regional Faculty Seminars in Economics. In 1967, he became a fellow of the Economics-in-Action Program at Case Institute of Technology. During 1967-68 he was a visiting lecturer in economics at Oxford University, England.